Dawn staggered to the bathroom, convinced that a warm shower would make her feel better. But when she shed her nightgown and looked into the mirror, her heart wedged in her throat. A fine red rash covered her arms and torso. She started shaking so violently that she had to grab ahold of the sink for support.

Dawn knew what the rash meant. She'd read too many pamphlets and booklets following her transplant. A rash was often the very first sign of bone marrow rejection.

NO TIME TO CRY

Lurlene McDaniel

SCHOLASTIC INC.

New York Toronto London Auckland Sydney
Mexico City New Delhi Hong Kong Buenos Aires

ISBN 0-439-69212-1

Text copyright © 1993 by Lurlene McDaniel. All rights reserved.
For information contact Darby Creek Publishing, 7858 Industrial Parkway,
Plain City, OH 43064. Published by Scholastic Inc., 557 Broadway, New York,
NY 10012, by arrangement with Darby Creek Publishing and Lerner
Publishing Group. SCHOLASTIC and associated logos are
trademarks and/or registered trademarks of Scholastic Inc.

12 11 10 9 8 7 6 5 4 3 2 1   5 6 7 8 9 0/0

Printed in the U.S.A.   01

First Scholastic printing, January 2005

Cover photo and design by Michael Petty
Petty Productions

One

"**H**EY Dawn . . . Dawn Rochelle! Wait up."

At the sound of her name being called in the jammed hallway, Dawn stopped suddenly and was almost mowed over by a group of kids hurrying to classes. She flattened herself against the bank of lockers and waited for her friend Rhonda to struggle through the crowd.

"Is this a mob scene or what?" Rhonda half-shouted above the noise.

"I never expected the first day of high school to be so crazy," Dawn admitted. "I think everybody's lost—even the seniors." Since she and Rhonda were only sophomores, they had expected to be hunting for every room on their assignment cards. But Hardy High was brand new and no one had attended classes there yet. Everyone seemed to be bewildered by the maze of halls and doors that looked all alike.

"According to the info packet, green room numbers mean science; red, math; brown, language; blue, the arts—"

"Enough already!" Dawn interrupted her friend. "Let's see if we have any classes together before the first bell rings."

They compared their schedules. Dawn was disappointed that the only class she and Rhonda shared was a final period Driver's Education class. They wouldn't even be in the lunch room at the same time. "I hate to admit it," Rhonda said, "but I miss our dinky old junior high school."

"Me too. At least we knew our way around."

"And we knew everybody and everybody knew us."

Dawn glanced around at the kids bustling through the hallway and realized that except for Rhonda, she didn't know a soul. In June, she'd been looking forward to attending a school where she could be anonymous, where most of the kids wouldn't know what the previous three years of her life had been like. She was tired of kids whispering behind her back and pointing to "that girl who has cancer."

Now, after the long summer she'd been through—her experience at cancer camp as a counselor, her months of being a friend to Marlee, one of girls in her cabin, of visits to Marlee in the hospital and watching the young girl die—now she longed to put the past behind her and be a normal girl with a normal life. That is, if there were such a thing for a victim of leukemia.

"I'm glad we're taking Driver's Ed together," Rhonda said.

"I'm just glad your parents are letting you get your permit at all," Dawn answered. Rhonda could have gotten her permit last year when she was a freshman, but her parents made her wait until she brought her grades up.

The blast of an electronic bell warned that classes would soon begin. Dawn quickly glanced at her card. "I've got English upstairs. Do you suppose that's a brown room number?"

"Beats me. I'm trapped in biology. Definitely green."

Both girls laughed. "See you last period," Dawn called as Rhonda scampered off.

Dawn made her way to the stairwell. She clutched her new notebook to her chest and tried to stay out of everyone's way. A group of boys wearing letter jackets—football players, she guessed—sauntered past her. One of them gave her the once-over, and her cheeks flushed bright red. His interest made her feel good in one way, but in another way, she wondered what his reaction might be if he knew she'd had cancer.

She thought of her brother, Rob. He'd played football once, but a knee injury in his sophomore year had ended his career. Now he was at Michigan State finishing his senior year. He was graduating early, in December, and Dawn was sure he'd be coming home. After all, Katie was still here, and anyone could tell that Rob was head-over-heels in love with nurse Kate O'Ryan.

"Watch where you're going!"

The sharp words drew Dawn up short. "Sorry," she mumbled, steering clear of a girl who was busy arranging information on a bulletin board.

"Probably sophomore sludge," Dawn heard the girl mutter under her breath.

Dawn tossed her head of thick auburn hair, attempting to shake off the girl's hurtful words. *Well, I wanted to start fresh*, she told herself. *Guess I'll have to put up with an insult or two*.

By the time she hooked up with Rhonda in the Driver's Ed room that afternoon, Dawn was relieved to see a familiar face. So far that day, she'd gotten lost twice, and it was hard not to feel overwhelmed by all the new faces. Although she'd seen a couple of her former classmates, always at a distance, she realized that the juggling of the school district lines had truly put her and Rhonda in another world, but in a way she was relieved. Now she wouldn't have a bunch of people asking her about her health all of the time.

"I've got the cutest guy in my French class," Rhonda blurted the moment Dawn slid into the desk next to her. "How about you? Any hunks?"

"I didn't notice," Dawn confessed.

"You didn't *notice*? Why not? Isn't that what high school's all about?"

"Silly me. I thought it was to take classes, get good grades, and prepare for college."

Rhonda rolled her eyes in exasperation. "Maybe I'd feel that way too if I had a gorgeous guy like Brent Chandler waiting in the wings, but I don't."

"Don't start on that. I told you he and I were only friends." Brent had called her from West Virginia the week before to say that he was on his way to West Virginia Tech for freshman orientation. "You will write to me, won't you?" he'd asked.

"You bet," she had assured him. Brent was handsome and nice, and they'd had a wonderful time together at camp. But she wasn't kidding herself. She figured that a high school sophomore couldn't possibly hold much interest for him once he was settled on campus. Dawn knew that it was their shared memories of his sister Sandy that had brought them together in the first place. But, like Marlee, Sandy was dead. Sandy, her best friend ever. And Dawn was left to carry on with everyday life.

"Well, then if you and Brent are only friends, all the more reason to check out the guys here at Hardy," Rhonda insisted. "The first football game is Friday night, and there's a dance afterward in the gym. I think you and I should go."

"Are you asking me for a date?"

Rhonda gave Dawn a murderous look. "Very funny. I'm just saying it would be fun to go and hang around and check out the prospects. What do you say?"

"Can we talk about this later?"

A teacher entered the room and wrote

"Mr. De Marco" on the board. Then he explained, "We've got eight weeks of classroom work, then we'll put it into practice in the driving area next to the school track. Each of you will drive solo with me, and if you pass all parts of the class, you can take your driving test when your birthday comes up."

"Freedom," she heard Rhonda sigh.

Freedom. Dawn wondered what it was like. Ever since she was thirteen, her life had revolved around leukemia. Hospitals, chemo treatments, remission, check-ups, relapse, a bone marrow transplant, more check-ups. She felt as if she'd spent forever fighting the monster that had invaded her body two and a half years before. But the battle scars were mostly on the inside. Surely, nothing showed on the outside now that she was going on sixteen and in total remission.

Her gaze darted around the room. Could any of the kids sitting in the class really tell what she'd been through by simply looking at her? And how would they treat her if they knew? She felt as if she'd been forced to grow up far too fast. She'd hardly had a chance to be a kid. Dawn promised herself right then that all that was truly behind her. She wanted her life back. And she didn't want to share it with anything having to do with cancer.

Two

"HOW was your first day?" Dawn's mother asked the moment she arrived home from school.

"It was fine, Mom." Dawn tossed her books on the kitchen counter and poked through the contents of the refrigerator.

"Don't spoil your supper."

"I won't." She took out an apple and bit into it, savoring the juicy sweetness. There had been times when she was so sick from chemo that she couldn't keep anything down, and other times, when she'd been taking cortisone drugs, that she couldn't get enough to eat.

"Tell me about it," her mom coached.

"I got lost a lot. Rhonda and I have Driver's Ed together. There's a football game Friday night."

"That's it, huh?"

Dawn wished her parents didn't expect her to spill her guts over every detail of her life. Didn't they realize that she liked her privacy? Instantly, she felt ashamed. She still had to take certain chemo medications and immune-suppressant drugs to keep her body from rejecting Rob's bone marrow. Her parents had stood by her through the worst of her ordeal. She knew she never would have made it without their support.

She smiled contritely. "Hardy's awfully big and I felt like a lost sheep most of the day. Except for Rhonda, I don't have any friends. The juniors and seniors all seem to have their own groups, and new kids aren't exactly invited in."

"I'm sure they'll warm up to you as time goes by. Are there any after-school activities that might appeal to you? Cheerleading?"

Dawn had been a cheerleader in seventh and eighth grade, but hadn't been able to keep up with the practices when she was in and out of the hospital. "Cheerleading's different in high school," she said. "You have to try out in the spring."

"Maybe next year," said her mother. "Anything else?"

Dawn toyed with the stem of her apple. "I'm not sure what I want to do."

"You're taking college prep courses. Maybe there's something fun for college-bound students."

"I have no idea what I want to study in college. My future's one big mystery."

"Something will come along that you'll like," her mother said cheerfully. She picked up a potato from beside the sink and started peeling it as she talked. "By the way, Katie called to remind you of your clinic appointment tomorrow at four."

Dawn felt the familiar twinge of apprehension. She'd been going for bloodwork regularly since her bone marrow transplant. And even though she had received a good report each time, she always felt a shiver of fear before every test. What if her white blood cell count was elevated? What if Rob's bone marrow stopped working and her leukemia returned? What if she had a severe episode of rejection?

"Did you hear me?" her mother asked.

"Of course I heard you." Dawn said peevishly.

"I'll pick you up from school at 3:30 and take you."

"I can grab a bus."

"Oh, honey, that's silly. I'll come and get you."

Stop treating me like a baby! Dawn had to bite her tongue to keep from saying it aloud.

"Katie wants to show you something," her mother said, smoothing over the awkward moment. "She says she'll bring you home."

"What's she want to show me?"

"She didn't say, but she was eager for you to see it. I invited her to stay for dinner tomorrow night." Dawn's mother sighed. "I know she misses Rob as much as he misses her. Maybe seeing us will help. I was a little worried that he might not want to finish up at Michigan State because it would mean they'd be apart for four months."

Dawn dropped her apple core into the trash. "Not too far apart," she said. "Rob told me he'd be home once a month no matter what."

"Love," her mother mused with a smile. "Isn't it wonderful? I can't believe that this is the same boy who washed his face because some girl kissed him at a birthday party. Of course, he was nine then."

Dawn suddenly remembered how badly Marlee had wanted to be kissed just once before she died. *"For real. Not like in my dream*," she'd told Dawn. It seemed like such a small wish. Now it would never come true.

She wondered how Marlee's grandmother was doing without her granddaughter around. Mrs. Hodges had raised Marlee and then lost her to cancer. Her own health was poor, and Marlee's hospitalization had been difficult on her.

Dawn told herself she should call the elderly woman and say hello. She'd looked so lost and alone after Marlee's funeral. But although Dawn went up to her room and even picked up the phone receiver, she didn't call. This was her first day of school and the start of a brand new year. All she wanted to do was leave the past behind and look to the future.

* * * * *

The next morning, Rhonda called in a panic. "Can you believe it? I overslept. Anyway, you'll have to walk to the bus stop without me. Mom will run me to school."

"See you in Driver's Ed," Dawn replied, feeling slightly dismayed as she hung up the phone. She didn't have anybody to sit with on the bus and wasn't looking forward to boarding it alone. *Grow up!* she told herself. After all, she'd never been one to travel in groups. It was another habit she'd missed out on because she'd been busy having cancer instead of collecting groups of friends. Being sick meant spending a lot of time by yourself.

When she was thirteen and diagnosed with leukemia, she'd felt like a freak. She'd looked like a freak, too, after all her hair fell out and sores had broken out on her skin. She'd worn scarfs and wigs to hide her baldness. In school, there had been plenty of kids who treated her as if she were contagious and stayed far away from her, but she'd had some good, loyal friend through it all. Rhonda had been one. Rhonda wasn't a friend like Sandy, of course. Only someone who'd been through hospitalization and chemo could truly understand what life with cancer was like.

Sandy had been through it all, Dawn reflected. She'd been there when Dawn first found out about her own cancer—barely thirteen and suddenly thrust into a world of pain and fear and confusion. Sandy had only been in the hospital two weeks herself, but she was a pillar of strength and reassurance for Dawn. Always optimistic, always encouraging. They'd learned about leukemia together—about staying positive and battling the cancer cells through imaging. They'd been through chemo together; their hair had even fallen out at the same time!

Dawn sighed wistfully. She would always miss Sandy. It seemed so unfair that their time together had been so short.

Her thoughts were interrupted by the phone ringing again. She stared blankly at it for a moment before reaching over to answer it.

"Me again!" Rhonda's cheerful voice snapped her back to the present. "Forgot to ask you—did you ask if you could go to the game and the dance Friday night?"

"Yep. I can go."

"Good. We'll have to figure out what to wear to impress the guys."

"Don't you ever give up about boys?"

"No way. This is my year. I can feel it."

Dawn was still smiling to herself over Rhonda's optimism while she walked to the bus stop. Overhead, the trees were still green, but Dawn could already feel the autumn in the air. In another few weeks, the weather would turn nippy and the leaves would begin to change color.

She hadn't gone far down the block when she began to notice a car following her. *It's your imagination*, she told herself. But it soon became obvious that it wasn't. The car was some weird shade of bronze. It was old, and its muffler was loud. Her heart began to beat faster.

The car pulled alongside her, and for an instant she considered bolting and running. The driver, a teenage boy, leaned across the passenger seat and slightly out the window. "Dawn?" he asked. "Dawn Rochelle? Is that you?"

Dawn stopped cold in her tracks and peered at him suspiciously. He looked familiar, but she couldn't see his face very well. How did he know her name? Taking a step closer, she could see that he had black hair and deep brown eyes—the color of rich chocolate. Suddenly she realized why he looked familiar.

"Jake?" she whispered.

His face broke out into a dazzling smile. "Yup, it's me—Jake Macka. Don't you recognize me?"

Three

Jake Macka! Memories of the past tumbled through her mind like scenes from an old movie. "Is it really you?" *Dumb question!* she told herself. Her heart thudded and her knees felt weak. "But you moved away almost two years ago." She instantly recalled how disappointed she'd felt when his family had left Columbus. It was just before her relapse.

"Well, a year and a half ago, actually. But my dad's company moved him back last month. We've got a house over on Claremont Avenue. I'm going to Hardy High. You too?"

"Yes."

"Hop in. I'll drive you." He reached over and opened the passenger side door.

Dawn thought for just a second about what her parents would say. But they knew

Jake and his family, so she figured it was okay to accept his offer of a ride. She climbed into the car, still numb with the shock of seeing him. She'd had a crush on Jake in the fifth grade that had lasted until he moved. Now, seeing him again, after more than a year, she could hardly think straight. He was taller, more muscular, and his shoulders were broader, but he had the same heart-melting smile and warm brown eyes that had always sent chills through her.

"When I saw you walking along the sidewalk, I couldn't believe it was you," Jake said. "I told myself, 'It's just someone who looks like Dawn.' But the longer I looked, the more I was sure it was you. It's the hair. I always thought you had the prettiest color hair." She touched her shoulder-length hair self-consciously. "You look great," Jake said, easing the car into traffic. "How are you?"

"I'm fine."

He pulled up at a stoplight and studied her carefully.

"No, I mean how are you, *really?*"

Of course, Jake would remember her first hospitalization and diagnosis. Her entire class had sent her get-well cards, including an unsigned one with an adorable teddy bear on the front, which she'd always suspected was from him.

"I heard you had a bone marrow transplant."

"You did?"

"One of your friends called and left a message about it. I called you, but I guess someone forgot to tell you."

Dawn vaguely recalled an entry Rob had made in her diary, when she was too sick to write in it herself, about calls from lots of friends. Jake had been one of them.

She felt a warm tingling sensation all the way down to her toes. Still, the last thing she wanted to discuss with him now was her health.

"The doctors think I'm cured," she said breezily, hoping to end the discussion.

His face broke into a smile. "That's terrific! I'd never known anyone with cancer and I thought you were brave—a real hero."

"Not me," she said with a self-conscious laugh. "You were the hero."

"When?"

"When you ran for the touchdown and Adams beat Harrison."

Jake laughed. "Talk about ancient history."

"Do you still play football?"

"I switched to soccer when we moved to Cincinnati. Soccer's a spring sport, but I'm the extra point kicker for Hardy's football squad this season." He glanced over at her. "You coming to Friday night's game?"

"I'm planning to. Do you remember Rhonda? We're going together."

"You're the person I remember best," Jake said.

Dawn's heart tripped, and she could feel a blush creeping up her neck.

"Remember the school carnival?" Jake asked with a smile.

"Of course! You dressed up like a clown and sat in the dunk tank to help us cheerleaders raise money," she replied.

"I almost drowned."

"You were a life-saver." He groaned at her little joke. "Is this your car?" she asked.

"My parents got it for me when I turned sixteen this summer. It's not much, but it's mine."

She patted the worn seat. "I hope I can get a car when I turn sixteen."

He swung into the school parking lot, which was teeming with morning traffic. In the distance she saw school buses pulling in and was glad she hadn't had to ride one that morning. "Thanks for the lift," she said when he'd found his assigned parking slot and turned off the engine.

"Maybe we can do it again." He walked with her toward the entrance and she couldn't help noticing that some of the girls were giving them curious looks.

"That would be fun." Because he was on the football team and because he was so good-looking, everybody would soon know who Jake Macka was, Dawn thought to herself. But this one morning, he was walking with her. In some ways, she felt like a thirteen-year-old again— like she had before she'd gotten cancer, when nothing was more important than being seen with one special person by all your friends.

"If you can hang around until I wrap up football practice, I'll take you home."

The urge to shout "Yes!" was on her tongue when she remembered that her mother was picking her up for a clinic appointment that afternoon. "I . . . um . . . can't today. I have someplace I have to go."

"Okay," he said.

She felt very disappointed. Once again, her stupid cancer had interfered with her life. If only she could be free of it forever. "It was really good to see you," she said, stopping beside her locker.

"You, too. I'd better go," he said. "I've got a bear for a geometry teacher. Rumor has it he gives detentions for tardies."

"Sounds mean."

He grinned, gave her a nod, and started off down the hall. She watched him disappear into the crowd and felt a bittersweet longing. Seeing Jake had stirred memories from a time when things were simple and life was uncomplicated. She sighed, wondering if life could ever be that way for her again.

* * * * * *

"All finished?" Katie asked when Dawn walked up to her at the nurse's desk on the fourth floor.

"The bloodletting is over," Dawn replied, holding out her arm to show off the Snoopy Band-Aid in the crook of her elbow.

"Since I was a big girl and didn't cry, the lab tech gave me a special reward."

She and Katie laughed together. "I guess you get used to it after you've been through it as much as you have," Katie said.

Dawn shook her head. "Over the past three years, I'll bet they've withdrawn a small ocean of blood from me. Believe me,

I never get used to it!"

Katie flashed her a look of sympathy. "Well, when the report comes back and you're given a clean bill of health, you'll be glad."

"Until the next time. And speaking of that, I'll have to have a bone marrow aspiration next time." She made a face. "I hate when they stick needles into my bones. It hurts."

"But it's necessary," Katie said.

"I still hate it." Dawn shrugged. "So what do you want to show me?"

"It's upstairs."

"Not on the oncology floor, I hope," Dawn said. "You know how I feel about going back up there, Katie." She hated going to the cancer floor where she'd spent so much time in isolation when she'd almost died.

"It isn't." Katie took Dawn's hand.

They rode up to the tenth floor and stepped off the elevator. Dawn could see that it was a floor full of offices. Because it was after five, most of the workers had gone home. A few doctors were still inside their cubicles, doing paperwork or talking on the phone. A janitor was emptying wastebaskets.

"Have they given you your own office?" Dawn asked, intrigued.

Katie laughed. "No—I'm still only a nurse. Here we are," she said, turning a corner to face a long wall. On it, a tree was painted. The trunk was thick and sturdy looking, its branches sprawled down the wall as if it were actually growing there. Each branch held plump green leaves. Every leaf bore a person's name.

"What is it?" Dawn asked.

"It's the Tree of Life," Katie explained. "It's dedicated to cancer survivors. Like you, Dawn Rochelle."

Four

DAWN stepped forward and examined the painted tree more closely. Several of the large green leaves were only outlines, as if waiting for names to be filled in. "I don't understand," she said.

"It's a new program we've started," Katie said eagerly, her blue eyes sparkling with enthusiasm. "It's a survivor support group, and they meet right inside this room." She gestured toward a closed door beside the trunk of the tree. "All the members of the group have their names painted on the leaves to announce that they're survivors. Think of it, Dawn. Before bone marrow transplants came into being, less than a third of all kids with leukemia were cured. Today, more than half can expect a normal life span. Kids with other kinds of cancers are living longer too."

"That's great, but why have a support group? I mean, support groups are super when you've just been diagnosed. It really helps to be able to talk about treatments and feelings and stuff like that when it's happening to you. But if you're doing fine, why keep bringing it up?"

"Discussion groups are helpful no matter what the problem. And just because something's over doesn't mean it's one hundred percent behind you. Don't you ever wish that you could talk to someone who's been through what you've been through?" Katie asked.

Dawn wasn't sure how to answer. A part of her *was* curious about other cancer patients' experiences. But a part of her was also glad that much of the ordeal was behind her. She wasn't sure she wanted to dredge up the past and all its heartrending memories of treatments and pain and uncertainty.

Then there was the heartache of losing your friends to cancer. She'd worked long and hard to get over the feelings of loss she had when Sandy died. Then the feelings had all rushed back when she'd watched helplessly as Marlee died. What good would it do to discuss it with a bunch of strangers?

"I've just started high school and I'm pretty busy with my studies. I want to make good grades and be involved with school stuff. I'm not sure I'll have time to come to some support group." She stepped away from the mural of the tree.

"They only meet once a month. There are doctors and nurses who help guide the discussions and answer questions. A lot of kids your age attend. You might enjoy getting to know them."

"I hardly have time to get to know the kids at my school," Dawn said with a nervous laugh.

"You don't have to come regularly unless you want to." Katie put her hand on Dawn's arm. "There're a lot of things pent up inside you about your experiences. Things that need to be talked about."

"But I feel fine," Dawn protested, beginning to feel pressured. Why didn't Katie drop it?

"Do you?"

Katie's question added to Dawn's discomfort. Of course she did. Hadn't she faced her reluctance to be involved with other patients that summer when she agreed to be a counselor at the cancer camp? It had been hard to go back and perform the same rituals she had during her very first summer. But she'd gone anyway and she ended up actually having a good time. "Look, Katie, I know you only want to help me, but right now I don't want to do anything that isn't connected with school. I want to have fun this year, you know, like a regular person."

"I understand. But will you just think about it? Just give it some thought?"

Dawn couldn't tell Katie no. She liked her too much. And she didn't want to hurt her feelings. But she didn't want to be forced into some cancer memory sessions either. "I'll think about it."

Katie smiled. "Good." She tucked her arm around Dawn's shoulders. "Now that that's settled, we'd better get you home. I'm starved for some of your mom's good cooking."

Dawn sneaked one final peek at the mural, at the leaves decorated with various names, and wished that Sandy's and Marlee's names could be listed.

But that was impossible. They weren't survivors. Sandy had leukemia, just like Dawn. Marlee had non-Hodgkins lymphoma, which causes tumors to grow on internal organs. Both had fought a tough battle with cancer, and both had lost. Dawn shook her head, trying to shake off the feeling of sadness that crept over her whenever she thought about Marlee and Sandy.

* * * * *

"Of course I remember Jake Macka! He was so cute! And he's here at Hardy? And he remembers you? Awesome!" Rhonda's voice bubbled. "Why didn't you *tell* me?"

"Calm down. It's not me he remembers. It's my cancer. I really didn't want to make a big deal of it."

Dawn and Rhonda were sitting in the stands. The football team had just jogged onto the field amid the cheers of the packed stadium.

"Where is he?" Rhonda craned her neck toward the field.

"That's him—number 6." Dawn had seen Jake instantly. It was as if her eyes had radar for him.

"Do you suppose he'll be at the dance?"

"How should I know?"

"You have all the luck," Rhonda grumbled. "First a college guy, and now Jake."

Dawn didn't remind Rhonda that her luck also included leukemia. "He was glad to see a familiar face. We had two years of information to catch up on, you know." Quickly, Dawn filled Rhonda in on what Jake had told her. "Once he gets popular at Hardy, he won't remember my name," she finished.

"We'll see," Rhonda declared.

After the game, Dawn and Rhonda shouldered their way through the crowd in the gym. "Let's grab a seat over there." Rhonda pointed to a section of bleachers reserved for general seating.

The center of the gym floor was jammed with dancers and a disc jockey was stationed at one end of the room. Colored spotlights reflected off the crowd. Music blared and Dawn had to shout to be heard. "Are we having fun yet?"

"Don't be a party pooper. We just got here." Rhonda grabbed Dawn's arm. "Maybe someone cool will notice us."

"Who? The janitor?" Even though she was giving Rhonda a hard time, Dawn was enjoying herself. She liked watching the dancers and feeling like she was part of things. The DJ announced "a blast from the past" and the mellow voice of Elvis Presley filled the gym. Couples glided together and swayed slowly to an old fifties love song.

The song jolted Dawn's memory, and suddenly she was back at camp, at the fifties dance with Brent. Brent had dressed as Elvis, and every female camper had flocked around him. She remembered walking in the moonlight with him, the feel of her hand in his. He'd pulled her into his arms and would have kissed her, but the girls from her cabin, hiding in the bushes, had begun heckling them.

All at once, she missed Brent terribly. She missed his easy and open personality and his low southern drawl. But what she missed most of all was the talks they'd had about Sandy. It had helped take away some of the pain of losing her.

"How about a dance?"

The voice above her jerked Dawn back to the present. But it wasn't Brent who was holding out his hand to her. It was Jake.

"She'd *love* to," Rhonda said, giving Dawn a shove.

Dawn was on her feet and in Jake's arms, still shaken by the powerful memories that had come upon her so unexpectedly. One minute she'd been having the time of her life, and the next, at the sound of a song, she'd dropped into a pit. What was wrong with her, anyway? "Great game," she said, trying to cheer herself up. "I'm glad we won."

"Thanks." His arms tightened around her. "Is everything all right?"

"Just fine." She offered him a breathless smile. His dark, chocolate brown eyes gazed down at her, and she felt an odd melting sensation going through her. *This is Jake!* she reminded herself. Someone she never thought she'd see again, and now, here they were dancing.

From the loudspeakers, Elvis's voice crooned, "Two different worlds, we live in two different worlds . . ." The words made perfect sense to her. Brent Chandler represented one of her worlds and Jake, another. Why did she feel as if she were caught between both of those worlds, but didn't fully belong to either?

Five

WHEN the song ended, Jake started to walk Dawn back to where Rhonda was sitting. Dawn tried to think of something clever to say—something to make him want to stick around awhile.

"Hey, Macka, wait up. I want to ask you something," a guy Dawn recognized as one of the senior players called out.

"Hi, Rich," Jake answered as the boy shouldered his way through the crowd toward them.

"We're going out for pizza and thought you might like to come along."

Jake glanced down at Dawn. "Gee, I don't know—"

"Go on," Dawn urged, not wanting him to feel obligated to her simply because they'd danced together.

A pretty girl with short dark hair

materialized beside Rich.

"This is my sister, Sharon," Rich said. Dawn recognized her as one of the Hardy cheerleaders.

"I've been wanting to meet you," Sharon said with a smile that flashed perfectly straight white teeth. "I thought you played an awesome game."

"Well, thanks." Jake smiled.

Dawn could tell that he was pleased by Sharon's attention.

Suddenly she felt like a third thumb. "I've got to run," she said.

"Are you sure?"

Dawn nodded. "Rhonda's waiting. It was great to see you again." She quickly made her way back to the bleachers, where Rhonda was tapping her toe impatiently. Dawn knew she wanted a full report.

"Let's go to the bathroom," Dawn said.

In the crowded bathroom, they found a small space next to a tiled wall. "I saw the whole thing," Rhonda announced. "Who does that girl think she is? Barging in on you like that."

"She's one of the most popular girls in this school and she can do anything she wants." Dawn's heart was pounding.

"Well, you didn't have to give up so

easily," Rhonda insisted. "You were there first. Jake asked you to dance, not her."

"He wanted to go with them. I could tell."

"You didn't give him any other choice." Rhonda eyed her. "What's wrong with you, anyway? You get offered a great opportunity and you run away. Jake Macka is so cool. I don't get it, Dawn. What's your problem?"

Dawn had no answer. She couldn't put her problem into words because she couldn't understand it herself. She wanted to have fun and act normal, but something was holding her back. "My problem is that I want to go home," she told Rhonda. "I'm sorry I'm such a drag, but I don't want to hang around any more tonight. I'm going to call my dad to come pick me up. If you want to stay, it's all right."

"I don't want to stay if you don't," Rhonda said limply. Dawn started for the door, but Rhonda caught her arm. "It's okay this time," she said, "but please don't be like this next time we come to a dance. How're we ever going to get noticed, if we never hang around?"

*   *   *   *   *

In October, Rob came home for a weekend.

"Hey Squirt," he said, giving her a hug. He pulled back and looked her over. "I guess I can't call you that anymore."

"That's right. I've added a half-inch to the four I grew over the summer." Dawn's chemo and radiation treatments had stunted her growth. It had taken her longer to mature in every way. All the previous year she'd felt extremely self-conscious about her lack of curves, but now, with Rob's bone marrow working and her drug therapies greatly reduced, she was finally growing and developing again.

"So I'll have to come up with a new nickname." Rob puckered his brow. "How about 'hotshot'? You *are* taking Hardy High by storm, aren't you?"

"Not quite. There's over a thousand students at Hardy. I'm afraid I'm just a speck on the wall."

"Not for long, I'll bet."

Dawn wished she shared his confidence in her, but she felt so ordinary. And except for Jake, who was busy with football, classes, and Sharon's attentions, she didn't see much excitement coming her way.

The phone rang and her mother called, "Dawn, it's for you."

She decided to take it in her room. "Don't

be too long," Rob said as she started up the stairs. "I have an important call to make."

"Really? Anybody I know?" she teased over her shoulder, knowing full well it was Katie.

"Just don't gab all afternoon."

She was still laughing when she picked up the receiver in her room.

"Got time for an old friend?" Brent Chandler asked.

Both surprised and pleased to hear his voice, she sprawled across her bed eagerly. "Brent! How are you?"

"I'm fine. And I've been thinking a lot about you lately."

"I thought college life was supposed to be exciting."

"Well, it is. But it's hard too," he confessed. "I've missed everybody. My family. Friends. I've been thinking a lot about camp this past summer. And all the great times you and I had."

She couldn't deny that being with him had made her time as a counselor extra special. "I thought you would have forgotten all about me by now."

"No way."

Goose bumps skittered up her arms. "I've missed you too," she said quietly.

"I was hoping you'd say that."

"Why?"

"I want to come see you over Christmas break."

Her heart skipped a beat. "You do?"

"Don't sound so surprised." His laugh warmed her. "I know it's a bit early to be making plans, but we have a long break, and I'd really like to see you. I was thinking of coming a week before Christmas, staying a couple of days, then heading home in time to spend the holidays with the folks. What do you think? Would your parents mind?"

Dawn knew that Sandy's brother would be welcome anytime. "I'm sure it won't be a problem," she said. "We have a spare bedroom in our basement. I'll ask and write you."

"Good. I'll be looking for your letter." She heard someone in the background yell for Brent to get off the phone. "Bye for now," he said.

She hung up, but the sound of his soft southern voice lingered in her head. She could barely contain her excitement. Brent wanted to come see her! She wanted to see him too—very much. She bolted to the door and took the stairs two at a time. She needed to talk to her mother. And then she had to tell Rhonda.

"Mom!" Dawn bounded into the kitchen only to see her mother, Rob, and Katie standing together in a huddle. She skidded to a stop. "Katie, you're here! I didn't know—" The words died on her lips as she glanced from face to face. "Something's wrong," Dawn said. "I can tell. What is it?"

"Oh, honey," Katie said, stepping forward from the group and taking both of Dawn's hands. Katie's big blue eyes looked troubled. "I came straight from the hospital because I wanted to tell you the bad news myself."

"What bad news?" Dawn's heart pounded and a queasy sensation filled her stomach.

"Mrs. Hodges, Marlee's grandmother, died this morning."

Six

THE October air felt crisp and cool. The thick green grass was clipped and neat, as orderly as the rows of bronze plaques and flower-laden vases that stretched as far as Dawn could see in the immaculate cemetery. It was the last place she wanted to be on a Saturday afternoon. But when her parents and Katie and Rob had said they should all go to Mrs. Hodges's funeral, she couldn't think of a way to get out of it.

The minister spoke highly of Mrs. Hodges and of her wonderful contributions to their community. Across from her, Dawn recognized the mayor, and she realized how important Mrs. Hodges must have been. Beside him stood Mrs. Hodges's attorney. He had surprised Dawn by knowing her name. "So, you're Miss Rochelle," he'd said. "Mrs. Hodges thought very highly of you."

Dawn swallowed hard, trying not to cry. Mrs. Hodges was very old and had been sick with a heart condition for a long time. She'd practically raised her granddaughter, Marlee, showering her with wonderful things. The two of them had lived in a mansion, and Marlee had been the only one at summer camp with designer sheets and a limo for transportation. But even though Mrs. Hodges could give Marlee anything money could buy, she couldn't make her cancer go away.

". . . ashes to ashes, dust to dust," the minister said.

Dawn kept remembering Marlee's funeral and how Mrs. Hodges had given her back her worn-out teddy bear, Mr. Ruggers, along with a farewell note from Marlee. At least now Marlee and her grandmother were both in heaven together. She tried to comfort herself with that thought.

"Hey Squirt, it's over." Rob's voice startled Dawn out of her thoughts.

Dawn glanced around and saw that people were beginning to disperse or gather in small groups. Her parents were talking to the minister, and Katie was talking to a fellow nurse. "Tell Mom I'll be waiting in the car," she said, struggling to hold back tears. She began walking toward their car, parked in a long line of cars from the funeral procession. More than anything, she just wanted to go home and forget all the sadness.

She was almost to the car when she heard a familiar voice.

"Dawn?"

Jake's voice so unnerved her that she dropped her purse on the ground. He stooped to pick it up.

"What are you doing here?" she asked in shrill voice. Although she was standing in wide open space, she felt cornered and trapped. Jake wasn't supposed to be part of this world, and his presence felt like an intrusion.

"I work here some weekends. I help with grounds maintenance," he explained. "You all right?"

"I'm fine," she lied, wanting him to go away and leave her alone. Her emotions were on a roller coaster, and she couldn't trust herself not to burst into tears in front of him.

"Did you . . ." Jake's voice caught a little. He started again, "Did you lose someone close to you?"

"No one. I mean, friend. Sort of . . ." she stumbled. Jake smiled a kind smile, but Dawn could tell he was confused by her response. She took a deep breath, forcing her racing heart to slow its pace. "It was the grandmother of a friend. A girl I knew."

"Knew?"

Dawn winced, hating her slip of the tongue. "It doesn't matter. They're both dead now."

"Listen, if you'd like to talk about it—"

"I don't! I don't want to even think about it. I just want to go home!"

Jake took a step backward, as if she'd shoved him. "Dawn, I'm sorry," he said softly.

Dawn felt tears brimming in her eyes. She was embarrassed by her outburst, but didn't know how to make him understand. She *had* to get away! She didn't want Jake to see her cry. She didn't want him feeling any sorrier for her than he already did. Without another word, she turned and jogged to the car. Once inside, she buried her face in her hands and sobbed.

* * * * *

"Come on, Dawn. It'll be fun." As they walked home from the bus stop on Monday,

Rhonda was urging Dawn to join her on the Hardy High Christmas Dance committee. "We can help with the decorations. It'll be a good way to meet some people—maybe even some cute guys."

"Don't you ever give up?"

Actually, helping out on the dance sounded like good idea to Dawn. It would give her something to think about besides the awful way she'd treated Jake on Saturday. She felt so embarrassed, she could hardly look at him in the hall. How was she ever going to apologize? He probably thought she was nuts.

"So I'll tell the head of the dance committee we'll be at the meeting," Rhonda said cheerfully. "This is going to be just like old times. Remember in eighth grade when we did stuff like this together?"

Dawn couldn't believe it had been that long since she'd participated in a school project with Rhonda. Yet, when she thought back, all she could recall were days and nights in the hospital or stuck in bed at home because her medications had made her so sick.

"I have lots to catch up on," she told Rhonda. "Maybe this is a good place to start."

On Friday, small group of kids gathered in the gym to plan the dance. Dawn recognized several cheerleaders, including Sharon Lewis, who constantly hung around Jake.

They voted to call the dance "The Snowflake Ball" and to decorate with giant, glittery snowflake cut-outs that would dangle from the gym ceiling. One of the girls announced, "My grandfather has an old-fashioned sleigh. We could put it in a corner and drape it with angel hair and fake snow. I think it would add atmosphere." They all agreed.

Dawn's brain was buzzing with suggestions, and she busily wrote them down for when they broke into smaller groups. As she was dragging her chair to the area where the decorations committee would meet, she noticed Sharon staring at her, as if she wanted to speak to her. Sucking up her breath, Dawn asked, "Is something wrong?"

"No, nothing," Sharon said quickly, but Dawn could tell something was definitely on the girl's mind.

"Are you sure?"

"Well, I do want to ask you something," Sharon confessed.

"What's that?" Dawn tried to look friendly, but somehow she just didn't trust Sharon.

Sharon glanced at the two cheerleaders who had walked up to stand next to her. "I hope you won't think this is too personal," Sharon began. "But I'm just dying of curiosity. Is that your real hair? Or is it a wig?"

Seven

CAUGHT off guard by the bluntness of Sharon's question, Dawn fingered her hair self-consciously.

"Your hair—is it real?" Sharon's face was the picture of innocence, but Dawn suspected her motives weren't innocent. "I was told you have cancer, and I thought people with cancer go bald, and so I was just wondering about your hair. If it's a wig, it looks real. If it isn't, then how come it didn't fall out?"

Dawn felt her cheeks flame red. But she held her head high, determined not to let Sharon get under her skin. "This is my 'real' hair. Sometimes chemotherapy makes hair fall out, but not always. Even if it does, the hair grows back."

"But you *do* have cancer?" Sharon queried.

The other two girls were watching closely, and Dawn wasn't sure how to answer. Saying yes would give Sharon some kind of perverse pleasure, but Dawn couldn't lie. She felt an urge to bolt for the door, but she didn't want to give Sharon the satisfaction. "I'm being treated for a form of leukemia," Dawn finally replied quietly. "I'm in remission and have been for well over a year."

"I was just curious," Sharon declared. "I've never known anyone with cancer before."

Dawn calmly headed toward her small group. She didn't look back, even when one of Sharon's friends said, "Honestly, Sharon, that was so totally rude of you."

"What's rude?" she heard Sharon ask innocently. "Can't a person ask a question around here?"

Dawn had lost her enthusiasm for the dance committee. She looked for Rhonda, but Rhonda was with a boy, staring raptly up at his face, hanging on his every word.

She scooped up her books and walked out the door. Once she was outside, her hands began to shake and her knees quivered. Hot tears rushed to her eyes. Now that Sharon knew about her cancer, all of

Hardy High would know. And she'd acted so hateful about it—as if cancer had been something Dawn had contracted to gain attention. Was this disease going to follow her everywhere for the rest of her life?

*　*　*　*　*

"Why'd you run off? Good grief, Dawn, you were there one minute and the next time I looked around, you were nowhere. Where'd you go?"

Dawn listened patiently on the phone while Rhonda fussed at her. "I remembered something I had to do," she replied.

"You could have told me."

"You were busy talking with some guy."

"You could have interrupted. *I* would have if I had to run off. I asked everybody where you'd gone, but no one knew anything. It was like you evaporated into thin air."

"Well, if you must know, I got blindsided by Sharon Lewis," Dawn confessed. Switching the receiver to her other ear, she quickly told Rhonda about her run-in with Sharon.

"What a cat. She's just jealous," Rhonda declared after hearing the story.

"Jealous? Of me? Get real! Why should she be?"

"Because she can't keep Jake Macka's undivided attention."

The thought of Jake reminded her of how she treated him at the cemetery. "That's hard to believe. Maybe Jake really likes her."

"Not by a long shot. The word is he's nobody's property. And that Sharon's making a pest of herself."

"How do you know these things?"

"I keep my ear to the ground."

The image of Rhonda down on all fours in a Hardy hallway with her ear plastered to the floor made Dawn giggle. "Don't get run over," she joked.

"And don't *you* run away every time someone like Sharon acts like an idiot."

"You don't understand," Dawn started.

"Then explain it to me."

Dawn knew that she couldn't. Sandy had understood completely. But Rhonda—well, Rhonda just wasn't Sandy.

"I mean, you can't get all bent out of shape whenever someone asks you about it." Rhonda made it sound as if Dawn should put off the past like one would take off a jacket.

"Rhonda, I actually died and got resuscitated. That sort of thing makes an impact on a person."

"You make it sound as if I should apologize for not having shared the experience. As if I missed out on something."

Rhonda's remark stabbed at Dawn. It made her feel much the same as Sharon's remarks had—like cancer was something she'd chosen in order to gain attention. She twisted the cord around her finger. "You missed a lot of pain. I wouldn't wish what I went through on my worst enemy. And I don't mean just having cancer. Do you know what it's like to have your best friend die?"

A long silence stretched between them. Dawn stared at the light from her bedside table lamp, reflecting off the wall. Beyond the puddle of light, shadows loomed. Rhonda broke the tension with, "I know what it's like to be afraid my best friend *would* die. I told you a long time ago that I was sorry about Sandy. I didn't know her, but I know how much you liked her."

Rhonda sounded hurt, which made Dawn feel bad for even bringing Sandy into the conversation. "Rhonda, this discussion is going no place. Why don't we just drop it?

I'm sorry I took off this afternoon without saying anything to you. I'm sorry I let Sharon get to me. I'll try not to let it happen again."

"Sure," Rhonda said. "Let's just forget the whole thing."

"So, when's the next committee meeting?"

"Monday. Does that mean you'll be back?"

"I'll be back." Dawn meant it, too. Sharon Lewis wasn't going to keep her away. And although she didn't like the idea of kids at Hardy knowing about her cancer, there wasn't anything she could do about it. It was a part of her life and nothing could make it go away.

* * * * *

By Thanksgiving week, plans for the dance were well underway, and Dawn and Rhonda had worked hard at cutting out hundreds of oversized snowflakes. Dawn stayed clear of Sharon, who let it be known that *she* was going to the dance with Jake. Dawn tried not to let it bother her. Jake was polite to her, acting as if the scene at the cemetery had never happened, yet he didn't attempt to call her or offer her rides to school.

"Don't be greedy," Rhonda told her. "You've got Brent coming to visit, and he seems much more interested in you than Jake does." Rhonda was right, of course. Dawn really was looking forward to Brent's visit, but still she couldn't control the funny way her heart beat every time she saw Jake in the halls.

The day before Thanksgiving, Dawn was in the kitchen helping her mother get a headstart on the holiday meal when the phone rang. Rob, home for the weekend, grabbed the receiver, then offered it to Dawn. "It's Katie and she says she needs to talk to you. Right now."

Surprised, Dawn took the phone. "Hi. What's up?"

"What are you doing Friday?" Katie's voice sounded excited.

"Hitting the mall bright and early with Rhonda to start Christmas shopping."

"Wrong," Katie replied. "You're coming with me to a special meeting of the hospital board. The administrator is making a big announcement, and he wants *you* to be there."

Eight

"**D**O I look all right? Is my hair messed up?" Dawn asked. She sat in the waiting area of the offices of Dr. Marcus Douglas, Executive Director of the Columbus hospital, where she'd spent so much of her last three years undergoing cancer treatments. Both Katie and her mother were with her.

"You look fine," Katie assured her. "Very pretty in that shade of green."

Dawn smoothed the skirt of her best dress. "Couldn't you find out what this is all about?"

Katie shook her head. "Every floor of the hospital is buzzing with some kind of theory, but no one knows anything definite."

"I'm sure it's something exciting," her mother added. Dawn couldn't imagine why she'd been summoned, and no amount of thinking or talking about it had turned up any possibilities. What could the hospital possibly want with her?

Just then the outer office door opened. A cameraman from a local TV news station stepped inside. Another man and two women, apparently reporters, followed. Dr. Douglas's secretary stepped forward, offering the guests a broad smile. "Welcome. I'll tell Dr. Douglas that all of you have arrived."

Moments later, the inner office door swung open and several distinguished looking men emerged. A round of introductions was made. The mayor was there, as well as several other politicians and hospital department heads. A man with a thick head of silver hair stepped up to her and held out his hand. "Hello, Dawn. Remember me? Franklin Chase. We met at Mrs. Hodges's funeral service. I'm her attorney and I'm handling her estate."

Dawn smiled and shook his hand. Dr. Douglas ushered the entire troop into his spacious office. Sunlight flooded the room through banks of windows along one side. At one end of the room, a table held a scaled-down model of the hospital. "This way," Dr. Douglas said, and he led the way to the model.

Dawn crowded around the table with the rest of the guests and studied the model, fascinated. It reminded her of an elaborate dollhouse, complete with miniature shrubs, lampposts, and parking lots. Then, off to one side of the model, she saw a sleek, modern-looking addition.

Dr. Douglas said, "It gives me great pleasure to announce that, thanks to the generosity of a benefactor, we will build the Marlee Hodges Cancer Treatment Center."

When the applause died down, Dawn could hear the TV camera whirl. A film of tears filled her eyes as emotion swept through her. So that was what Mrs. Hodges did with her money—she funded a much-needed treatment center in honor of her granddaughter. She had wanted so badly for Marlee to be cured, and though Marlee couldn't be cured, she had dedicated her wealth to a center for other cancer patients in the hope that they could.

Dawn felt her mother's hand slip into hers and squeeze.

"That's right," Mr. Chase, the attorney, added. "It was Amanda's wish that a special unit be built and dedicated to Marlee—a unit to treat even more kids with cancer."

"We definitely need the space," Dr. Douglas said. "This addition will give us a hundred more beds and several outpatient areas, as well as the newest, most technologically advanced equipment available to treat all forms of cancer in children."

"When will it be opened?" one of the reporters asked.

"We'll break ground on Easter weekend. The facility should take about eighteen months to complete."

Dawn hardly heard other questions. She kept gazing down at the scale model, thinking about Marlee. Marlee was such a puzzle. She had wanted so much to be part of the gang, yet she was so aloof—sometimes downright mean. She would probably have had something smart-aleck to say about the whole project. But Dawn knew that Marlee would have been very pleased; the smart remarks would have been her way of covering up her pleasure.

". . . Dawn Rochelle." At the sound of her name, Dawn startled. Mr. Chase was smiling and everyone was looking at her, including the man with the TV camera. "Dawn, I know you must be very curious as to why you were invited today."

"Yes, sir," she said, feeling her heartbeat

accelerate.

"It was Amanda Hodges's wish that you say a few words at the groundbreaking ceremony."

Dawn swallowed hard. Her? Say something with a bunch of important people watching? She was thinking of a way to get out of it when Mr. Chase added, "More than that, she also wanted you to help gather artifacts that will be placed in a special box. This box will be sealed and buried beside the building's cornerstone and will act as a kind of time capsule. It won't be opened for one hundred years."

An excited buzz went through the room. *A hundred years!* "But—but what will I put in it?"

"That will be left entirely to your discretion. Mrs. Hodges felt that when it is opened, people from the twenty-first century should have a glimpse of what was important to young cancer victims of today. She wanted you in charge of the project, Dawn, because of your kindness to Marlee and because of your own fight against leukemia."

Dawn was speechless. She didn't know what to think. For one thing, she certainly didn't feel qualified for such an important task—she didn't want to be responsible for selecting the items to be sealed inside some time capsule. And for another, she wanted to forget about her cancer, not be reminded of it. Frantically, she searched for a way to beg off. Then she saw her mother's face, glowing with pride. And Katie's, beaming with pleasure.

Dawn's objections died on her lips. Against her will, she heard herself say, "I'll do it." A flash went off in her face and several of the dignitaries stepped closer to her. Her head was swimming, her stomach tied in knots, but she managed a smile for the hard round eye of the TV camera.

Later, when the interviews were over and the pictures had all been taken, Dawn, her mother, and Katie retreated to the hospital coffee shop. "Oh, Dawn, I'm so proud of you!" her mother gushed.

"What will I say? What will I put in the time capsule?"

"You've got five months to think about it," Katie replied. "I'm sure you'll come up with something that's absolutely perfect."

Five months didn't seem long enough. Five *years* hardly seemed time enough.

"Mrs. Hodges wouldn't have selected you if she hadn't been confident of your ability,"

Dawn's mother said, scooting away from the table to get another cup of coffee.

Once she had walked to the coffee urn, Katie gazed at Dawn with a thoughtful expression. "What is it?" Dawn asked.

"I was just wondering if you ever gave any more thought to coming to the survivor support group I told you about."

Immediately, the sprawling tree with painted leaves along the corridor wall sprang to Dawn's mind. She glanced down at the half-empty cup of hot chocolate. "I've been busy."

"Perhaps meeting with some of these people, others like yourself, could give you some ideas for your project. I know for a fact that they're meeting three weeks from today—"

"Oh, I can't. That's the night of the big Christmas dance."

Katie looked disappointed, but brightened and asked, "Are you going with anyone special?"

"No. Rhonda and I volunteered to help the photographer. We have a sled all decorated with bells and artificial snow. We think it'll make a good backdrop for memory photos." She didn't add that Jake would have been the only boy she'd have wanted to go with, and he was taking Sharon.

"There's another meeting after New Year's," Katie suggested. "How about coming in January?"

"Maybe," Dawn said evasively. "I'll see. I mean, who knows what the New Year will bring?" But privately she knew why she wasn't giving a straight answer about attending the meetings. It was more than putting the past behind her. It was more than not wanting to hash over her past experiences with cancer, to dredge up old memories, and mourn the loss of old friends. Deep down, inside the deepest part of her heart, in spite of all the encouraging lab reports from her doctors, she wasn't a hundred percent sure she could call herself a survivor and a winner. With the ongoing tests and medications and the possibility of a relapse, she simply wasn't *sure*.

Nine

"**D**OESN'T everything look wonderful?" Dawn asked Rhonda as they stood together in the gym.

"It's hard to believe we were still running around hanging snowflakes and icicles at four this afternoon," Rhonda said with a chuckle. "Looking at you now, one would never know."

Surprised, Dawn looked down at herself. The dress she wore belonged to Katie. It was an incandescent green color that shimmered in the dim light. She'd worn her hair long, clipped back on one side with a green bow. With Rhonda standing next to her in a brilliant red dress, Dawn thought they complemented each other quite well.

The gym looked like a winter wonderland. At the main entrance, twin igloos stood on either side of the doorway. Tables, draped in white paper cloths and adorned with centerpieces of styrofoam snowmen, ringed the dance floor. The refreshment table was heaped with frosted Christmas cookies, chocolate brownies, bowls of red punch, and a large frosted gingerbread house. Lights had been lowered and colored candles glimmered from every table. A mirrored ball spun overhead, reflecting light on the dancers below.

"I wish I were with someone special," Rhonda said with a sigh.

"There's always next year," Dawn told her, determined not to let Rhonda start feeling sorry for herself because she didn't have a boyfriend. "Come on. The photographer's setting up his gear."

They wove their way around the tables where groups of kids sat, all decked out in satin, lace, and suits. Dawn forced herself not to look for Jake and Sharon. She didn't want to start feeling sorry for *herself* either.

The photographer gave them each a task. It was Dawn's responsibility to make certain that names and addresses were correct on cards of couples wanting photos of themselves, and that each card was filed to coincide with the correct frame of exposed film.

The sleigh looked picture-perfect with its leather bench seat and dark wood sides. The runners were decorated with tiny twinkling lights. It all looked so inviting that couples began to line up early for photographs. Dawn went to work and in no time was completely involved in her job.

She began to notice that many kids spoke to her by name, which surprised her. If she hadn't been so busy, she might have tried to figure it out, but the line for photos kept growing longer, and she found herself taking information as fast as she could write.

"Macka," a boy's voice said, above her shoulder. "Jake Macka. Hi, Dawn."

Dawn almost dropped the pencil. Jake wore a charcoal-gray suit and white shirt, set off by a red silk tie. He was smiling, but Dawn couldn't shake the image of the hurt expression she'd seen on his face at the cemetery.

"And Sharon Lewis," Sharon cooed from beside him. Sharon was dressed in pure white. Her hair sparkled with gold glitter but was stiff with hairspray. Her smile seemed forced and a little too perfect.

"Proofs will be mailed in two weeks," Dawn said as she wrote their names on the

cards. She handed them each a form to give
to the photographer and tried to look the
other way when they stood together in
front of the sleigh, arms around one
another for the camera.

Once the photo was taken, Jake and
Sharon stepped out of the bright lights.
Dawn resolved to ignore them and the
crazy way her heart was thudding. From
the corner of her eye, she saw Rhonda
approaching, carrying two cups of punch.
Somehow, when Rhonda was directly in
front of Sharon, she tripped and spilled
bright red liquid all over the bottom of
Sharon's dress.

"You idiot!" Sharon cried. "Look at what
you did!"

Rhonda gasped, set the cups down on the
registration table, and exclaimed, "Oh, good-
ness! Klutzy me. I'm *so* sorry." She hastily
tried to wipe off the dress with a blank
registration card.

"Get away from me," Sharon demanded,
shaking the soggy, stained hem of her dress
while glaring at Rhonda.

"You should wash it off right away," a
helpful bystander offered.

Sharon's face was the color of the punch
as she told Jake, "I'm going to try to undo

some of this damage. Wait for me at our table."

Dawn thought she sounded awfully bossy. "I'll hang around," Jake mumbled, and Dawn could have sworn he was attempting not to laugh out loud over the incident.

Rhonda fanned herself with the crumpled card as they all watched Sharon stalk off in a huff. "It was an accident," Rhonda said, her eyes all wide with innocence. "She didn't have to bite my head off."

Dawn knew she saw mischief in Rhonda's eyes and vowed to ask her later whether it was really an accident. Rhonda hauled Dawn out of the chair. "Take a break," she said. "Let me do this for a while." She held up the empty cup. "Maybe you'd better get us another drink. I'm positively parched."

Jake took Dawn's arm. "Come on, I'll walk you over to the refreshment table." They were skirting the edge of the dance floor when Jake stopped and said, "Let's dance."

"But I should get back."

"Rhonda's handling things. You can take time for one dance." He put his arms around her. "You look lovely tonight," he said. "And your hair looks so soft."

Dawn was glad she hadn't weighted it down with hairspray, so it still looked and felt soft and natural. "I'm really sorry about Sharon's dress," she said.

"I'm really sorry about Sharon."

"What do you mean?"

"Look, Dawn—I didn't *want* to come with her. I sort of . . ." Jake studied his toes. "Well, I sort of got tricked into it. I'm sorry."

Dawn took a deep breath and added, "And I'm really sorry about that afternoon at the cemetery, too."

"Ancient history," he said. "I forgot all about it.

He might have forgotten, but she hadn't. "I felt bad about the way I acted. I should have said something before now, but . . ." she let the sentence trail off, embarrassed and tongue-tied.

"I know about your friendship with Marlee."

"You do? How?"

"Rhonda." He gestured toward the photo table. "I cornered her and talked her into telling me."

"She never said a word to me." Dawn was shocked and a little angry, too. She knew what a gossip Rhonda could be. She hated knowing that Rhonda and Jake had discussed her and her private feelings.

"Please don't be mad at Rhonda," Jake said, as if sensing how she felt. "I would have rather have heard the story from you, but you were so upset at the funeral, I wasn't sure how to bring it up again."

Dawn's anger passed, but she wasn't sure what to say next. Jake must have sensed how she was feeling. He held her a little closer and said, "That was a pretty cool article about you in the newspaper. My mom said you were on TV, too, but I didn't see it."

"Well, it wasn't really about me. It was about the new cancer wing of the hospital."

"All I know is that Mom showed me the paper and there you were on the front page. Everyone in school saw it, too."

That explains why everyone acts like they know me, Dawn told herself. "Well I'd rather be in the paper because I did something great," Dawn told him. "Like kicking the field goal that put Hardy into the state play-offs."

"And missing the one that knocked us out of the championship," Jake added ruefully. "So what are you going to say at the ground-breaking ceremony?"

"I only wish I knew." Dawn noticed that the music had ended, but Jake was still holding her close. "I guess it'll be like a term paper—I'll figure it out the night before it's due."

He laughed, making her feel clever. "You have a busy Christmas break planned?" he asked.

She couldn't tell him about Brent coming, and didn't want to mention her upcoming appointment for a day-long visit to the clinic. "My brother's graduating early from Michigan State and my family's going up for the ceremony. How about you?"

"My family's going out to visit my grandparents. We'll be gone until New Year's Day."

She felt the keen edge of disappointment and told herself she was being silly. She couldn't wait to see Brent, couldn't wait to talk to him, spend time with him. So why did her emotions get so confused whenever she was with Jake? "I'd better get that punch before Rhonda sends out a search party," she said.

Jake walked her to the refreshment table, picked up a full cup, then walked her back to the table where Rhonda was happily writing names and flirting with every cute guy. "It's about time," said Rhonda. "I thought the two of you had been kidnapped." She gave Dawn a sly wink.

"We wanted to make sure we didn't trip and spill any on the way." Dawn turned to face Jake. "So, I guess I'll see you in January."

"I guess so." Jake caught her hand. "Have a great Christmas, Dawn."

"You too, Jake." Dawn watched him walk away, feeling a letdown she couldn't explain.

Ten

ROB Rochelle graduated from Michigan State University on the third Saturday in December in a ceremony held on the campus. Dawn sat with her parents and Katie in the stands, watching with awe and a sense of pride. The University Chancellor, dressed in the distinctive dark robe and colored hood that designated his academic position, led the dignified procession of professors, graduates, and baccalaureate students. Stately music played over the sound system while Dawn's gaze followed the long line of black graduation caps down the aisles to the front of the auditorium.

Because Rob had told them his approximate location, Dawn was able to pick him out in the steady stream of bobbing flat black hats and dangling green-and-white tassels. A lump rose to her throat as she watched him. *Rob, my big brother.* Without him and his gift of bone marrow, she would certainly be dead.

Hi, Squirt. His pet name rang in her ears. His was the first face she remembered seeing when the doctors had resuscitated her. He had looked ghastly pale and terrified. She would remember the look always, because she'd never seen him look that scared before. She hoped she never had to see such an expression on his face again.

Her mother reached over and squeezed Dawn's hand as Rob's name was called. Dawn held her breath as he crossed the stage, took the offered diploma, shook the Chancellor's hand, and walked back to his seat. From the corner of her eye, she saw her mother dabbing her eyes with a tissue and her father smiling broadly.

She knew that she had a long way to go before she would get a college diploma. *Besides, you don't even know what you want to study*, she reminded herself. A shadow of doubt flickered across her mind. *Will I even be alive?* Would Rob's bone marrow continue to function? Was her battle with cancer truly over? Dawn refused to speculate. Anything could happen in the next few years.

"Wasn't it fabulous?" Katie asked when the ceremony was complete. They were waiting in the crowded lobby for Rob to find them.

"I can't believe my baby boy's all grown up." Dawn's mother sighed.

"Mom, he's hardly a baby."

"You'll both always be my babies," she insisted.

Dawn watched the crowds surging around them. Suddenly, she caught sight of a small blond woman posing for photographs nearby. She jabbed Katie in the ribs. "That's her! There's Darcy Collin, the girl Rob used to be engaged to."

Katie's eyes narrowed as she studied Darcy. "She sure is pretty," Katie said. "No wonder Rob fell in love with her."

"Looks aren't everything," Dawn reminded her, wanting to find a way to make her feel better. "She's not half as nice as you are."

"I remember when Rob and Darcy broke their engagement. You were in isolation, fighting for your life when it happened. He was awfully depressed."

"He told me how you talked to him. And you've helped him get over her totally," Dawn replied with a confident smile. "You have nothing to worry about."

"I really care for Rob." Katie cast a long glance toward Darcy who was talking excitedly with several people. "But when I see how pretty she is . . ."

Dawn immediately thought about Sharon. "Why do we always feel inferior whenever a prettier girl comes around a guy we like?"

Katie arched her brow. "Is there somebody in your life you've never mentioned to me?"

"Not exactly. I mean there's a guy at school who makes me crazy sometimes. But then Brent's coming next week and I know I like him. And—and—" she threw up her hands in frustration. "I don't know what to think. How can I like two guys at the same time?"

"It isn't hard," Katie said with a laugh. "You're lucky you have choices. Tell me about the boy at school."

Dawn wished she'd never brought it up. The crowds around them were beginning to thin out, and she didn't want her parents overhearing her. She saw that they were in a conversation with several other parents. Hesitantly, she said, "His name's Jake, and I've known him since fifth grade. I had a crush on him. You know—elementary school stuff. But I've been through so much these past few years, he could never understand. Brent does, though, because he went through it with Sandy, and he was a counselor at camp. I like the comfortable way he makes me feel."

"Have you ever given Jake a chance to understand?"

"I don't know how to talk to him about it. It's like I have two separate lives. One of me has been through all this stuff with cancer. The other me is just a regular person who's almost sixteen and trying to get on with her life. It's hard being in two worlds at once. I . . . I'm not sure I want to involve Jake in the cancer world."

"Maybe that's a choice he should make."

Dawn was uncomfortable with the discussion. It was difficult to put her doubts and feelings into words. "It probably won't matter anyway. I think he might like somebody else."

Katie gave Dawn a compassionate look. "You know, before I met Rob, I was dating a guy pretty seriously."

"You were?"

"Tony and I were a steady item. I even thought about marrying him."

"Do you still like him?"

"I'll always *like* him." She put her hand on Dawn's arm. "He's a wonderful friend. But I don't love him."

Rob had thought he was in love with Darcy, but their love hadn't worked out. Dawn found it all very confusing. "How do you know whether you're in love with somebody or not?"

"It sounds corny, but you just *know*." Katie offered a smile. "Love isn't *only* body chemistry, you know. It's a lot of other things."

"So what should I look for?"

"I'm hardly an expert," Katie said with a laugh. "But I do know that love is patient and trusting; it doesn't hold a grudge when somebody hurts you, and most of all, it endures. The Bible says that love is greater than even faith and hope. That sounds pretty big to me."

"I wonder if I'll ever find it. And if I do, I wonder if I'll recognize it."

"You have plenty of other things to do first," Katie said. "You have school to finish and a career to plan. I think you even have to get your driver's license first."

Dawn burst out laughing. "I guess you're right. I don't have to settle on anyone right now." She glanced toward Darcy, who was walking off with a good-looking dark haired man. "And you don't have a thing to worry about. You're the one Rob thinks about, talks about, probably dreams about."

"I'd better be," Katie said with a grin. "I know he's the one I think about."

* * * * *

Dawn fidgeted with the curtain at the living room window and peered out into the cold darkness. She'd been anticipating Brent's arrival all day. He'd called around suppertime to say he was about an hour away. She glanced at the mantel clock and wondered why time seemed to be moving so slowly.

Behind her, the Christmas tree twinkled and glittered with decorations. A few packages lay underneath, including the one with the thick, cable-knit sweater she'd bought for Brent. The scent of bayberry and evergreen hung in the room and Christmas music played softly on the CD player.

She was more nervous than she'd ever imagined she'd be. She hadn't seen Brent since June, when camp ended. They had stood together on a cabin porch, watching the rain pouring down, and he'd taken her in his arms and kissed her. She could still recall the soft feel of his lips on hers.

A bright beam of headlights swept across Dawn's face, startling her. Out the window, she saw a car in her driveway. Her heart thudded in renewed anticipation—Brent Chandler had arrived.

Eleven

DAWN waited for Brent to ring the doorbell. She didn't want to seem too anxious, after all. When she opened the door, the icy December air rushed inside, but she hardly felt it. Brent was dressed in jeans and a leather jacket. His blond hair spilled low on his forehead and his slow, easy grin warmed her. For a moment they stood looking at one another.

"Don't I even get a hug?" Brent drawled.

She threw herself into his arms. "I'm so glad you're here!" She pulled him into the coziness of the living room. "Are you all right? Did you have a good trip? Do you want a soda?"

"Whoa," he said with a laugh. "One thing at a time. "Yes, yes, and not right now." He held her at arm's length. "You sure look pretty, Dawn."

In spite of herself, she blushed. It was as if no time had passed since they'd last seen one another. At that moment, her parents, who'd stayed out of the way and in the kitchen, came into the room. Dawn made a round of introductions.

"We've heard a lot about you," her father said, making Dawn feel self-conscious. She didn't want Brent thinking that all she'd done was babble about him.

"We're glad to have you stay for a few days," her mother added. "Your sister meant a great deal to Dawn, and we will always cherish her memory."

"Thank you," Brent murmured.

Dawn wished that they hadn't mentioned Sandy, especially when she saw a look of sadness cross Brent's face. "Let me show you where you'll be staying," she said hastily.

"Can I help you bring your things in?" her dad asked.

"I'll get them. There's not much—a duffle bag and a big wrapped box." Brent winked at Dawn. "The box is for under your tree."

Eventually, she was able to lead the way down to the basement to the rec room. Just off the rec room her dad had transformed an area into a guest bedroom and bath. She pointed to a plate of cookies on a small table next to the bed. "I baked these myself, in case you get hungry in the middle of the night."

He sampled one of them. "They're delicious."

"How's college?" she asked.

"If it weren't for having to go to classes and studying, I'd like it just fine."

She laughed. "Isn't that what college is all about?" She remembered what he'd told her last summer. "Are you still planning on being a doctor?"

Brent gave a little shrug. "Pre-med looks like it's going to be a lot tougher than I thought. I'm not sure I'm cut out for it."

For some reason, Dawn felt disappointed. She had wanted him to be a doctor and to treat kids with cancer. "What else, then?"

"It's too soon to tell. There are so many courses freshmen have to take that it's hard to think about a major this early on." He gazed down at her. "How's high school?"

"Not all it's cracked up to be. Hardy's so big, a person gets lost."

"No excitement at all?"

She puckered her brow. "One thing." She told him about the new cancer wing dedication and her role in it.

"I'm impressed."

"Don't be. I'll probably embarrass myself by going blank when I have to stand up there and give my speech. Not to mention coming up with something important for the time capsule."

He took a bite out of another cookie. "So what's the game plan for my three-day visit? You going to show me around Columbus?"

"I've got lots of places to take you. Don't worry, you won't get bored."

"I never figured I would be." His blue eyes glowed, and he reached out and ran his thumb along her cheek. A shiver of delight shot up her spine. "Not for a single minute."

* * * * *

The next day Brent drove around Columbus, with Dawn pointing out special sights. In the late afternoon, they stopped by the largest mall, crammed with Christmas shoppers hurrying from store to store. A gigantic tree stood near the entrance of the food court. They stood and watched a tiny train run its course around the tree.

They skirted a long line of small kids

waiting to sit on Santa's lap and miraculously found an empty table. "You hold our place and I'll get us some drinks," Brent told Dawn.

She was watching clusters of people scurry past when, to her surprise, Rhonda called to her. "Help!" Rhonda flopped dramatically onto a chair. "My mother's holding me prisoner and won't let me go until we've bought something for every relative on her list." She straightened. "What are you doing here? I thought you'd be off alone with Brent." She looked around. "Where is he, anyway? I want to see this hunk with my own eyes."

Dawn thought Rhonda was acting overly dramatic. "He went to get us something to drink."

"Is it great having a guy drive all the way from college to visit you? What's it like having him *sleeping* under your roof?"

"Slow down." Dawn glanced up. "Why don't you ask him for yourself? He's right behind you."

"Ask me what?" Brent wanted to know.

Rhonda fairly shot out of the chair, almost knocking Brent backward. "Oh— sorry! I . . . I didn't see you. Hi. I'm Dawn's best friend."

Rhonda appeared so flustered, it was hard for Dawn to keep from laughing. "This is Rhonda. I've mentioned her to you in my letters."

Brent grinned. "You take my drink and I'll get another."

"No, no," Rhonda said. "I—um—was just leaving." Behind Brent's back, she made a face like a panting puppy, again causing Dawn to almost burst out laughing. All at once, Rhonda jumped up and down and started waving. "Yoo-hoo! Sharon," she yelled across the crowded food court. "Why look, Dawn, it's Sharon Lewis."

Dawn turned in time to see Sharon and a group of her friends. Sharon glanced coldly from Rhonda, then to Dawn, then to Brent. Her mouth almost dropped open. Dawn groaned and buried her face in her hands. Rhonda was obviously trying to get Sharon to notice Dawn and Brent together.

Sharon tossed her head and marched off into the crowd. "Gee, maybe she didn't see us," Rhonda said with a silly grin. "Oops—my mom's signaling to me. Got to run." She waved good-bye and made her way toward the Christmas tree.

"What was that all about?" Brent looked puzzled.

Bemused, Dawn shook her head. "Believe me, Rhonda defies explanation."

He took a long swig from his cup. "So, she's your best friend?"

"I've known her since the fifth grade and she's pretty much always been there for me." She stopped herself short, realizing who she was talking to and why he might be asking. *Sandy had been her best friend.* She didn't want Brent to think her disloyal. "Not like Sandy, though. Look, all this noise is giving me a headache. Why don't we head for home?" Dawn grabbed her cup and purse and stood up.

Slowly, Brent rose beside her. "Sure," he said. "This place is bugging me too."

He was quiet all during supper. She wasn't sure how to break through his silence. She wasn't even sure if anything was wrong. But she felt anxious, as if they were somehow out of sync.

Dawn slept fitfully and woke very early. She saw a stream of light beneath her door and heard someone moving downstairs. Slipping on her velour robe, she padded down the staircase. In the living room, the Christmas tree lights had been turned on and Brent was sitting on the sofa, staring moodily at the tall evergreen. "Is something wrong?" she asked, coming into the room.

"I didn't mean to wake anyone," he said guiltily.

She sat beside him on the couch. "What's wrong, Brent? Please tell me."

He turned his face and she saw his sadness instantly. He said, "I can't stop thinking about my sister."

Twelve

DAWN longed to make Brent's hurt go away. "I'm sorry if what Rhonda said at the mall about being my best friend upset you."

He shook his head. "That's not it. I mean, I know how you felt about Sandy, and I'd never expect you to not have other friends. And I don't want you to think that I think about my dead sister all the time, because I don't." He shrugged his shoulders and gazed back at the tree. "Maybe it's just 'cause it's Christmas."

"How do you mean?"

He didn't explain right away, but when he did, his voice sounded thick and soft. "Our family's always been big on Christmas. When we were younger, we never had a lot in the way of presents 'cause we never had a lot of money. But we kids never noticed. Mama and Daddy put on a fine celebration. All the kids would sneak into my room on Christmas Eve and we'd talk half the night about what Santa might be bringing us.

"I had a flashlight, and we'd make a tent under the covers and talk about how rich we'd be when we grew up, and how we'd take turns coming to visit each other different Christmases in our mansions." Dawn saw a soft smile cross Brent's face. "Sandy always said she'd have a big white house with a red roof and a big green lawn with a lake in the back. She said she'd have enough bedrooms so that we'd never have to share like we did in our house. And that she'd even build a little house out back for Mama and Daddy to live in when they got really old."

In her mind's eye, Dawn could see Sandy's dream perfectly. It caused a lump to form in her throat, knowing that her friend's dreams could never come true. "She used to talk to me about getting married," Dawn offered. "She said she wanted a big family."

Brent nodded, making the reflection from the tree lights bounce off his blond hair. "That first Christmas . . . after Sandy was gone . . . well, that was the hardest one. We went through the motions. We tried to do all the things we usually did for the holidays, but without her, it just wasn't the same."

Dawn's heart was breaking for him. She knew exactly how he felt. She had cried off and on for months after Sandy died. It hadn't mattered where she was or what she was doing. If something brought the memory of her friend back to her, her eyes would fill with tears. "I wish she were here," she said softly.

Brent stared at the tree and continued. "That first Christmas, late in the afternoon, Daddy and I went out to the cemetery where she's buried. It was really cold. The sky was all gray and the wind kept whipping through the tree branches. There were some snow flurries. Daddy and I just stood there looking down at her headstone. I kept thinking that it wasn't right for the dates of her birth and her death to be so close together. Thirteen years. That's all she had." Brent linked his fingers together and hunched forward on the sofa. "It was the only time I ever saw my dad cry."

The lump in Dawn's throat had grown impossibly large and her eyes swam with tears. "I wish I knew what to say . . ."

He smiled at her wistfully. "There's nothing anyone can say. I had a sister and she died too young." His expression changed. "I really don't sit around thinking about it all the time. I don't want you to think I'm morbid or anything. It's just that it's Christmas, and this is the hardest time of the year for me. I wish I could talk to her one more time, you know?"

Dawn sniffed. "I know what you mean about wanting to talk to her. I'd give just about anything to hear her voice." Brent nodded. All at once, Dawn was struck with an idea. "Wait right here," she told him, scooting off the couch. "I'll be right back."

She hurried up the stairs to her room and rifled through her closet shelf until she found what she was looking for. Quickly, she descended to the living room and returned to the sofa, thrusting a shoebox into Brent's hands. "I want you to have this."

His brow puckered. "You said my Christmas gift was under the tree."

"It's not your Christmas present." She took a deep breath. "It's—it's some of Sandy's things. The stuff she left to me."

He shook his head vigorously and thrust the box onto her lap. "I couldn't. She wanted you to have this stuff."

"I know she gave it to me," Dawn said. "But I think you should take it now. It's a way for you to hold on to her."

Slowly, he took the old shoebox and lifted the lid. The reflection of the tree lights twinkled on the glitter from the popcorn necklace Sandy had made during her stay in the hospital. "Looks pretty bedraggled," Brent said with a half-smile as he held it up.

"It's a work of art," Dawn countered, returning his smile.

His hands played over the combs and hair ribbons. "She sure liked fixing her hair. I remember how she cried when all of it fell out from the chemo." He held up a handful of the colorful ribbons, gently brought them to his nose, and sniffed. "They still smell like her hair," he said in wonderment.

Dawn wasn't so sure. After all, they'd been shut inside the box for years and stored in her attic until this past summer. But if the items smelled that way to him, she didn't want to take away from the comfort they might provide.

"You sure you want me to take these?" he asked. "She gave them to you."

She felt her heart clutch, and for a moment she almost backed down. But seeing his fascination with the items and understanding how much they meant to him gave her courage. "I'll just hold on to a few things for memory's sake. I want you to take the rest. You're her brother and someday you can show them to your kids and tell them all about their special aunt."

Dawn saw that his eyes looked misty. She glanced quickly down into the box and rummaged through it. Finally, she settled on one set of combs, the popcorn necklace, and the page from the Bible imprinted with Ecclesiastes 3.

He closed the lid and laid the shoebox next to him on the sofa. He raised his hand and stroked Dawn's hair, all the while gazing into her eyes. "Thank you, Dawn."

"We both loved her," Dawn said. "It's only right we should share her."

He pulled her into his arms and they clung to each other with a soft and quiet tenderness. Dawn had the feeling that Sandy was somehow in the room with them, holding them in arms big enough for both.

* * * * *

She'd opened the gift from Brent the night before he left, and she was crazy about the book bag and sweatshirt bearing the emblem from his college, West Virginia Tech. Once he had left for home, she moped around, but by Christmas morning, she woke up excited about the holiday ahead of her.

All the time they were opening gifts that morning, Rob seemed distracted. He left early to pick up Katie and bring her back for Christmas dinner. "We're going to open our presents to each other together," he explained, grabbing his keys and darting out the door.

When Katie and Rob came back, they came in through the kitchen, where Dawn was helping her mom and dad prepare Christmas dinner. "Just in time to peel potatoes," Mrs. Rochelle announced.

Dawn took one look at Katie and knew something was going on. Katie's face looked radiant. Dawn looked to her brother, who appeared equally happy. "Okay, you guys, what's up? You both look like you're ready to bust." Her parents stopped their work and came over to investigate.

Katie glanced at Rob and he nodded. She held out her hand. "Rob asked me to marry him, and I said yes," Katie announced. From her finger, a diamond glittered.

Thirteen

"**E**NGAGED! Yikes! You mean your brother went and got engaged? Does that mean he's definitely not going to wait for me?" Rhonda asked. Rhonda and Dawn were sitting in Dawn's bedroom the day after Christmas, checking over her gifts, when Dawn broke the big news.

"I know it's hard to accept, Rhonda, but you'll just have to. You're a big girl now." Dawn kept a straight face as she spoke. Rhonda's hopeless crush on Dawn's older brother had long been a standing joke between them.

"I'm wounded." Rhonda flopped dramatically on the bed. "But if it can't be me, then I'm glad it's Katie."

"Me too." Dawn shifted to the bed and sat cross-legged. The news had really lifted her spirits, especially since she'd been missing

Sandy so much. The terrible sadness of the one was offset by the joy of the other. Marriage meant a new beginning, and Dawn was thrilled about the engagement.

"The wedding was all we talked about yesterday. Me and Mom and Katie spent the afternoon making plans and lists. It's going to be so much fun, because this time things are just right."

"In other words, you mean Darcy, the snob, isn't his fianceé."

"That's not nice," Dawn scolded.

"You never liked Darcy and you know it."

"She just wasn't the one for Rob." Dawn also knew that Darcy had never cared much for her. Nothing had ever been said outright, but deep down, Dawn had always suspected that Rob had broken his engagement to Darcy because she couldn't accept Dawn's illness.

"So when's the wedding?" Rhonda wanted to know.

"At the end of June. And they're holding the reception in the Conservatory gardens."

"Oh, that's *soooo* romantic."

"Everything's romantic to you."

"I guess you'll be in the wedding."

"Katie's asked me to be the Maid of Honor." Dawn beamed a smile.

"June's six months away. It seems like *forever*," Rhonda lamented.

"Katie and Mom say there are a million things to do. Katie has to shop for a gown and the bridesmaids' dresses. She and Rob have to make out a guest list, reserve the church, hire a caterer, decide where to go on their honeymoon, and find an apartment."

"A honeymoon. How romantic." Rhonda was beginning to sound like a broken record. "I *will* be invited, won't I?" She sat up and leaned into Dawn's face.

"I doubt they'll want you on their honeymoon."

"Very funny." Rhonda scooted backward. "I mean, I want to come to the wedding."

"How could we leave you off the list? Impossible."

"Good. I have to plan what to wear. Who knows if a cute guy will show up or not?"

Rhonda would never change. "Good thing we've given you plenty of time."

"Have you heard anything from Brent?"

"He called to wish me a merry Christmas." She'd already told Rhonda about Brent's visit, leaving out the part about their discussion of Sandy. Their conversations about Sandy had been too personal, too private. Why was it so easy for her to discuss Sandy with Brent and yet she felt unable to even mention her name to Jake? She knew it went deeper than the fact that Brent was Sandy's brother. It was as if she were protecting Jake from the realities of her cancer. As if the truth would somehow drive him away.

"I'm actually looking forward to school starting." Rhonda changed the subject. "We get to practice driving during Driver's Ed. In another two months, I'll get my license."

"Lucky you." Dawn was excited about school starting again too, but not because of Driver's Ed. Dawn couldn't wait to see Jake again. She wondered if he thought about her half as much as she thought of him.

* * * * *

School had been in session for a week before Dawn saw Jake long enough to talk to him. She was on her way to Driver's Ed and he was on his way to the gym. "How was your holiday?" she asked.

"All right. And yours?"

"Fine." The day was blustery and cold, even though the sun was shining. She hugged her coat closer. "My brother got engaged," she added, then immediately felt dumb. What could Jake possibly care? He didn't even know Rob.

"But *you're* still unattached, aren't you?"

She glanced at him quickly and saw that he was teasing her.

"Of course I am." She felt her cheeks flush and hoped he'd think the redness was due to the wind. "Doesn't soccer season start soon?"

"The first of March. But the team's practicing every day after school. I heard they're holding cheerleading try-outs in March. And I remember that you were a great cheerleader. Are you going to try out?"

Dawn hadn't even considered it. She figured that since Sharon was the captain, she'd never have a chance. Plus, she still had clinic visits to work into her schedule. "Not this year. I'm not sure I'm one of the squad's favorite people."

Jake stopped and looked at her with surprise. "You're wrong. A lot of kids in this school admire you. Since that article came out in the paper, plenty of them have asked about you."

Terrific, she thought darkly. She was a celebrity because she had cancer. "I can think of other ways I'd rather be remembered."

"People are curious. They want to know more about you."

Dawn groaned. It was the *last* thing she wanted. "Well, do me a favor and tell them it's not worth knowing about. It was horrible and now it's over—end of story." Nervously, she peeked at her watch. "I've got to run or I'll be late to class."

As she hurried off, she realized that she'd probably made a bad impression on Jake. *What does it matter?* she thought. After all, he had only been making polite conversation on his way to the gym. He'd always think of her as "that girl who had cancer."

* * * * *

"Don't you just *love* it?" Katie asked as she led Dawn from room to room in the empty apartment.

February sunlight poured through double banks of windows in the living room of the old Victorian house that had been converted to apartments. The oak floors needed polishing and the walls needed painting, but Dawn could see the potential in the spacious rooms with high ceilings and carved doors. "I think it's super. When will you move in?"

"Rob and I figure that I can move in next month and together we can fix it up, buy some furniture, then he can move in with me after the wedding."

Dawn poked her head into one of the rooms. An old-fashioned bathtub with claw feet stood in the middle of the floor, and a pedestal sink stood beside it. "There's no shower."

Katie laughed. "We're lucky to have working plumbing. This place is over a hundred years old. But we both think it's so neat."

Since graduating, Rob had been working for a local engineering firm, and Katie still had her job at the hospital. It seemed that all they ever talked about was their future. Dawn walked through the bathroom into a smaller area that led to the room Katie had said was the master bedroom. "What's this space for? It's too big for a closet."

"That's the nursery. In Victorian times, it often adjoined the main bedroom so the baby could be tended to in the middle of the night."

"Cool. Does this mean you and Rob are

going to have a baby right away?"

Katie laughed. "No way! We plan to wait awhile."

"Don't wait too long. Who knows, maybe I'll get married and have a baby right away. Then mine and yours will be close to the same age. Think about it—I'd be an aunt and a mother all at once." Dawn was joking, but even as she was speaking, she saw Katie's expression change from one of smiling to one of concern. "What did I say?" Dawn asked. "What's wrong? Are you thinking I'll never find a guy who'll want to marry me?"

"It's nothing like that," Katie said. She took Dawn's hand sympathetically. "I thought you knew."

"Knew what?"

"Honey, with all the chemo and radiation you've had, it's highly unlikely you'll ever be able to have children of your own."

Fourteen

"IS what Katie told me the truth, Dr. Sinclair? Will I never be able to have a baby?" Dawn sat in her doctor's office, her hands gripping the arms of her chair. She'd finished her latest round of bloodwork that afternoon in the outpatient clinic. Then she'd gone directly to his office to ask him the question that burned in her mind.

The doctor studied her with a kind face. His hair was gray at the temples, and the lines around his eyes looked deeper than when she'd first become his patient, almost four years before. "Some of your earlier chemo and radiation protocols will have an effect on the reproduction process," he said.

She felt a sinking sensation in the pit of her stomach. "Then it's true."

"More than likely. It's possible that you will be able to have children, but it still might not be advisable."

Tears sprang instantly to Dawn's eyes. She glanced quickly away. She'd never thought much about having children. She'd simply figured it was something she'd do eventually—if she got married. If she lived. "Why didn't anyone tell me?"

"Frankly, it never came up. We were never attempting to hide it from you, but you were so sick that it hardly seemed important." He sighed and leaned back in his swivel chair.

"Later on, when it becomes necessary, there will be tests you can take to determine your fertility."

"But to never have a family!" she blurted.

"Dawn, hundreds of couples never have children and still have a very satisfying married life. And there are other options— like adoption, for instance."

She almost put her hands over her ears. She didn't want to hear about "options." In fact, she didn't even want to discuss it any further. Here she was, not quite sixteen, and already she was being forced to look into a future that was upside-down and backward. Dawn stood up. "It's later than I thought. My mom will be looking for me."

"Don't run off. I think you should talk

about this. We have trained professionals on staff who can help you come to terms with it."

She knew what he was suggesting. She should see one of the hospital's counselors. Well, she didn't want to. She didn't want to face prodding and questioning about her innermost feelings with a stranger. "I've got to go." She left his office as fast as she could.

In the car, Dawn stared gloomily out the window. Her mother interrupted her dark mood. "Rhonda called to say that she passed her driver's test and wanted to go out for pizza tonight. I told her you were getting bloodwork done and that you'd call her when you got home. Would you like to go off with her tonight? She sure sounded eager."

Dawn had forgotten that this was the day Rhonda was going for her driver's license. How could she have? Rhonda had talked about nothing else for days. "I'll call her, but yes, I'd like to go."

"Honey, what's wrong?" Her mother's voice sounded concerned. "Did everything go all right at the hospital?"

"Everything went fine."

"But I can tell something's bothering you." In spite of telling herself not to cry,

Dawn felt a tear trickle down her cheek. Alarmed, her mother pulled over into a grocery store parking lot and turned off the engine. "What's wrong? Tell me."

Haltingly, Dawn revealed what she'd learned. She'd been carrying it around inside of her for weeks, and the discussion with Dr. Sinclair hadn't helped at all. "I feel like I've been robbed," she told her mother. "As if someone stole something from me and I can't get it back."

Her mother said nothing.

"You knew, didn't you?" Dawn asked. "You and Daddy knew all along. Why did you keep it a secret? Why didn't you say something to me?" She couldn't hide the sense of betrayal in her voice.

"You were thirteen, Dawn, and fighting for your life. It hardly seemed relevant. All that mattered was that you lived. If you'd had a kind of cancer that meant you'd lose an arm or a leg in order to save your life, we'd certainly have agreed. We knew that the medications they were giving you were potent enough to damage or possibly destroy your reproductive system, but at the time, it didn't matter."

"Maybe it would have mattered to me!"

"Think back. You were a scared little girl,

still collecting teddy bears. How could you have made such a choice at that time?"

Rationally, she knew her mother was right. They'd made the only choices they could. She wasn't angry with her parents. Or her doctors. She was simply *angry* over what she hadn't had any choice about. It was the same kind of anger she'd felt when Sandy had died. And Marlee. Helpless, frustrated anger—anger at life because it just wasn't fair.

Her mother took a deep breath and touched Dawn's shoulder. "I'm so sorry, honey. I'd give anything if it had been me instead of you."

"You would have traded places with me?"

"In a heartbeat. You're my daughter and I love you very much."

Dawn felt a softening inside her. She saw that her mother was hurting, and for the first time, she realized how much her illness had affected her whole family. Yet they had survived it. All of them. And for the most part, they were happy. Her parents were together, Rob was getting married, and she was alive. "If some guy ever wants to marry me, what do I tell him?"

"The truth. If he loves you, it won't matter." Dawn couldn't imagine it not mattering. "Listen," her mother added, "when I was pregnant with Rob, all my doctor could tell me was that the baby was big and had a strong heartbeat. Now, they can tell if it's a boy or a girl, if there are genetic defects—why, doctors can even operate on a fetus while it's still in its mother's womb.

"Think about it, Dawn. Who knows what kind of technology they'll have available by the time you're completely grown and ready to get married and have a baby! Don't consider childbirth for you a closed book. You've got to think positively. You've got to think about what you do have, instead of what you don't."

Hesitantly, Dawn nodded. She knew her mother was right.

"All right," she said softly. "I won't think about it any more."

"You have a wonderful future ahead of you. You're alive. That's worth everything."

Her mother started the car, and together they drove the rest of the way home in thoughtful silence.

* * * * *

Hardy High's soccer season started on a

chilly, sunny Friday afternoon in March. Jake Macka scored a hat trick and three goals, and Hardy won four to one. Dawn cheered from the stands and when the game was over, Jake called her over to the side of the field.

"I'll wait for you," Rhonda said, juggling her car keys.

Rhonda's mother had allowed her to use her car that day so that she and Dawn could stay for the game.

Jake was all smiles as Dawn approached. "You played a great game," she told him.

"Help me celebrate."

"Me?"

He made a production of looking around. "I don't see anybody else. You were cheering for me, weren't you?"

Her heart began to hammer. "How can I help you celebrate?"

"Go to a movie with me tomorrow night."

Words seemed trapped in her throat. "All right," she managed.

He grinned. "I'll call you tomorrow."

She watched him jog off to rejoin his team on the way to the locker room. *Jake had asked her out!*

"What's up?" Rhonda asked, coming up beside her.

"Jake asked me for a date."

Rhonda's eyes grew large. "Wow! Lucky you."

Dawn couldn't stop smiling. "Yeah. Lucky me." And in her heart, she meant it.

Fifteen

D AWN scarcely saw the movie on Saturday night. She only remembered the complete sense of contentment she felt sitting in the dark theater, sharing a jumbo bag of buttered popcorn with Jake. Sometimes their hands brushed as they went for the bag together, and once, during an especially tense part of the movie, he put his arm around her. When the film was over, he took her hand and led her up the aisle and out into the damp, chilly March night. "How about a soda?" he asked. "All that popcorn made me thirsty."

Since she didn't want the evening to end, she agreed quickly. He drove her to one of the popular hangouts, and she didn't mind one bit when heads turned as they entered. From the corner of her eye she saw Sharon, but she was with another guy, so Dawn figured that whatever had been going on between her and Jake was long since over.

Jake showed Dawn to a booth toward the back and slid in beside her. After the waitress took their order, he smiled and asked, "What did you think of the movie?"

"It was good." She hoped he didn't ask any details, since she couldn't remember any. "How's soccer going?"

"Great. We play twice next week. Will you be there?"

"I wouldn't miss it." An awkward silence fell and she racked her brain for something witty to say. Why did her brain turn to mush every time she was with Jake? He probably thought she was a real dope.

"I guess that big ceremony's coming up soon." He broke the strained silence. "The one I read about."

"Next month—the weekend after Easter. I'm glad Easter comes late this year. It gives me more time."

"Do you know what you're going to put in the time capsule yet?"

For a moment, Dawn wasn't sure she wanted to be discussing this with him. After all, it did have to do with her cancer. But she quickly decided to pretend that the capsule wasn't connected with cancer at all.

She would pretend that it was more just a place for preserving fragments of the past for posterity. "I've been thinking hard about it. It's a big responsibility. What do you think people would want to know about us a hundred years from now?"

"How about a story on Hardy's great soccer team?" He grinned impishly.

"People may not even play sports in a hundred years. We may all be video game freaks and never leave the front of our television sets. We'll all have fat rear ends from sitting all the time and fat thumbs from pressing game buttons."

He grimaced at her suggestion. "Let's hope not."

"Do you have any suggestions? I'm willing to hear them."

"How about some music?"

"Explain."

"You could make a cassette of today's top hits. That way kids in the twenty-first century can hear what kids from today thought was cool."

She liked his idea. "They'll probably think our stuff is weird. I know when I hear the music my parents liked, I can't believe it."

"You should try listening to what your grandparents liked. Talk about weird!"

They laughed together. "I could use some help making the cassette," she said. "Would you help me?"

"Sure." His brown eyes reminded her of melted pools of dark, rich chocolate. "Do you have a tape deck that can make dubs? Maybe I could come over and bring some blank tapes. How about next Saturday?"

"That's fine with me." If he'd suggested they start at two in the morning, it would have been fine with her.

He drove her home, and at the door, she secretly hoped he would kiss her. He looked as if he might, and her heart thudded in anticipation. But at the last moment, he backed off, said goodnight, and left.

She went to her room and relived every moment of her date with him as she undressed for bed. Impulsively, she opened her desk drawer and fumbled for her diary. She had two. The first was full of her thoughts and impressions from when she was first diagnosed with cancer. Absently, she thumbed through it, rereading the details of her ordeal, her times at camp, her memories of Sandy, her relapse and readmission to the hospital for her bone marrow transplant.

She saw the parts Rob had entered on

her behalf, when she'd been too sick to write anything. She reread the entries about Marlee and Brent, and Marlee's funeral. It didn't seem right to put something about Jake and her new life in it. She tossed aside the older diary and opened the newer one.

March 18

It's strange to write about Jake. Who would have thought that he would ever come back into my life? Even though so much has happened to me in the past years, even though I've met so many new guys—Mike, Greg, Brent—Jake is still the one. I don't know why, but ever since fifth grade, I've liked him. It's the brown eyes, I think. None of the others had brown eyes. Whenever Jake looks at me, I feel like melting. Go figure!

I wonder where Brent fits in all of this? I still care about him. Every time he calls, it's like we've never been apart. We pick up right where we left off the last time. How can that be? How can I like Brent so much and still feel the way I do about Jake?

I guess Katie's right. Sixteen (almost!) is too young to decide anything about a boy. Now if only I can get the message through to my heart . . .

* * * * *

Dawn woke up Monday morning with a scratchy, raw throat. Her mother insisted she forget about school and spend the day in bed. She didn't want to. She wanted to go to school to see Jake, but there was no changing her mother's mind.

By that night, Dawn was running a fever and felt weak and achy all over. She was too sick to even talk to Rhonda when she called. All through the night, Dawn tossed and turned, and by the next morning she had a hacking cough and a tightness in her chest that made it difficult to breathe.

She staggered to the bathroom, convinced that a warm shower would make her feel better. But when she shed her nightgown and looked into the mirror, her heart wedged in her throat. A fine red rash covered her arms and torso. She started shaking so violently that she had to grab ahold of the sink for support.

Dawn knew what the rash meant. She'd

119

read too many pamphlets and booklets following her transplant. A rash was often the very first sign of bone marrow rejection.

Sixteen

"**D**ON'T panic," Dr. Sinclair told Dawn as he listened to her chest through his stethoscope in the Emergency Room.

"I *am* panicking." Dawn's voice sounded raspy. She wadded the sheet covering her with her fists. On the other side of the door, her parents and Rob waited for Dr. Sinclair to finish his checkup. She'd seen how scared they looked when she showed them the rash along her arms. They'd left for the hospital immediately, and Dr. Sinclair had met them in the emergency room. "Am I rejecting? Please tell me the truth, Dr. Sinclair."

"I don't like what I'm hearing. I want some X-rays, but I'm sure you've got pneumonia."

He had avoided answering her question. "Am I rejecting?"

"It's too soon to tell." He straightened. "I'm checking you in."

Tears swam in her eyes. "I don't want to be back in the hospital. Everything's been going so well until now."

"No choice, Dawn. As you know, the immune-suppressants make you more vulnerable to infections. You need to be here for your own safety. I'm going to increase your suppressant medications and start antibiotics and oxygen. I want you here where I can keep a close eye on you." He gently squeezed her shoulder. "You'll have to go into isolation, too. I'm sorry. There's no other alternative. I'll go tell your family and start the paperwork to move you upstairs."

She tried to hold back her tears. Breathing was already difficult enough without crying. *Why? Why is this happening to me?* For a while, things had been going so smoothly that she'd almost forgotten about her health. She was doing well in school, she'd had a date with Jake—she suddenly remembered another reason to feel bad—her birthday was coming up. She'd made plans to go take the test for her learner's permit. Now, she'd be spending her birthday in the hospital. And if she *had* rejected the bone marrow, there was no hope left for her at all.

* * * * *

The oxygen tent, with its fine mist of oxygen mixed with decongestants, did help Dawn's breathing. From inside the plastic enclosure, everything outside looked fuzzy to her, as if people were moving around in a fog. IV lines, inserted in the back of her hand, regulated a controlled flow of potent medications into her bloodstream. The pain medication she was taking made her feel spacey, but it did help her deal with the pain left over from her most recent ordeal— a spinal tap, which would tell the doctors whether there was cancer in her system.

The only visitors allowed were her immediate family, and they had to wear masks and green paper gowns and head coverings. Germs—any kind of germs—were her enemies. Because Katie was a nurse, and because Rob had called her from the emergency room, she and Rob came in together. Dawn reached out for Rob. He took her hand and held it tightly. "You're going to lick this thing," he said. His voice was upbeat, but she saw genuine fear in his eyes.

"Dr. Sinclair said my bone marrow needs a little extra help. He said that the pneumonia is taxing it to the max, but I know it's going to hang in there for me." She wanted to assure him that he wasn't responsible for what was happening to her. The bone marrow—*his* marrow—wasn't at fault for her troubles.

"It had better hang in there. But if you need more, just say the word."

"Katie, I'm sorry we can't go shopping for bridesmaid dresses this weekend, the way we planned."

"That's not important. All that matters is you getting well." Katie's blue eyes looked serious above her mask. "I've asked my supervisor to assign me to your case, and I'm going to move some things into the nurses' quarters so I can be close-by."

Knowing that Katie was going to take care of her made Dawn feel secure. "Just like you did before," she said. "Will you call Rhonda for me? Will you tell her I'll call just as soon as I can?"

"Of course I will. Is there anyone else?"

She thought of Jake and Brent. As much as she hated Jake knowing, she realized Rhonda would tell him. As for Brent, she didn't want him called yet. There was nothing he could do but worry. "I'll tell my other friends," she told Rob and Katie. "I don't want them to freak out over this. I'm sure it's only a temporary setback."

"Whatever you want," Katie said. What Dawn wanted was to be well, to be back home, to have this nightmare behind her.

"You get some rest," Rob added. "Just concentrate all your strength on recovering. You've come too far to be sidelined now."

Over the next week, Dawn practiced the imaging techniques she'd been taught. She imagined the pneumonia virus being tracked down by her white blood cells—her non-leukemic white blood cells—and zapped into oblivion. Focusing on the destruction of the virus *did* make her feel better emotionally.

Cards began to arrive for her. Several from Rhonda and girls in her classes, and one from Jake. He'd even scribbled a note inside. It said: *"We won both matches, but I only scored one goal. See what happens when you're not in the stands for me to impress? Get well, Jake."* She traced his signature with her fingertips and wished with all her heart that things could be different, that she could be normal and healthy.

At the end of the week, Dr. Sinclair took down the oxygen tent but insisted she remain in isolation. Her condition was still too vulnerable to ordinary germs, and her bone marrow needed all the help it could get. Katie saw to it that she got a phone in her room. It had to be specially sterilized, but Dawn loved being able to connect with the outside world again. She called Rhonda. "When can I come see you?" her friend asked.

"Dr. Sinclair says that I can have outside visitors anytime, but they'll have to garb up."

"You mean dress in those funny little paper outfits?"

"Yes. I know they're hardly a fashion statement."

"I'm glad you still have your sense of humor." Rhonda went on to fill Dawn in on all the latest from school, but all the news only depressed her. She felt like a runner who'd been yanked out of a race and now had to play catch-up. Life was passing her by, and there was nothing she could do about it. A wave of pity swept through her, and after Rhonda hung up, she had a long cry. She was tired, so very tired, of standing on the outside, looking in.

When the phone rang later that night, she was still feeling low. She didn't feel like talking to anyone, but she answered it because she couldn't think of any other way to make it stop ringing. Her caller was Brent.

"I called your house to say hi, and your mom told me how to reach you. Why didn't you let me know what was going on?"

His voice sounded hurt and she was sorry. "I wanted to tell you myself. Once I was better."

"Are you better?"

"I think so. But I sure don't look so hot." Her face and lower limbs were retaining fluid, so she looked plump and puffy.

"You getting out soon?"

"Dr. Sinclair won't say. I hope so. I'm so far behind in school and all."

"You sound really down."

"I am." There was no use hiding the truth from Brent. If anyone understood, he did. "I'm just sick of the whole mess."

"Now, you're not giving up, are you?"

"No," she said, but without much conviction.

" 'Cause one of the reasons I called was to tell you that the committee in charge of that dedication ceremony has invited my whole family to come."

Dawn's grip tightened on the receiver. Up until that moment, she'd forgotten all about the upcoming ceremony.

"You're all coming?"

"I didn't think Daddy would want to at first. He's always held a grudge against the doctors and the hospital for not making Sandy well. But he surprised me and said he wanted all of us to go." She heard him pause. "So, I reckon the bottom line is that you have to get well and get out of the hospital, Dawn. We're all coming to that ceremony, and we want to hear your speech."

Seventeen

THE next afternoon Dawn looked up and saw Jake standing at her doorway. For a moment, her breath caught and she could scarcely breathe. He looked handsome, even with a green mask on.

He looked healthy—and so out of place. "Hi," he said. "Up for a visitor?"

No! her mind screamed. "I—I—sure. Come in," she replied hesitantly.

He entered the room cautiously, eyeing the equipment and hospital paraphernalia. "I—um—I've never been in a hospital before," he confessed.

"I don't recommend it," she said. In her mind she was thinking, *Welcome to my world, Jake.* She felt awkward and self-conscious and wished she were wearing one of her cute nightshirts instead of the hospital gown that tied behind her neck.

"Sorry, I have to wear this thing." She apologized for the mask that covered her mouth.

"Rhonda said you had pneumonia."

Dawn was a tiny bit relieved. At least pneumonia was something that could happen to anybody. Maybe she wouldn't have to make a big deal about her cancer. "It's clearing up," she said.

"I brought you something." He pulled a small shopping bag from behind his back and grinned sheepishly. The tips of his ears were bright red, and Dawn could tell he was self-conscious, unsure of himself.

"You brought me a present?"

"Only one's a present. The other is something we talked about doing together."

Mystified, she opened the bag and took out a small, cuddly white teddy bear. She rubbed her cheek against the soft fur.

"He's adorable. Thanks."

"I remembered that you liked teddy bears."

"I had a whole collection once. And I still have Mr. Ruggers."

"Mr. Ruggers?"

"He's my favorite. Left over from my crib days."

Jake laughed. "I had a stuffed football and a blanket that I dragged around."

Imagining Jake as a toddler made her go all soft inside. She thought back to when they'd been in fifth grade and how crazy she'd been about him. And then she'd gotten leukemia. Five years was a long time to have a crush on somebody. "What else did you bring me?" She poked inside the bag.

"It's that cassette of today's top hits for the time capsule. I hope you don't mind that I taped the songs without you. I—um—didn't know if you'd still want to do it. If you don't want to use it, it's okay. I only wanted to help out."

She had completely forgotten their discussion about it! She cleared her throat. "I appreciate it. Really. It's just that I don't know if I'll be attending that ceremony." She fiddled with the cassette, wishing he'd drop the subject.

"Why not?"

"I'm not sure how all this is going to turn out, Jake. I don't know if I'll be released by then or not." Telling him felt awkward and painful. It was an admission that her hospitalization was more complicated than pneumonia.

"Oh." He sounded shocked. "I didn't think . . . I mean, I just figured you'd be fine."

"It's no big deal. Relapses happen."

"But you will be all right again, won't you?"

"Probably so. I'm used to this, you know."

"Are you saying it can happen again after this?"

"Maybe. No one knows." She hated having to tell him the truth. All of a sudden, she wished he'd never come to visit her.

"The truth is I'm getting sick and tired of it all."

"You sound as if you're giving up."

Dawn felt a flare of irritation. "You don't understand what my life is like! You're healthy and you can come and go as you please. There's nothing holding you back. I *hate* going through this over and over. Sick. Well. Relapse. Sick. Well. Sick." She ticked her hospitalizations off on her fingers. "Don't you understand that every time it happens it gets harder and harder to keep on smiling?" Dawn felt tears filling her eyes. Quickly she glanced away.

"How could I know what you've been through? You never talk to me about it. You just tell me everything is 'fine.' You make me feel like I should apologize for being well," Jake said.

"That's dumb!"

"No, it's not." Jake sounded angry. "What's

dumb is you giving up. What's dumb is you acting like this setback is the end of the world. What's dumb is me standing here arguing with someone who won't even *try*."

"Well, at least you're free to *leave*," she snapped.

"Is that what you want?"

"You bet. I didn't ask you to come, and I'm not asking you to stay."

"Then fine. I'm leaving."

She watched him turn on his heel and stalk out of the room. For a moment she sat in stunned silence while waves of pain washed over her. The pain wasn't the same as the pain from chemo and needles and cancer. She was accustomed to that kind of hurt. This was a deeper kind of pain. This was the pain of feeling her heart breaking in half as Jake Macka walked out of her life.

Eighteen

"HI, Little Lady," a man's voice said from Dawn's doorway. "They told me down at the nurses' station that you were a patient. And they told me that today was an especially good day to visit. The word down at the nurses' station is that it's your birthday—your sixteenth, they say."

"Dr. Ben! What are you doing here?" Dawn struggled to sit up in bed. She hadn't seen Dr. Ben, director of the cancer camp, since the previous summer, when she'd been a counselor in training.

"Occasionally, I work here." He came alongside her bed and took her hand. "I just admitted a newly diagnosed patient from my private practice. She's twelve and a cute kid. Reminds me a little of you."

"Poor kid."

He laughed. "Poor *me!* I can't imagine

having another Dawn playing pranks on me."

She couldn't help smiling. "We got you pretty good, didn't we?"

"You and that Chandler girl first. Then you and Mike. And I can't forget Marlee Hodges either."

"I didn't have anything to do with that one."

"She was in your cabin." He dragged a chair over and sat down. "How are you feeling?"

"Better." That was partly true anyway. She was feeling physically better. But inside, she still hurt over Jake. And she couldn't make that hurt go away, no matter how hard she tried.

Dr. Ben studied her thoughtfully, then asked, "You're feeling a little blue, aren't you?"

His perception surprised her. "You're a hard person to fool."

"Want to talk about it?"

His white lab coat and necktie made him look too professional. She was used to seeing him in a T-shirt, shorts, and his favorite baseball cap. Then she noticed that his ballpoint pen had left a glob of ink on the pocket of his lab coat. Somehow, the stain made her feel more comfortable, less formal. "No one understands what my life is like, Dr. Ben. The only people who really understood—Sandy, even Marlee—are dead." Dawn picked at her blanket. "When I got sick this time, when I saw that rash, I freaked. I—I thought I was rejecting, and I knew I couldn't take it anymore. I'm so tired of this hospital. I want to be well. You know—normal, like other sixteen-year-olds."

Dawn sighed. She had tried to forget that this was her birthday. She and Rhonda had made great plans—shopping, a movie, and dinner, and knowing Rhonda, she would probably work in some boy-watching, too. Now the whole thing had been postponed indefinitely. She looked at Dr. Ben's kind face. "I just want to have a normal life," she said wistfully.

"Hmmm. I think I know what you mean," he said. "Do you know why I decided to be a pediatric oncologist, Dawn?"

She shook her head. "I can't understand why anyone would want to be. How can you watch kids die?"

"I had an older brother who died from leukemia. That was back in the 60s, when the diagnosis was usually an automatic death sentence."

"I didn't know . . ." She thought of Rob and wondered how she would have felt if this had happened to him instead of her.

"Peter was athletic and smart. I was puny and bookish. Watching him die, seeing how it affected my parents' lives, really influenced me. I thought that by becoming a doctor, I might be able to help kids like him."

"That's the way Sandy's brother feels," Dawn said softly.

"It's hard to stand by and watch people you love suffer," he continued. "You feel like there's something you should be doing to make a difference. You watch people you love die, and you feel guilty because you're still alive."

Dawn felt her cheeks redden. Hadn't she'd felt *exactly* that way? Hadn't she wondered why she'd been left alive while her friends had died?

"Sometimes it's hard to be left behind," she replied.

"We doctors wish we could cure everyone. Every time we lose a patient, it hurts, because it reminds us that we're only human too. The good news is that because of research, because of all kinds of new drugs, some forms of leukemia have a

137

seventy percent cure rate. In Peter's day, it was less than thirty percent."

"You mean we're human guinea pigs."

"When traditional therapies fail, when there's no other choice, yes. People are given experimental drugs and techniques. Your bone marrow transplant was highly experimental in the 70s. Today, such procedures are far more common. And because of immune suppressant drug research, we have successful transplants between non-blood-relative donors. There's the National Marrow Donor Registry to help make genetic matches between organ donors and recipients. If a person wants to be a marrow donor, all he has to do is take a simple blood test. The results are programmed into the data banks, and doctors can search for possible matches for their most critical patients. Sometimes we get lucky and find a match. Believe me, it's a gift of life to someone who needs it."

His eyes looked owlish behind large-framed glasses. "Did you know that we have a survivor support group here at the hospital?"

"Katie told me about it." Dawn didn't want to admit that she'd resisted attending.

"Believe it or not, now that the cure

rate's gone up in cancer victims, so have problems of adjustment."

"What do you mean?"

He placed his hand on her shoulder. "It's sort of like soldiers attempting to readjust to civilian life after the trauma of war. That adjustment can be tough. Sometimes it helps to talk to others who've had similar experiences, so the adjustment can be made more easily."

"I just don't know where I fit in, Dr. Ben. I'm tired of having cancer. I want it to be over forever."

"You should check out the group. You're good at helping people. I remember the first time I saw you at cancer camp. You were with the little Chandler girl, and the two of you made quite a team. You befriended Greg and Mike—no small feat. Mike was a very angry, bitter kid about having his leg amputated. But somehow you two cut through his armor and drew him out."

"That was mostly Sandy's doing."

"It was the two of you. He came back to camp even after Sandy was gone. And you were the person Marlee wanted with her during her hospitalization. No, Dawn." His eyes sparkled mischievously behind his thick glasses. "Like it or not, you have a gift for working with people. You have the gift of caring. You'd better watch out. You may end up becoming a doctor too."

"What's this? Are we adding a new medical recruit to our staff?"

Dawn and Dr. Ben looked up to see Dr. Sinclair in the doorway. He waved some papers at her. "These are the results of your latest bloodwork. It looks perfect. So you can take the worried look off your face and call your mother to come get you. I'm kicking you out, Dawn Rochelle."

Nineteen

A balmy April breeze ruffled Dawn's hair as she sat on the stage, facing an audience seated in folding chairs on the hospital lawn. At the podium, the mayor was giving his speech, but Dawn scarcely heard him. She would be next, and her mouth felt cotton-dry. Other dignitaries sat on the stage with her. A photographer and a TV cameraman skirted the audience of a hundred, taking pictures and a videotape of the event.

On a table beside the podium Dawn saw the metal box that was to be the time capsule. Her fingers brushed the edge of the bag by her feet, holding the treasures for the capsule. Propped next to the capsule was the gold-plated shovel the mayor would use to scoop out the first spadeful of dirt, marking the groundbreaking for the new cancer wing.

In the distance, she saw green, manicured grounds and patches of daffodils waving in the soft spring breeze. Overhead, the sky sparkled blue, freshly washed by an April shower. Dawn's eyes skimmed the audience. Her parents, Rob, Katie, and Rhonda were sitting in the front row.

Right before spring break, Dawn had decided to fill out a schedule card for the next school year. But when she'd shown it to Rhonda, her friend looked aghast. "Why all the science and math courses? I *hate* science and math. We'll never have any classes together if you stick to this schedule!"

"I need them for college," Dawn explained with determination. "I'm thinking about going into medicine."

"You want to be a *doctor?*"

"Don't look so shocked. I know more than most first-year med students already. Heck, I figure I'm halfway to a degree by now."

"All right—I won't complain," Rhonda told her with a grin. "I'm just glad you're making plans again."

From the front row, Rhonda fluttered her fingertips and made a face at Dawn up on the stage. Dawn quickly glanced away. She didn't want to have a giggle fit, and if anyone could start one in her, it was Rhonda.

Her gaze fell on Jake, who sat in the very end seat in the last row. Dawn had almost fallen over when he'd asked if he could come for the ceremony, especially after the harsh words they'd had at the hospital.

"I'm sure it'll be fine," she'd told him stiffly over the phone.

"Good," he'd replied. "I'll see you there."

On the other side of the makeshift aisle, she saw the Chandlers. It had been hard talking to them right before the ceremony began. She hadn't seen them since the time they'd picked Sandy up from camp, when she and Sandy were thirteen. Mr. Chandler looked older, more weathered, and uncomfortable in his suit. Mrs. Chandler was slim and blond, and Dawn could see traces of Sandy in her mother's features.

Brent caught her eye. She rolled her eyes, a subtle protest to the mayor's long-winded speech, and Brent grinned. Dawn kept remembering the night before, when he showed up at her door, saying, "My family's holed up in a hotel downtown, but I've managed to escape. Can I come in?"

Laughing, Dawn threw her arms around him. "You should have brought them along."

"Are you nuts? I've been plotting my escape all afternoon."

They went down to the rec room and settled on the sofa. He wanted to hear every word about her hospital stay. She wanted to know all about college. Haltingly, he told her about a girl he was dating. She was glad for him, and said so.

Then he took her hand and said, "I'll never forget Christmas. The talk we had that night about my sister, the things you gave me . . . I took them to the campus with me and sometimes I take them out and hold them. It's like she's there in the room with me."

Dawn touched Brent's cheek. "Sandy's the glue that holds us together," she said, knowing it was true.

"I care about you," Brent said.

"And I feel the same way about you," she replied.

"Will you be a camp counselor next summer?" he asked.

"I made up my mind at Marlee's funeral that I would. And you?"

"I'm not sure." He looked long and deep into her eyes, put his arms around her and hugged her tightly. "I'll never forget you, Dawn."

"You'd better not."

He kissed her lightly and left. She went to bed feeling as if a chapter in her life had closed.

Now, looking into Brent's face, she knew the past was truly over.

". . . speaker, Miss Dawn Rochelle."

Dawn jumped at the sound of her name. The audience burst into applause. She took a deep breath, picked up the bag and walked to the front of the stage.

"It's a real honor to be up here," she began, glad her voice didn't crack. "Marlee and her grandmother meant a lot to me. I'm just sorry they can't be here with us today."

The audience murmured and Dawn forged ahead. "I got leukemia when I was thirteen. In the hospital and at camp, I met others who also had cancer. We became great friends. Forever friends." She saw Mr. and Mrs. Chandler take each other's hand.

"Many of them are gone now." Dawn held her head high. "But I'm still here. I'm still alive. And according to my doctors, many of the kids who come to this new cancer clinic to be treated will be alive twenty—even thirty—years from now.

"So I brought some things to put in this

capsule in the hope that when it's opened a hundred years from now, people will see them and ask, 'What was cancer? Did people really die from it?'"

Dawn saw her mother dab her eyes with a tissue. "These things will remind them that people did die, but they will never be forgotten." She opened the bag, reached in, and pulled out the newspaper from the day the new cancer wing was announced. "I thought they might want to read the news of the day, to see what was important to us."

Dawn noticed people in the audience nodding and smiling, and she continued. "And a friend of mine made a cassette of today's top hits, so kids from tomorrow can talk about our weird taste in music." A ripple of laughter went through the listeners.

"I'm also including some items entrusted to me by my two most special friends. From Marlee Hodges, a letter she wrote to me before she died. She knew she was dying, but she was no longer afraid. And she asked that we carry on for her. And from Sandy Chandler, a page from her Bible. The verse says: 'For everything there is a season . . . A time to live and a time to die.'" She looked up. "Nobody gets to pick their time to die, but living every day to the max is something we all get to do." Dawn took a deep breath to control the slight quiver that had crept into her voice.

"And I'm putting in my personal diary. In this diary, I wrote down all my thoughts and feelings about having cancer. And I wrote about watching my friends die, one by one." Dawn saw Rob nod with approval, and Katie wipe her cheek.

"Also, I'm burying Mr. Ruggers." She pulled out her old, rumpled teddy bear, with its one missing eye and bald spots. "He's been loved a lot, but I figure it's time that he had a long rest. Maybe some kid from the future will love him as much as I have." She gently placed the tattered bear into the box on top of the other things.

Her hand trembled as she removed the final item from the sack. "And last of all, I want to put in this box of ashes from the bonfire at cancer camp. We're supposed to bring the ashes back each year and sprinkle them onto the new fire, for the kids who can't come back, for the ones who've died. But I think they belong in this capsule to remind people that we all eventually turn to ashes, even if we don't have cancer." She picked up the now-empty bag and said into the microphone, "So that's about it. I want to say thank you for giving me this privilege. Thank you for helping us win this war."

People began to applaud, then to stand. She felt a lump clog her throat and tears mist her eyes. She gazed out at the audience, at the faces of the people she loved most in the world—her family, her friends, Sandy's family. All at once, through the din of the applause, she heard birds singing in the trees. Their song, new every morning, gave her a special sense of peace.

Twenty

THE remainder of the ceremony moved quickly. Dr. Douglas dug up a spadeful of dirt while cameras clicked. The time capsule box was taken away to be permanently sealed. It would be buried by the construction crew, who would start the excavation on the new building Monday morning. Then it was announced that refreshments were being served in the hospital lobby.

People swarmed around Dawn as she made her way into the hospital. Reporters shoved mikes into her face and asked for more comments. Once inside the lobby, she grabbed a cup of punch, but before she could take a sip, the Chandlers came up to her.

"Thank you for remembering our little girl," Mr. Chandler said.

"She was my best friend. I'll never forget her," Dawn replied.

Mrs. Chandler opened her purse. "I found this in a drawer and had a copy made for you." She handed Dawn a photograph. It was a snapshot of Sandy and Dawn at camp that Mr. Chandler had taken. The two of them had their arms around each other and were mugging for the camera. Their balding heads were covered with scarves, and Sandy held Mr. Ruggers under her arm.

Dawn stared at the picture, trying to fight the tears that were springing to her eyes. How young she and Sandy looked at thirteen! And how very happy—in spite of having cancer. "Thank you," she said. "I'll treasure this always." She slipped it into the purse that was hanging from her shoulder.

Rhonda rushed over, all smiles. "Your speech was *so* fab! I mean it, Dawn, I had a huge lump in my throat the whole time." Rhonda's gaze darted to one side. "Oops. Cute guy alert to our left. I'd better go check this out."

Dawn shook her head as she watched Rhonda scurry away. Her parents and Rob and Katie came up and hugged her. "When are we going bridesmaid's dress shopping?" Dawn asked Katie.

"Is that all you can think of at a time

like this?" Katie asked, grinning.

Dawn smiled back. "Yep! Let's go next weekend! Promise?"

Rob slugged her arm playfully. "I'm proud of you, Squirt. How'd you get to be such a good speechmaker?"

"It's in my blood," she joked, and they all groaned.

Finally, the crowd thinned, the reporters and cameramen left, and the dignitaries vanished into expensive cars. Dawn leaned against a wall, sapped by the crazy tangle of emotions that had been pouring through her. "Tired?" a voice asked.

She turned and faced Jake. She'd forgotten he was there.

"Yes, but it's a good tired."

He took her empty punch cup and placed it on a table. "Come on. I'll take you home." She glanced around for her parents.

"I asked your mom and dad if I could drive you," Jake explained. "They said it would be all right."

"That was nice of you."

"Hey, I'm a nice guy." He grinned. "Besides, I'm not about to let some hot-shot college guy ace me out."

"Brent? He's just a friend. I didn't know you cared."

"I care, all right," Jake said. He took a deep breath. "And I'm sorry I yelled at you in the hospital. That was no way to treat a friend."

"I guess I needed it," she said, feeling her mouth go dry. "Pity parties aren't my usual style."

"Well after hearing your speech today, I'm able to see some things through your eyes. I can't imagine watching my friends die the way you have. And I can't imagine how you deal with knowing it could happen to you too."

Dawn shrugged. "I really try not to dwell on that part, Jake. No matter how down I feel, I try to concentrate on living, not dying."

"Well, even though I'm sorry for the way I said it, I'm not entirely sorry for what I said. You do make me feel like an outsider sometimes, as if I don't belong in the cancer part of your life."

Dawn experienced a pang of guilt. Is that what she had been doing to him? "I never meant to make you feel like an outcast because you're healthy. It's just so hard trying to live in two worlds."

"When we were in seventh grade and the teacher told the class that you had leukemia, I felt really rotten. It scared me. I felt sorry for you, but I didn't know how to tell you."

"That's part of the problem," Dawn said. "People like me, who are sick or hurting, don't want pity. We just want to be accepted."

"I stopped feeling pity for you that day at the school carnival. I wanted you to notice me. That's why I volunteered to go into the dunk tank."

If he only knew how much she'd noticed him! "I couldn't believe it when you showed up here at Hardy this year."

"Me either. But I'm glad we moved back to Columbus. And I'm glad I got to know you again. I wasn't sure how to treat you at first. I wasn't sure you'd want to be around some guy you'd known since the fifth grade."

"I felt the same way," she said. "I'd changed so much and been through so much while you were gone. I didn't want you to feel as if you owed me anything just because you'd known me for a long time."

His voice became low and soft. "I always liked you, Dawn. And I have a feeling I always will."

Her heart skipped a beat, and she felt so

giddy and lightweight that she thought she might float off the floor. "I always liked you too."

For a minute they stood staring into one another's eyes. Finally, Jake said, "We'd better get going."

They had only walked a few steps when Dawn stopped. "I just thought of something I need to do before I leave," she said. "Will you come with me?"

"Lead the way."

She crossed to the elevator and punched the button for the top floor. She and Jake rode up in silence and when the doors slid open, they stepped off into a deserted section of offices.

"Where are we?" Jake wanted to know.

"Follow me." She led the way past a bank of windows, down the dimly lit hall, and stopped in front of the mural of the Tree of Life. Its long branches and green leaves seemed alive.

"Cool," Jake commented. "Whose names are on the leaves?"

"Survivors. They're people who've beaten the odds against cancer. They're part of a support group that I'm going to join."

He studied the tree carefully. "Where's your name?"

Dawn took a deep breath. "It's not there yet."

He glanced at her quickly. "Why not?"

"No good reason. Come on, pick a leaf for me."

Jake pointed to a leaf near the top of its furthermost branches. Dawn dug in her purse until she found a felt-tip pen. She stepped forward, took a deep breath, and wrote her name in bold black strokes. "There. What do you think?"

"I think it looks terrific."

She stepped away from the wall and looked up at him. Jake reached out and gently raised her chin with his forefinger and gazed into her eyes. "You know that old saying 'This is the first day of the rest of your life'? I always thought it was kind of corny, but now it seems to fit. What do you think, Dawn? Is that true?"

She felt her heart pound at jackhammer speed. *The rest of her life!* No one ever knew what the future held—even kids who never got leukemia. Perhaps her cancer would be permanently cured. Maybe she'd go to medical school and become a doctor and help others, like Dr. Ben had done. Maybe she'd get married. And maybe she'd be able to have children someday in spite of the grim prognosis. Maybe life was for living. She said, "Yes, Jake Macka. It's true."

He brushed his lips lightly across hers, then tucked her under his arm, against his side. "Then let's go live it."

She hooked her arm around his waist, and together they walked down the deserted hallway toward the light streaming through the windows.

Claude
offers yc
profita

Hindsight + Foresight = Success

In *Stock Market Primer* he gives you the basic facts you need to know in buying stocks and bonds, the background and foundation for intelligent investment—the first part of the formula, *hindsight*. It also provides you with guidelines for arriving at the right investment decisions in the future—*proper foresight*. His approach to investment emphasizes low-risk, high-reward situations—and his own unusual success has stemmed from his ability to uncover many stocks which have multiplied ten-, twenty-, and thirty-fold. Most important, his philosophy is one that discourages an investor from selling good stocks too soon.

Mr. Rosenberg spent 15 years with the investment firm of J. Barth & Co. in San Francisco (now a part of Dean Witter & Co., Inc.)—the last eight years in the capacity of General Partner. His Research Department there, which became the largest in the western part of the United States, was one of the most respected in the world. In 1970, Mr. Rosenberg founded Rosenberg Capital Management, which has become one of the country's most successful investment advisory organziations. His stock market comments and ideas are widely read and quoted in this country and abroad.

Stock Market Primer

Claude N. Rosenberg, Jr.

REVISED AND UPDATED EDITION

WARNER BOOKS

A Warner Communications Company

Contents

Contents

From Writer to Reader

This book was originally published in 1962 at the "blue chip" price of $12.50. At that time—and every year since—I have heard from countless people who have told me that they consider *Stock Market Primer* the most understandable and worthwhile book they have ever read on the subject of stocks and the market. I hope they are right—and I hope that you, too, find it useful.

The *Primer* is now fully revised. What encourages me most is that the revision entailed almost no change in basic approach. What seemed basic and important eighteen years ago still holds today. This successful aging gives me confidence that the substance is there and that the reader can gain lasting benefit from its use.

The stock market! One very learned man I know calls it "the greatest dice game in the world." "What," he asks, "makes Exxon worth two points less—or over $400 million less—today than it was yesterday? Has the company really changed by almost a half billion dollars in one day? And then, what makes the same company worth three points more—or over $600 million more—next week?"

Indeed, if you approach the market on this basis, it does appear to be a senior Las Vegas. Yet there is far more to the stock market than these day-to-day fluctuations. From the average investor's viewpoint, it is of much greater importance to know what makes Standard Oil or Zenith Radio or XYZ Electronics Company worth double or triple or quadruple or ten times its value five or ten years ago.

The answer to this is relatively simple. After all, hindsight is *always* 20–20! The important thing is that we can learn from our hindsight.

Anyone connected with investment securities will agree that it is a very *in*exact science. Like many other pursuits, it involves a certain amount of luck. But luck is often enhanced by placing yourself in the right strategic position. Hence, you *can* improve your probabilities. You can *prepare* yourself to take better advantage of luck than the next person and achieve far superior results.

Is there an exact formula that will provide *you* with superior results? Well, I know of one. A man I know determined forty years ago that he would retire in forty years with $100,000. Believe it or not, he succeeded. The formula that allowed him to retire after forty years with $100,000 involved four factors:

1. Hard work.
2. Economical living.
3. Occasional saving.
4. The recent death of an uncle who left him $97,000!

I don't know how many of you can depend on such a formula to cushion *your* future. But I do know that there is a serious approach to investing money and achieving success. If this formula were boiled down to its essential elements, it would look something like this:

$$Hindsight + Foresight = Success$$

This book gives you the basic facts you need to know in buying stocks and bonds. It provides the background and foundation for intelligent investing. In essence, it attempts to give you the first part of our formula—hindsight. As to foresight—the *in*exact part of investing—an important portion of this book is devoted to providing you with it so that you will arrive at the right investment decisions for your personal future.

Stock
Market
Primer

PART I
An Introduction to Investments

1

Investment Channels

A simple definition of the word "investment" would read: "setting money to work to earn more money." Yet simple definitions are seldom enough, and the case of investments is no exception. A few more words should be added to our definition, namely that "any investment involves risk." And before you argue that certain investments are risk-free (e.g., savings accounts under $100,000, U.S. government bonds), let's take a look at the two basic risks that exist:

1. The risk that you might lose your capital (this is the ordinary risk that you take when you go into business, buy real estate, stocks, etc.).
2. The risk that your investment will not keep up with the purchasing value of the dollar.

The first of these risks is, of course, obvious and always has been. The second has become widely publicized in the United States in recent years. It involves that dreaded word *inflation* and the chance that $1 invested today will not buy the same $1 worth of goods and services in the future. Those of us in the investment business have done our best to warn of the declining purchasing power of the dollar and to advise people to provide themselves with a "hedge against inflation." The statistics bear us out. From 1939 to 1959, for example, the purchasing power of the dollar was more than cut in half; the next ten years saw "only" a further 20% deterioration; but the ensuing four years heated up and produced a further 35% inflation, which was followed by staggering cost-of-living increases from 1973 through 1980.

The people who suffered most from inflation were the conservatives—those who concentrated on safety and avoided the forms of investment that involve more risk. Those who preserved cash or who bought future protection through insurance, those who depended on social security or pensions—all were left behind by the soaring cost of living.

Before discussing the different types of investment and how they rank in risks and rewards, let me point out one more "risk" that we in the United States especially are prone to. Some people might call it the risk of "not keeping up with the Joneses"; suffice it to say that our population enjoys a high standard of living and should not be denied such pleasures. Certainly we are accustomed to a steadily increasing standard of living, and we must make our money work to keep us up with this progress. Luxuries turn into necessities as time flies, and we have to make our money grow to buy these new necessities. For example, twenty-five years ago, a television set was a luxury; today it is a necessity. As one philosopher so aptly put it: More and more we find ourselves pondering how to reconcile our *net income* with our *gross habits*.

WHERE TO INVEST?

Let's take a look at the various forms of investment and see where they fit in a discussion of risks. The most obvious investment channels are:

U.S. government obligations (bonds, notes, bills, etc.).
Savings deposits in commercial banks.
Savings deposits in savings and loan associations.
Life insurance and annuities.
Real estate mortgages.
Real estate.
Corporate securities (corporate bonds, preferred stocks, and common stocks).

U.S. Government Obligations

Certainly U.S. government securities do not carry the so-called ordinary risk. You should not have to worry about the government defaulting on its obligations (if you worry about this, then there just isn't any investment suitable for you). Without getting into a detailed discussion of "governments," let's look at the two basic forms of government securities that are of interest to the average investor:

1. Government obligations that can fluctuate in market price.
2. Government obligations that are *not* traded and therefore do not fluctuate in market price.

In the first category are all government securities *with the exception of savings bonds.* Treasury bills (which always come due within one year), Treasury notes (one- to ten-year obligations), and Treasury bonds (issued only for a term of ten years or more) all sell after their issue on a supply-and-demand basis and thus are subject to changes in market price.

Savings bonds, on the other hand, are not transferable and cannot be sold. Instead, holders must turn them in to the government if they want cash and will be paid a fixed amount depending on how long the bonds have been held.

In either case, investors know that they will eventually get what they deserve and that their income from these securities is completely secure. Thus government obligations fall into the category of investments that do not carry the ordinary risk of losing capital. What these fixed-income securities lack is protection against the rising cost of living; therefore they do carry the second risk mentioned. For an illustration of this risk, see the chart on p. 6.

The conclusion, of course, is that—considering taxes and the increased cost of living—savings bonds bought in any year from 1935 to 1946 would *not* have kept up with inflation. Savings bonds purchased from 1947 to 1958 (after World War II) did better. Bonds maturing from 1957 through 1968 just barely kept abreast of the rising cost of living for the lowest tax-bracket individual. But, as might be expected, a high-bracket taxpay-

RETURN ON 1935–1946 SAVINGS BOND ISSUES AFTER INCOME TAX AND "INFLATION TAX"

Bought for $75 in	Maturity Value of $100 in	Initial (Lowest) Personal Income Tax Rate	Income Tax on $25 Interest	Maturity Value Less Income Tax	"Inflation Tax"— Increase in Cost-of-Living Index over the 10 Years (%)	Amount of "Inflation Tax"	Maturity Value Less Income Tax and "Inflation Tax"	Dollars of Original Investment Lost	Average Annual Rate of Loss (%)
1935	1945	23.0%	*	$100.00	35.9	$26.42	$73.58	$1.42	0.19
1936	1946	19.0	*	100.00	44.2	30.65	69.35	5.65	0.75
1937	1947	19.0	*	100.00	55.7	35.77	64.23	10.77	1.44
1938	1948	16.6	*	100.00	70.5	41.35	58.65	16.35	2.18
1939	1949	16.6	*	100.00	71.4	41.66	58.34	16.66	2.22
1940	1950	17.4	*	100.00	71.6	41.72	58.28	16.72	2.23
1941	1951	20.4	$5.10	94.90	76.5	41.13	53.77	21.23	2.83
1942	1952	22.2	5.55	94.45	61.2	35.86	58.59	16.41	2.19
1943	1953	22.2	5.55	94.45	51.3	32.02	62.43	12.57	1.68
1944	1954	20.0	5.00	95.00	47.7	30.68	64.32	10.68	1.42
1945	1955	20.0	5.00	95.00	43.5	28.80	66.20	8.80	1.17
1946	1956	20.0	5.00	95.00	34.0	24.10	70.90	4.10	0.55

* The interest on savings bonds bought from 1935 to 1940 was not subject to federal income tax.

SOURCE: First National City Bank of New York monthly letter, May 1956, p. 57.

er would have suffered a loss of purchasing power. And the small after-tax, after-inflation gains made by the low-bracket bond owners were hardly sufficient to provide them with an improved standard of living. The 1969–1980 experience was disastrous for investors in both low and high tax brackets. With inflationary pressures in the United States (and abroad) expected to continue at high levels, it is doubtful that savings bonds of the future will be any more suitable than those of the past for real protection against cost-of-living hikes.

Savings Accounts in Commercial Banks

Here, too, we find an investment that lacks the ordinary risk (because of insurance with an agency of the federal government on savings accounts up to $100,000 in any one bank), but we assume the risk that our dollars will not keep up with the rise in the cost of living. Savings accounts can only grow through compounding interest, and the interest paid by banks has been well below that available from other investments.

Savings Accounts in Savings and Loan Associations

Here, again, we have a "static" investment and we take the chance that inflation may well eat away at our dollars. Savings and loan deposits (also insured up to $100,000 by a federal agency) normally pay $\frac{1}{4}$ of 1% more than savings accounts in commercial banks, but it is questionable whether the return from such accounts will be sufficient to overcome inflation over the years.

Insurance

A discussion of the countless insurance plans available could fill many volumes. So I will simply summarize a few pertinent points:

1. Insurance with the top companies carries no ordinary risk because of the huge reserves set up for the policy holder.

2. Life insurance should be purchased as *protection*, not as investment. It should protect the family from death, but should not be counted on to accomplish much for you while you're living. (Life insurance has been aptly described as "a plan that keeps you poor all your life so you can *die rich*.")

3. Life insurance and annuities carry the very definite risk of not keeping up with the dollar. In both cases, you are buying a guarantee of a specified number of today's dollars *for a future date*. For example, people who bought annuities in 1939 (or any time thereafter) and protected themselves with what looked like adequate income at that time found themselves far short of a living income fifteen or twenty years later.

4. Annuities, like life insurance, have their use as a protective device, but they constitute a very poor form of investment. For one thing, they provide no hedge against inflation. Second, they are an extremely low-yielding investment. Annuity policies written many years ago assumed that the insurance company would earn a very low 3–5% for the holder; even in recent years, with interest rates skyrocketing, earning assumptions by the insurance writers have seldom exceeded 7–8½%— hardly generous. Annuities are a convenient savings medium, but frankly I don't recommend them.* The advent of "variable annuities" (wherein future payments to the policy holder will *vary* according to the value of an investment portfolio managed by the insurance company) may overcome the weaknesses I have mentioned.

Real Estate and Real Estate Mortgages

Like insurance, real estate is a broad field that is a study in itself. For the sake of our discussion, ownership of property

*The exception is if you live an abnormally long life. In 1960, for example, one of our country's largest insurance companies pointed proudly to the fact that certain (fifteen) policy holders had collected over two and a half times their investment in annuities. These people were all between 99 and 102 years of age, however, and not many of us can count on this kind of life span.

(whether improved or unimproved) carries the ordinary risks of losing part of your capital, but well-chosen real estate should more than compensate for inflation. I believe that real estate constitutes a wonderful investment vehicle. Just a few attributes of real estate ownership are:

1. Depreciation from a building provides certain tax advantages and enables the owner to receive a tax-free cash "throw-off" to pay off his investment; likewise, the fact that property taxes and interest payments are deductible items for income tax purposes is of sizable benefit to the property owner.
2. Rate of return (yield) may or may not be higher than on corporate securities. In 1980, for example, the average going-in returns to real estate purchasers who borrow (mortgage) were about equal to dividend yields on most common stocks but well below yields from bonds and other fixed-income instruments.
3. An investor can borrow more heavily to buy real estate, thereby affording considerable "leverage" (described in Chapter 18).
4. There may be a limited supply of land and/or property in a given area. In a growing region, this creates a very favorable supply-demand relationship—and leads to increasing property values.
5. An owner can trade properties without incurring a capital gains tax.

Unfortunately, real estate is not generally available to the smaller investor (other than home ownership, that is) and it does require management. Faucets leak, pipes occasionally break, and tenants often move. Furthermore, neighborhoods and property values change and real estate, like the stock market (or, for that matter, anything in life), is not a "one-way street."

This discussion involves actual ownership of property, not mortgages. Mortgages (especially second mortgages) can carry considerable ordinary risk and it is debatable whether they constitute a completely adequate hedge against inflation, although certainly when they are bought at sizable discounts, the return may be more than sufficient to account for any increased living costs.

Corporate Securities

Chapter 3 describes the various types of corporate securities. Suffice it to say here that bonds and preferred stocks both carry the purchasing power risk, as they have not provided a hedge against inflation over the years. Common stocks generally have successfully protected investors against the rising cost of living, although selection here is all-important.

CONCLUSIONS

Not everyone can afford to concentrate solely on ordinary risk investments such as real estate and common stocks. Later on, after we have discussed the stock market, growth stocks, and other topics, we will come to more conclusions on investing, but it is important to point out here that most people should *balance* their investments to include a certain portion of ordinary-risk ventures and a certain portion of ventures that are safe from ordinary risks, even though they do carry the purchasing power risk. Emphasis, however, should decidedly be on equities—on *ownership* forms of investment such as real estate and common stocks. As a matter of fact, aside from the protection of life insurance and cash reserves, investors who are thinking longer term should concentrate almost solely on equities.

2

Forms of Business Organization

Because this book is devoted almost exclusively to *corporate* securities, it seems only proper to distinguish a *corporation* from other forms of business organization.

There are three basic ways of going into business in our country: (1) by yourself (as sole proprietor); (2) in partnership with one or more associates; and (3) by forming a corporation.

SOLE PROPRIETORSHIP

This is the simplest way of going into business. No legal papers are needed, no extra expenses—you have only yourself to blame if things go wrong, and the profit is all yours if you succeed. Tax consequences are the simplest. Whatever you earn you simply report to Uncle Sam and pay the prevailing income tax on this amount.

PARTNERSHIP

This, too, is easy to form. You and I can go into business as partners with only a verbal agreement (but don't ever do it that way). Legal papers are relatively simple, so these expenses are minimal. And there are no extra expenses in the way of state fees and the like. Taxes are also simple. You and I merely take our agreed portion of the year's profits and report that portion to Internal Revenue and pay our taxes.

There are two distinct disadvantages to a partnership. First, the death of one partner automatically dissolves the partnership, necessitating the drawing up of a new partnership agreement. Of greater significance is the fact that each partner assumes unlimited liability for debts incurred *in the business*. And I mean *unlimited personal liability*. For example, let's assume you and I go into partnership. I buy some heavy machinery and make other expenditures for our business that do not work out. In a short time, we're broke and we owe considerable money. Our creditors press us for the money and bring suit to get it. Nothing is left in the business, but they *can* sue us personally for these debts *because it's a partnership*. Frankly, partner, I haven't a dime. I put all my eggs into the business. Fortunately for our creditors, *you* have other assets. The court can take those assets away from you to pay *our* debts, and there's no limit to how much they can take. They won't take the mattress out from under you, but they will grab almost everything else. So you can see that a partnership is a business marriage. And I don't recommend becoming partners with just anybody, any more than I do your marrying Lucy Vonderkronkle, whom you just met last night after consuming sixteen martinis at the local pub.

CORPORATION

This is a separate entity legally set up for business purposes. A corporation is quite different from a partnership. First of all, it is not as easily set up (it can't possibly be done verbally or in a matter of minutes); establishing a corporation takes legal know-how, and naturally involves the corresponding fees.

Of great importance is the liability limitation from being incorporated.* You simply can't lose any more money than you put in. The company can go broke and owe millions, but the creditors can't get any more money from the stockholders. The

*Assuming stock is nonassessable and that's the only kind of stock under discussion in this book.

obvious question then is: Why in the world doesn't everybody in business incorporate to protect themselves? The answer: *Double taxation.* A stockholder is actually taxed twice in a corporation: first, in the form of a corporate income tax (maximum rate 46%), and second, in the normal manner when the stockholder declares to Internal Revenue how much in dividends he received during the year. For example, let's assume you and I are considering the purchase of a business carning $100,000 a year and that we're both in the 50% tax bracket. If we go in as equal *partners*, each of us will report $50,000 in income from the business and Uncle Sam will take almost $25,000, leaving us $25,000 apiece (for a total of $50,000 net after taxes for us both). If, instead, we incorporate, the $100,000 will be subject to the corporate tax (let's round it out to be 50%), leaving us $50,000. Then (assuming all earnings are paid out in dividends) we have to declare our share of this—$25,000 each—and pay tax on it (in this case, $12,500 each*). So we are left with $12,500 each after taxes, for a total of $25,000—exactly half of what we would have retained as partners. The following table shows this rather clearly:

	PARTNERSHIP		CORPORATION	
Total net income	$100,000		$100,000	
Less corporate income tax	None		50,000	
Balance available for owners	$100,000		$ 50,000	
	Your Share	My Share	Your Share	My Share
	$50,000	$50,000	$25,000	$25,000
Less income tax paid personally	25,000	25,000	12,500	12,500
Income left after all taxes	$25,000	$25,000	$12,500	$12,500

*Actually, the tax on dividends—which is so-called "preferential" (as opposed to "earned") income—can run as high as 70%.

This broad generalization lets you see the major advantages and disadvantages of partnership versus incorporation. It does not allow for the possibility of stockholders receiving salaries from their corporation (thereby minimizing the effect of double taxation), nor does it discuss new tax regulations (such as one that allows certain corporations to elect taxation as a partnership). In short, an attorney is the best judge of whether you should incorporate or form a partnership.

Now that we know more about corporations, we can go ahead and talk about the securities they issue.

3

Corporate Securities

To commence business and to remain in business, a corporation needs capital. There are three basic means of obtaining this capital, namely through the sale of bonds, preferred stocks, and/or common stock. Let's take a look at these three and see how they differ from one another.

BONDS

Bonds are issued in exchange for money loaned to a corporation (or to a federal government, state, city, etc.). The *lender* of money *becomes a bondholder and a creditor* of the company. As in any loan, the lender expects to receive a fixed rate of return on his money—called *interest*—and to receive back the full amount of his loan at some future date, called the *maturity date*. Let me emphasize that bondholders are creditors of the company; they have *no ownership* and have nothing to say about the running of the business unless the company gets way behind in interest payments and is forced into bankruptcy or recapitalization. Therefore, bondholders do not share in the success of a growing company, other than knowing that their interest is being better covered by earnings and through more assurance that they will get their original investment back at maturity. Thus bonds (unless convertible into common stock—discussed in Chapter 11) are bought for their fixed income; they do not provide a hedge against inflation because you will never get back more than a set amount at maturity. Incidentally, the *maturity date* serves to limit both the loss and gain in market price of a bond over the years. Assuming a bond is sound and that it will definitely pay off at maturity, this factor keeps a bond from going down indefinitely or from plunging too far below its value at maturity or from rising very far above this price. The longer the maturity, however, the greater the potential fluctuation in interim market price levels.

PREFERRED STOCK

The term "preferred" makes this security sound glamorous and attractive. Nothing could be further from the truth! Although a preferred stock ranks ahead of common stock both as to payment of dividends and as to disposition of assets if a company goes out of business, a preferred stock is a "hybrid" security; it carries neither the extreme safety of a bond nor the chance for growth of a common stock. Like a bond, a preferred issue carries a fixed rate of annual payment (called a *dividend* in the case of a preferred stock and *interest* in the case of a bond) and this payment will *not* be increased.* No dividends can be paid on preferreds until all bond interest has been paid. Dividends are usually *cumulative,* meaning that the preferred stockholders are entitled to any omitted payments; that is, if preferred dividends are not earned and subsequently not paid, the corporation still has an obligation to pay all those accrued dividends when its earnings do recover. Naturally, the corporation has to pay off all its accrued dividends (called "arrearages") before it can pay any dividends on the *common stock.*

Like bondholders, preferred stockholders generally have no choice in management of the company (no voting power). Most bonds and preferreds have a *call price* (redemption price), which is the price at which the *company* can call the issues back in if it chooses. This call price limits any large gains in market

*Unless it is a "participating" preferred, in which case the preferred holders, after receiving their stipulated regular dividend, then share in the earnings available for the common stock.

price for bonds and preferreds. An investor is not going to pay 115 for an issue that has a call price of 105, because the day after he buys it at 115, the issue could be called at the 105 figure. The bond or preferred that has no call price does not have this disadvantage.

One of the big differences between bonds and preferred stocks is that the latter have *no maturity date.* At least bondholders know they are entitled to a certain sum at maturity. Preferred stock holders have no assurance of getting their investment back. They have to depend on market conditions and could conceivably hold their stock for 100 years and never see it back where it started. At least with a bond investors know that in 10, 20, or so many years they will have their money back. On the other hand, a preferred stock that is bought for its high yield at least guarantees owners a yield for as many years as they desire, with no "interference" from a maturity date.

COMMON STOCK

Here we come to the actual ownership of a company. Whereas bondholders are lenders of money and holders of preferred stock are in-beween investors, common stockholders supply permanent *equity capital* and own the company. They have voting power, elect the board of directors, and thereby indirectly control management of the company. For this privilege, they have last claim on dividends and are the last to collect in case the company goes broke and is forced to liquidate. On the other hand, common stockholders are the ones who benefit if the company is a success. As earnings increase, they get higher dividends and their corporate security goes up in market price.

CONCLUSIONS

Bonds represent a creditor's interest in a corporation. Bonds generally provide a high degree of safety—a fixed rate of return in good times and bad. This fixed rate, however, means that they are vulnerable to inflation when investors are demanding higher and higher returns.

Preferred stocks represent a very limited form of ownership. They carry ownership risks with very little opportunity for appreciation of capital. Long unpaid preferred dividends are seldom settled satisfactorily and preferred stocks, because they have no maturity date and are not of the same quality as bonds, have greater price instability than bonds, yet they usually provide only slightly higher yield. After this glum discussion you're probably wondering who buys preferred stocks. They are bought mainly by institutional investors, who want the higher return, and they are especially attractive to investing corporations, who get a tax advantage from receiving dividends from another corporation. Individuals, too, occasionally own preferred stocks, but I would generally advise against this, except for an elderly person not interested in growth who needs that "last ounce" of current income. Why, for example, should an individual buy Pacific Gas and Electric preferred with a return around 13% when he can buy the common to yield only 1% less? Pacific Gas and Electric is a stable utility company; its common stock dividend should be safe. Assuming the company is granted sufficient rate increases to bring about higher earnings over the years, dividends will rise, too, and chances are the ultimate return to the common shareholder will exceed that of the preferred holder. True, there is more market risk on the common, but anyone looking more than a few years ahead for the benefits of his investment would be better off with the common stock.

Common stocks represent ownership. If it is growth of capital or a hedge against inflation you are seeking, here is where you are going to get it.

Now, before we learn to distinguish between attractive stocks and those we should leave alone, let's see how corporate securities are bought and sold.

PART II
How the Stock Market Functions

4

How the Stock
Market Works

One of the great advantages of owning corporate securities is that they are liquid. By that I don't mean you can drink them. Only that they can be sold at a moment's notice and converted into cash. Contrast that with trying to sell your business or a large piece of property. The best example of this liquidity is that provided by the New York Stock Exchange. Here we have as close to a "perfect market" as there is anywhere for investments.

Open five days a week from 10:00 A.M. to 4:00 P.M. (Eastern time), the New York Stock Exchange enables a buyer in Connecticut to get together with a seller in California in a matter of minutes. The New York exchange is essentially a communications system. It is a central marketplace connected with offices throughout the world by about a half a million miles of telephone and telegraph wire.

From the gallery, the exchange looks like a wild mass of confusion. But it's the most organized mass of confusion I know of. For those of you who have not seen the New York exchange, picture a floor about two-thirds the size of an ordinary football field. Around the floor are the countless telephone stations that connect about 1,000 stock exchange members with their offices. These are the brokers who are handling orders for their customers. Also stationed around the room are numerous "trading posts," each one manned by specialists. In early 1980 the exchange had 392 specialists on the floor.

Each specialist is assigned certain stocks. It is his business to see that a proper market is made in each and every one of these stocks. It is his job to take care of orders to buy and sell for brokers. And it is his job to buy and sell for his own account to assure a good market at all times. In other words, the exchange expects there will always be a buyer for any stock within a close proximity of the last sale that took place in that stock. (The same rule applies for expecting to find a seller within close range of the last sale.) But sometimes there will be no buyer (or seller) from the public, and this is when the specialist must step in and bid to buy (or offer to sell) the stock for his own account. Specialists are closely regulated by the exchange and by the Securities and Exchange Commission (SEC).

Your broker can buy and sell for you and trade on the floor of the exchange because he owns a "seat" on the exchange. The number of seats available is limited and a new broker desiring one must buy it from a present holder, much as you buy a stock from another person. Also like individual stocks, these seats vary in price according to supply and demand. Over the past sixteen years, for example, there has been great variance in the price of New York Stock Exchange seats:

Year	High Price	Low Price
1979	$210,000	$ 82,000
1978	105,000	46,000
1977	95,000	35,000
1976	104,000	40,000
1975	138,000	60,000
1974	105,000	65,000
1973	190,000	72,000
1972	250,000	150,000
1971	300,000	145,000
1970	320,000	130,000
1969	515,000	260,000
1968	515,000	385,000
1967	450,000	220,000
1966	270,000	197,000
1965	250,000	190,000
1964	230,000	190,000

Aside from the seat price, the exchange has certain capital requirements and other standards that must be met by members.

There are a few thousand persons on the floor of the exchange, including stock exchange members, clerks, and employees of the NYSE itself. The clerks must turn over orders to the specialists, while exchange members can choose to turn over orders to the specialists or attempt to transact the orders themselves.

Before seeing how an order is transacted on the exchange, let's distinguish between the various orders that can be placed by an investor to buy or sell stocks. The most common order placed is the *market* order, in which the investor is telling his broker to go ahead and transact the order *just as soon as he can* and *to buy it at the prevailing market* at that time. The broker is obligated to complete the order when he reaches the specialist's post, regardless of what the stock is selling for at that time. (Remember there may be considerable differences in price between the time a client places his order and the minute or so later when the broker reaches the post.)

There is a distinction between a market order and an order giving *market discretion.* In the latter situation the client is also instructing the broker to complete an order to buy or sell, but in this case the broker does not have to transact at the prevailing price. Instead, the broker is given the discretion to wait and attempt to get a better price for the customer. You might ask now why everyone doesn't use this order instead of a plain market order. The answer is that you take a chance in giving market discretion that the broker's judgment may prove incorrect. He may elect to wait to buy or sell instead of transacting the order right at the moment, and his waiting may cost you money in the form of a higher price when you are buying or a lower price when you are selling. When you give a broker discretion, *he is not held* for his error of judgment. Of course, his discretion may prove correct and save you money, but there is no guarantee of this.

A third type of order placed is the *limit* order. In this case, you give your broker a price limit *that he cannot exceed* when buying the stock for you (or cannot lower in case you are selling the stock). For example, say you want to buy 100 shares of XYZ Company, which is currently selling at $10, but for which you are not willing to pay over $9. In this case, the broker is prohibited from paying any more than your designated limit of $9 for your intended purchase of 100 shares. When you put such a limit on a stock, you usually have to wait for the stock to reach that level; therefore most limit orders are put in for a period of time and are called *open limit orders*. In the case of this XYZ purchase, you might instruct your broker to leave the order in for a week, two weeks, a month, or any period of your choice. In the meantime, of course, it is your privilege to change your limit price at any time; for example, you can raise the limit to 9½ or lower it to 8 or 8½ anytime—or you can cancel the order completely. After the designated period of the open order is over, it automatically expires, unless you renew it. You may place a limit order good for only one day, in which case it is called a *day order*.

I insist there is one basic rule for limit orders. *Don't place a limit order only a fraction of a point away from the present price.* If you think a stock deserves to sell either far below or far above its going rate, then it may well pay you to wait for it to reach such a level, but when you are trying to save only a fraction of a point it's a bad gamble. Why? Because while the very most you can save is the fraction you are trying to squeeze out, you may lose a great deal by not transacting the order "at the market." For example, assume you are thinking of buying XYZ Company, whose stock is presently selling at $10. If you put your order in with a limit of, say 9¾, the very most you can save is ¼ of 1 point or 25 cents a share *if the stock declines to 9¾*. But if the stock does not decline to that level, what can it cost you? There's no limit! The stock may advance from 10 to 20 or 30 or more and you may "lose" a potential doubling or tripling of your money—all for a measly 25 cents a share. The same thing goes for selling a stock. If you think a stock is fully valued and that it should be sold, what can you gain by putting in an order a fraction above the market? Once again, only a few pennies, and if the stock never reaches your fractionally higher level and commences to go down in price, you could lose many points— and this is out-of-pocket loss from not selling it at the market.

To illustrate the same point, it's a basic rule of investing or speculating that you should see a possibility for a good-sized gain from any venture before plunging. *Never risk a lot of dollars to make a few!*

It's a different philosophy if you believe that a stock is overvalued now but that it represents a good buy at considerably lower levels. Here is where limit orders are most valuable, because you get yourself in line early to buy the stock where you think it represents a good buy. You give your broker your limit order and then it's there when the stock reaches that price. The advantage is that you are not influenced by your emotions at that time, whereas were you to wait for the stock to get to that level, chances are the declining nature of the market would make you say to yourself, "I think it's going lower yet." And this is probably just the time you *should* be buying!

THE SPECIALIST'S BOOK AND HOW ORDERS ARE HANDLED

Let's assume you want to buy 100 shares of XYZ Company and you instruct your broker to do so "at the market" for your account. Your broker writes out a tag with these instructions; this tag goes to his order department, which relays it to the floor of the exchange. The broker's partner on the floor receives the order and proceeds directly to the specialist's post where XYZ stock is traded. He asks the specialist what the going price is for XYZ. The very last sale price is easy to determine (it is posted on an electric board at the post), but the *next* sale price is still a mystery. The specialist has a guide to what the next sale will be, because he keeps track of all limit orders for the brokers. Of course he can't keep them in his head, so he puts them down in what is known as the *specialist's book*.

The specialist keeps a separate book for each stock he follows and each page in the book keeps track of open orders at various prices. For example, let's set up the specialist's book on XYZ Company:

XYZ COMPANY

Orders to Buy	Broker Placing Order	Date Order Expires	Price of Stock	Orders to Sell	Broker Placing Order	Date Order Expires
100 shs.	Laurel	Feb. 26	9			
200 shs.	Hardy	Mar. 1	9			
100 shs.	Abbott	Mar. 15	9			
100 shs.	Costello	Feb. 12	9			
200 shs.	Lunt	Mar. 15	$9\frac{1}{8}$			
100 shs.	Fontanne	Feb. 13	$9\frac{1}{8}$			
100 shs.	Gilbert	Mar. 1	$9\frac{1}{4}$			
100 shs.	Sullivan	Mar. 3	$9\frac{1}{4}$			
500 shs.	Smythe	Mar. 5	$9\frac{3}{8}$			
	No orders—		$9\frac{1}{2}$	—No orders		
			$9\frac{5}{8}$			
			$9\frac{3}{4}$	100 shs.	Chase	Mar. 20
				300 shs.	Sanborn	Mar. 1
			$9\frac{7}{8}$	100 shs.	Crosse	Mar. 3
			$9\frac{7}{8}$	200 shs.	Bl'ckw'll	Feb. 4

Your broker approaches the specialist and asks for a "quote," which is a request for the highest order to buy (the bid) and the lowest order to sell (the offer) that are open on the specialist's book. In this case, the quote would be "$9\frac{3}{8}$ at $9\frac{3}{4}$," which means that there is someone bidding $9\frac{3}{8}$ and no higher, and someone offering stock for sale at $9\frac{3}{4}$ and no lower. Your broker can also request the "size," meaning the number of shares wanted at $9\frac{3}{8}$ and the number for sale at $9\frac{3}{4}$. In this case, the size would be 500 and 400, meaning 500 shares bid for at $9\frac{3}{8}$ and 400 shares offered at $9\frac{3}{4}$.

Now, if you have given your broker a market order, he is obligated to buy the stock at the lowest offering showing, which would be $9\frac{3}{4}$. Actually the specialist can help out your broker by "stopping" him at $9\frac{3}{4}$ (meaning that he will guarantee to sell him 100 shares at $9\frac{3}{4}$ if there is another purchase at $9\frac{3}{4}$ by someone else—after all, he is carrying open orders to sell 400 shares at 9¾). In this way, he allows your broker to step in and try to get you a lower price. Let's assume the specialist does "stop" your broker at 9¾. Then your broker will probably step in among the other brokers milling around the XYZ post and call in a loud and clear voice, "9½ for 100 XYZ" (which means "I'm willing to pay 9½ for 100 shares"). Chances are there are both potential buyers and sellers of XYZ in the crowd who have not entrusted their orders to the specialist. They haven't "tipped their hand" and are waiting to hear new orders for XYZ. When your broker bids 9½, he changes the quote from "9⅜ at 9¾" to "9½ at 9¾." Another broker hears the higher bid and decides he'll offer 100 shares for sale at 9⅝ (remember, if he waits for 9¾, he has to get in back of line behind Chase and Sanborn, who are already on the book for 9¾). Your broker is satisfied that he won't do much better than this and yells, "Take it," at the 9⅝ offerer and a sale has taken place.

The specialist has served his function of handling buy and sell orders and of seeing to it that a good market exists in his stock at all times.

This bidding and offering goes on all day in front of the post. The result is a continuous market that reflects the supply and demand for the stocks. You would be amazed how efficient the system is, especially if you have watched, as I have, thousands of shares of a particular stock being bought and sold in a brief period of time without affecting much of a change in the price of the stock.

RECORDING OF TRADES AND THE TICKER TAPE

Whenever a transaction takes place on the exchange it is recorded immediately and, within a minute, is sent over the wires and appears on the ticker tape in the office of every exchange member. Every stock has an abbreviated symbol and the transactions are shown as follows:

XYZ	GM	X
9⅝	2s 50	4s 25.24½

Our previous 100-share trade of XYZ is the first example; whenever a transaction involves 100 shares, no mention is made of *anything but the price*. When more than 100 shares are traded, though, the price of the stock is preceded by the volume; in GM (General Motors), the "2s" means "200 shares"; in X (U.S. Steel's symbol), the "4s 25" means that 400 shares traded in one block at the price of 25, then the "24½" means that the 25 trade was followed by a 100-share transaction at 24½.

There are other peculiarities to the ticker tape. I won't list them here—your broker can explain them if you are interested and have the time to spend in his office watching the tape. The main thing is that trends of the market and of individual stocks show up on the ticker tape—nothing is hidden from you.

THE CENTRAL MARKET SYSTEM

Thus far you have heard only about the New York Stock Exchange. There is more to come on the American Stock Exchange, regional exchanges, and the over-the-counter markets. By the time you read this book, all these markets should be combined, *from a reporting-to-the-public standpoint,* into one reporting body, called the Central Market System. In short, the various mechanisms described here may not be altered, but their combined results will be centralized and communicated to investors through one "tape." In 1980, for example, we already have a consolidated ticker tape that includes trades completed on all markets. Whether an American Telephone transaction takes place on the Pacific, Philadelphia, or New York exchange, or, as to be explained, in the so-called Third and Fourth markets, the result is flashed for all to see on one centralized recording (and reporting) device—one tape.

Additional facets of the Central Market System are still to be worked out, such as: (a) a composite quote system (so you can find the most reasonable market wherever it is); (b) a consolidated limit order book; (c) centralized trading rules and regulations; and (d) an integrated clearance and settlement system (which, it is hoped, will someday become computerized to the point where the bulky stock certificate will become obsolete).

ODD LOTS

Up to this time we've been talking only about buying and selling stocks in 100-share lots—called round lots. Actually considerable business in stocks is not in round lots but rather in less-than-100-share units—called odd lots.

For many years the various exchanges had specialists who dealt exclusively in odd lots. To take care of the buyer or seller of 39 or 62 or 3 shares of any security, these specialized odd lot dealers guaranteed to sell or buy all the stock necessary to complete odd lot orders—in exchange for a set fee (called the odd lot "differential"). All these transactions were determined by the price of round lots. Thus if you were a buyer of 10 shares of XYZ stock, the odd lot dealer waited for the next 100 shares of XYZ to sell and then executed your order at that price plus the differential, which was either $\frac{1}{8}$ or $\frac{1}{4}$ of a point. If you were a seller of XYZ, the differential would be deducted from your sale price rather than added.

In 1976 the procedure was changed. Odd lots are no longer executed at any set differentials from round lot transaction prices. They are instead executed as separate orders, with the resulting price a competitive one—which could be the same, more, or less than the last sale.

Most important, odd lot purchasers and sellers are assured of good markets for their securities, and at reasonable costs. Therefore the conclusion on odd lots is as it was in previous *Primer* editions: Whatever fee is charged is small and should not be a deterrent to investing in odd lots.

COMMISSIONS

Commission rates were once set by the various stock exchanges but charges made for buying and selling are now negotiable. Different brokers charge different amounts for different types of transactions, so you simply have to check to determine what your costs will be. This, incidentally, does not imply that you should deal through the lowest-cost broker; brokers provide varying services and you should expect to pay some premium for these. In addition, you want to be certain that the broker with whom you deal is financially stable. Low cost does not necessarily signify best value.

SHORT SELLING

One of the interesting types of speculation in the stock market and one of the most difficult to comprehend is the "short sale." When a person *buys* a stock, he does so with the hope the stock will go *up* in value so that when he sells it he will make a profit. When a person sells a stock "short," he is *selling something he doesn't now own* with the hope that he will make a profit by buying it back later at a lower price.

Now, don't think yourself dense if you are asking, "How in the world can a person sell something he *doesn't own*?" Let me give you a practical example.

I own a 1955 Chevrolet. You and I are talking one day and I tell you how I just turned down an offer to sell my car for $1,000. It's only worth $500, but I'm sentimentally attached to the old buggy and I want to keep it. Well, it so happens that I'm going away tomorrow for a month and leaving my car here. Your eyes light up: If only you could "borrow" my car for the month, find that fool who was willing to pay $1,000 for my car, sell it to him, and then buy a similar car before I return. The result would be a profit of $500 to you:

$1,000 received by you when you sold my car
   -500 paid out to put similar car back in my garage
$ 500 net profit to you

What you have done is sell my car "short." You don't own it, but you've sold it just the same with the idea of replacing it at a lower price in the future.

Actually it's easier to sell short in stocks than in cars. How could you be sure the $500 1955 Chevrolet you put back in my garage would be the same exact color and have the same dented fenders as my original? You couldn't! But in stocks, it's easy. Any 100-share certificate of General Motors is exactly the same as any other. Thus, if you think that the present market price of GM stock is too high and that it will go down, why not sell it now for $80 (your broker will arrange to borrow it for you to deliver to the buyer) and then simply buy it back when it goes lower, say to $60.

Short selling does serve a function. It allows one to speculate that the market is too high and thus has a stabilizing influence. After all, if we had buyers of stocks by a great majority, stocks would quickly become inflated and priced too high. And then we'd be in for a sharp drop someday. Since most investors are conscious of *buying* stocks, short sellers can at least have a restraining influence and keep stocks from becoming overly inflated. And remember that every short seller is a potential buyer later on, and this buying when the market is sinking is also a stabilizing factor.

I don't recommend short selling for the average investor. For one thing, the risks are unlimited. There's no end to how much you can lose. If you sell a stock short at $10, who's to say it won't go to $100 or $1,000, in which cases you would lose 1,000% or 10,000% on your money, if you didn't buy back before.

This possibility is exactly what enters the short seller's mind and often panics him into buying back as quickly as possible when the market is rising. This sudden buying by short sellers (called "short covering") is one reason for occasional rapid upswings in various popular issues.

In contrast, if you *buy* a $10 stock, what is the worst that can happen? That the company will go bankrupt and the stock be worth nothing, in which case you've "only" lost your original investment (you've lost 100% of your money). And chances are that it will never go to zero; perhaps $2 or $3 or $5 is the lowest you can visualize, even under the worst circumstances.

A second disadvantage to short selling is that you have a minus return on your money to start with. Whereas when you *buy* a stock you receive dividends that give you a certain annual return on your money, in a short sale you have to *pay* out dividends as they are declared to the person from whom you borrowed the stock to make the short sale (you never come into contact with the person who owns the stock you are borrowing—your broker handles all this for you, and generally there is no cost to the borrowing).

The third reason for avoiding short selling is psychological. If you have sold short and the market goes down, you're a hero. But I can think of little worse than being short when the market is rising. Everyone you know is either buying stock or selling what he already owns. Ninety-nine percent of your friends are happy as a lark when the market is rising. To be losing money while all your friends are reaping the harvest is tough to live with.

A fourth criticism of short selling involves taxes. No matter how long you wait to buy back a stock you have sold short, any gain from the transaction is considered by Internal Revenue *to be a short-term gain, and thus you can never benefit from the advantageous long-term capital gain tax rate (see Chapter 30) in short selling.*

Short selling is for the real *speculator,* not the *investor.* And if you are one of those highly speculative individuals, remember that risk factor. And recall the old adage:

> *He who sells what isn't his'n*
> *Must eventually buy it back or go to prison.*

If you're short and the stock is rising, you're going to have to put up more money* right along—or eventually buy it back. So be sure you have ample cash on hand if you decide to become a short seller.

---

*Short selling requires original capital, too. In spite of the fact that you receive money from your short sale right away, you are required to put up this amount out of your own pocket (or at least the existing margin requirement; i.e., in 1980, 50% of the total amount). Then when you buy back the stock ("cover the short sale"), you can withdraw your cash plus the profit or minus the loss incurred from the short sale transaction.

TWO "PROTECTION" ORDERS ON THE STOCK EXCHANGE

We've already discussed limit orders, but there are two other types of limit orders that should be mentioned briefly. These are the stop-sell and stop-buy orders.

Stop-Sell

Suppose you own a stock that is now selling at $60. You think the stock will go considerably higher, but in case you are wrong you want to be sure you sell it at $55 on the way down. You can place a stop-sell order at $55, and if the stock retreats *to that level,* your stock will be automatically sold "at the market" after the $55 price is reached (since it becomes a "market order" there is no guarantee your stock will be sold at the $55 figure; you might receive $54\frac{1}{2}$, $54\frac{1}{4}$, or even less if numerous other stop-sell orders are touched off at the same time as yours). If the stock never retreats to $55, it won't be sold at all. The stop-sell order, therefore, allows you to limit your loss or protect your profit to some extent if it declines.

Stop-Buy

This order is intended mainly for the short seller. If a person sells a stock short at $60 and wants to be sure he loses no more than 5 or 6 points, he can place an open stop-buy at $65. Then if and when the stock goes up to $65, his order automatically becomes an order to buy the stock "at the market."

The stop-buy order can also be used to buy stocks as they rise or as they break through technical "resistance points." Some chartists use the stop-buy in this way to accumulate *stocks as they are rising.* The protection features of both the stop-sell and stop-buy orders make them sound very useful. Actually, these orders are most practical for the short-term speculator. They are not very suitable for the long-term investor, who is less concerned with day-to-day fluctuations and who is investing for large, long-range benefits. Stop orders tend to make an account too active (constantly in and out of the market). I will discuss in Chapter 31 on stock market "trading," considerable activity is to the definite detriment of the investor.

5
Regional Stock Exchanges

Chapter 4 dealt with procedures on the New York Stock Exchange. While the New York Stock Exchange is by far the largest, it is not the only central marketplace for securities. The American Stock Exchange is another, and there are numerous regional exchanges throughout the country, including the Pacific Coast; the Midwest-Philadelphia-Washington, the Boston, and the Detroit exchanges. Listing requirements are the strictest on the New York exchange, but these other markets serve an important function and the stocks traded on the other exchanges may equal or even be superior in quality to many issues traded on the New York board.

None of the regional exchanges in the United States opens before the New York exchange; the regionals all coincide their opening hours with that of the "Big Board." Because of differences in time, however, some exchanges are open after others have closed. The Pacific Coast exchange, for example, opens at 7 A.M. Pacific time, which is the same as the 10:00 A.M. Eastern time opening of the New York exchange, but the Pacific exchange does not close until 2:30 P.M. Pacific time (equivalent to 5:30 P.M. New York time)—or an hour and a half after the close of the Big Board. Many times significant news will be released *after* the close of the *New York* exchange but *before* the close of the *Pacific,* and a great deal of activity will take place on the latter exchange. Assume, for example, that XYZ stock closed at 45 on the Big Board and that shortly after the 4:00 P.M. New York closing an important announcement affecting XYZ is made. Provided that XYZ stock is traded on the Pacific exchange, too (many stocks are traded on more than one exchange), a person wanting to buy or sell XYZ can still do so on the Pacific because of the time differential. The idea, of course, is to make the purchase or sale before the news spreads so that you will be ahead of those who hear the news later and are forced to act after you on the Pacific or have to wait until the New York opening the next day. I must point out, however, that it may be dangerous to pay a big premium on the Pacific over the closing price in New York the same day (or, in the case of bad news, to sell well below what the last sale was in New York) because a great deal of "emotional action" takes place on the Pacific after the New York close. Suppose that after XYZ closes at 45 in the East, some good news suddenly appears and a few frantic people put in market orders to buy the stock; perhaps the first order results in a purchase at 45½, the next at 47 or so. Unless your order is the first or second, you might pay a premium of a couple of points over the New York close. My experience has shown that when frantic buying such as this appears on the Pacific after the New York close, the resulting prices are *usually inflated* and that a *person wanting to buy this stock in the limelight will be able to do so cheaper the next day in New York.* By the same token, a person who engages in emotional selling on the Pacific at prices well below the close in New York the same day would generally realize a higher figure by selling in New York the next day.

While we're on this discussion I should clear up one bit of confusion that exists in the minds of many investors, namely why prices sometimes vary so widely between the New York exchange and any of the regional exchanges in the same stock during the same day. Let's assume you are following the stock of Hercules, Inc., which is listed on both the New York and the Pacific Coast exchanges. You are eager to know what happened to Hercules in today's market and rush to buy the evening newspaper. Frantically you turn to the financial section and look for Hercules in the long list of New York stocks and find the following:

Sls	High	Low	Close	N'Ch
146 Hercules	39	38	38	$-\frac{1}{2}$

Then you notice how the stock traded on the Pacific exchange:

2200 Hercules	$38\frac{3}{4}$	$38\frac{1}{4}$	$38\frac{1}{4}$

Now perhaps the following legitimate questions come to your mind:

Q. Why did Hercules close at 38 in New York and at $38\frac{1}{4}$ on the Pacific?

A. The closing price on the NYSE was at or near 3:30 P.M. New York time (12:30 Pacific time), while the very last sale that took place in Hercules on the Pacific may have been either well before or well after the New York close. In other words, the Pacific close may have no relationship in time to the New York.

Q. Was the volume higher on the Pacific than on the NYSE?

A. No. The "146" on the NYSE means 14,600 whereas the 2200 on the Pacific really means 2200 shares traded.

Q. Hercules never sold as high as 39 on the Pacific. Does that mean that a person could have bought it cheaper there than in New York?

A. No. The volume of trading on the Pacific is small compared to that in New York. It happens that at the time Hercules was selling at 39 in the East, there was no trading at all in the stock on the Coast.

CONCLUSIONS

Regional exchanges serve a vital function in our country. For one thing, they provide a good market for many stocks—some of which have a local following—that do not qualify or do not wish to qualify for listing on the American or New York stock exchange. Regional exchanges are closely regulated; they have specialists and other conveniences and safeguards that are provided by the larger exchanges. In addition, they provide markets for many stocks that are also listed on the major exchanges—though it is fair to say that the great preponderance of trading exists in New York and thus the best market exists there. Prices of stocks listed on both the New York and a regional exchange are determined by activity and trading in New York. Prices on the local exchanges are arrived at in sympathy with what is going on in that central marketplace.

6
The Unlisted
(over-the-Counter) Market

Though listed stocks include most of our country's largest enterprises, *in number alone* listed securities are actually a small minority. Of approximately 55,000 securities traded in the United States today, only about 3,000 are listed on any exchange. The rest are *un*listed, or traded "over-the-counter" (please, not "*under*-the-counter"). The fact that a stock is unlisted does *not* mean that a good market doesn't exist for it. Take, for example, four companies from the San Francisco Bay Area—Pacific Gas and Electric, Syntex, Hibernia Bank, and Hexcel Corp. An active market exists in all four, yet PG&E is listed on the New York and Pacific Coast exchanges, Syntex is listed on the American and Pacific Coast, Hibernia Bank is only on the Pacific Coast, and Hexcel is traded over-the-counter (OTC).

Most of our country's top industrial concerns were originally traded OTC—and many experienced their greatest appreciation before they were listed. Many blue chip companies are still unlisted (Alexander and Alexander, Betz, Chubb, A. L. Nielsen). All the bonds of our cities, counties, and states (called municipal bonds) are unlisted, as are almost all U.S. government securities. More than 75% of all corporation bonds and all mutual funds are OTC. And, of course, all new issues start out trading in the unlisted market.

The main differences between listed and unlisted markets are:

1. There is no one central marketplace OTC. Whereas an order to buy stock on the New York exchange goes directly to that one spot, the OTC involves numerous dealers throughout the country who "make a market" in that stock.

2. There is generally a wider "spread" between the bid and ask price OTC than for a stock traded on an exchange (although there are many exceptions: i.e., the spread on Chubb, unlisted, is normally narrower than that on Iowa Beef, listed).

3. Large-volume orders to buy or sell are more easily handled on the exchange.

4. An investor can only margin (borrow to buy) a select number of unlisted stocks through his broker. This list of marginable OTC issues is set by the Securities and Exchange Commission. An unlisted stock not on this list must be paid for in full by the buyer; he may be able to borrow from his bank on such a security, but this availability is limited— if you are considering this or any other kind of borrowing on securities, you should check with your broker or banker for up-to-date regulations.

5. Unlisted stocks do not fluctuate as much as listed ones on an *hour-by-hour basis.*

6. There are no "stop" orders in the over-the-counter market, and short selling is impractical (in fact, it can seldom be accomplished by an individual).

Tracing through an actual transaction OTC might clarify a few things. Let's say you want to buy 100 shares of Apple Computer stock. If the stock were listed, the order would go through the procedure explained in Chapter 4 at the Apple post. But Apple is not listed. So your order will go to the OTC department of your broker (usually called the "trading department"). The OTC clerk receives the order and looks on the national quotation sheet, or on an electronic visual display, which shows which brokers throughout the country "make a market" in this stock. Let's assume there are four firms "trading" Apple. The clerk proceeds to get a quote from each of them as follows:

Clerk: "How's Apple?"

Broker B: "25 at 25½." (This means that B is willing to buy at least 100 shares of that stock at the bid price of 25 and stands willing to sell at least 100 shares at 25½).

Broker C gives his market as: 25⅛ at 25½.

Broker D gives his market at: 25 at 25¼.

Broker E gives his market as: 25⅛ at 25⅝.

The clerk has now checked the market and finds that the lowest offering is 25¼ by Broker D. He calls D back immediately and, if he finds that his market has not changed, he tells D, "Buy 100 from you at 25¼." Actually, the clerk may try to get the stock a little cheaper by bidding 25⅛, but he takes a chance that D may then change his offer. If the clerk decides that 25¼ is a fair price, the transaction is completed and you will be billed at this price plus commission.

Certain firms make a business of "making a market" in OTC securities. They stand ready to buy and sell, and naturally hope to make a good living from the spread that exists between the bid and ask. For example, if a broker can buy and sell the same number of shares without the market changing, he can make good money (in the Apple example, if broker D buys 100 shares from another firm at his bid price of 25 and then sells your broker this 100 shares at 25¼, he makes himself $25). The difficulty is that these OTC dealers can't count on buying and selling the same number of shares each day—and the price is always fluctuating. Take the theoretical case of a firm making a market in the technology company, Raychem. Let's say he quotes the stock 65 bid, 65½ offered. In the course of the day he buys from other brokers 500 shares at 65, without selling any at the offer of 65½. The next day more selling comes in on Raychem and the price drops to 63½ at 64 (that is, the other dealers in that stock have lowered their price to 63½ bid, 64 offered). This dealer naturally has to adjust his market to approximately the same level. Now another broker comes in and buys 500 shares at the current offer price of 64—this is the same 500 that the OTC dealer purchased only yesterday at 65 and thus he lost $1 per share on 500 shares, or $500. As you can see, "making a market" in OTC securities is risky business.

HOW DO UNLISTED SECURITIES SHOW IN THE NEWSPAPER?

We'll see in Chapter 11 how stock prices show in the daily papers. Whereas nearly all the stocks listed on the various exchanges show in the paper every day, there would not be room for the many thousands of unlisted securities. Therefore it is normal for the papers to show only the most widely traded unlisted issues and those that have a local following. Many papers print quotations on fifty to one hundred stocks total. *The Wall Street Journal* shows daily prices of a few hundred.

Now, suppose you own one of the many stocks that are not shown in your local newspaper or in The *Wall Street Journal* (or in a long list of weekly quotations shown in *Barron's*). How do you know where your stock is selling? Well, the only way to determine the stock's price is by asking your broker, who can get you a quote at any time.

Let's assume, however, that your unlisted stock or stocks are printed *daily*. They will show like this:

	Bid	Ask
Apple	25	$25\frac{1}{2}$
Raychem	$63\frac{1}{2}$	64

Preceding the over-the-counter prices is usually a statement such as: "These quotations, supplied by the National Association of Securities Dealers, are bids and offers quoted by over-the-counter dealers to each other as of approximately 3 P.M. (Eastern time). The quotations do not include retail markup, markdown, or commission, and do not represent actual transactions."

In other words, these prices are only a range; they are not the exact prices. Also notice that the prices are as of "approximately 3 P.M."; thus the time of compilation can differ greatly from that for the prices shown on *listed* securities. So these over-the-counter quotations are not as accurate as quotations from the exchanges.

Also notice that there is no column denoting the change in price from the previous day: there are no plus and minus signs to look at.* This is one reason why many banks and insurance companies have preferred to keep their stocks unlisted. You can imagine the effect of large minus signs on people who have money on deposit in the Thriftiman's Bank, for example. After three or four days of −3, −2, −5, a depositor might start thinking, "Say, what's going on in that bank of mine? Maybe I'd better run down there and take my money out!" The same psychology applies to insurance policy holders. People simply don't notice the ups and downs of unlisted securities so much when the plus and minus signs are missing.

CONCLUSIONS

Some of the best money-making opportunities exist in the OTC market because it contains not-so-recognized stocks that may become the blue chips of tomorrow. Many times you will find an OTC stock that is not so well known, that is much more reasonably priced in relation to its earnings, dividends, or book value than a comparable listed security. If and when this OTC stock becomes better known, it may rise in price very rapidly just because it is "catching up" and beginning to sell on the same basis as better-known comparable stocks.

Certain securities in the OTC market do not have a "good market." For these stocks, you have little assurance that you will be able to find a buyer when you want to sell. If you are considering investing in this type of stock (which, incidentally, is the exception), you should realize that you are sacrificing marketability or liquidity.

For the most part, however, you can be sure of reasonable marketability in unlisted stocks. A general rule: If a stock looks very attractive to you, don't let the fact that it is unlisted deter you from buying. Many very interesting situations will present themselves in OTC securities, so don't be prejudiced against them for that reason alone.

---

*Actually, the recent trend is toward showing plus and minus signs for OTC stocks, too. The *Wall Street Journal* makes a practice of this and other periodicals at least show what the previous day's bid price was, for the sake of comparison.

7

The "Third" and "Fourth" Markets

For many years a sharp distinction existed between so-called listed (listed on a stock exchange) and unlisted securities. The stock exchanges insisted that a security that had listing privileges on their exchange(s) could only be traded on those exchanges.

The trouble with this doctrine was that commission rates on those exchanges were fixed; if you wanted to buy American Telephone stock, you had to pay that set commission rate.

Such monopoly was not to persist forever. Certain entrepreneurial brokers recognized a potential opportunity—they were willing to take over-the-counter type positions on American Tel and other listed issues and attempt to effect transactions that would result in lower net costs to their customers than if these buyers and sellers went through exchange member brokers. Thus was born what came to be known as the Third Market.

The exchanges were constantly battling what they considered to be "intruders," but the cost elements were simply too attractive, so the Third Market flourished handsomely. Its major thrust was with large institutional-type investors, although some also had profitable business with individual investors. Weeden and Company, Jeffries, and other companies soon became very important market makers; they combined the function of specialist and broker and they transacted large amounts of business.

Later on, another market appeared—this one strictly oriented to institutions. This was labeled the Fourth Market. Without going into great detail, this new competitor offered a clearing house arrangement for such large investors. By paying some minimum fee, the institution (a large bank, insurance company, mutual fund, investment adviser, etc.) would communicate to the Fourth Market broker its desire to buy or sell certain securities. The Fourth Market broker would see if there was a "match" with any of his other customers, and if so, would attempt to arrange a transaction price between the two—with little or no cost to either side for this service. Thus if Bank A had registered an interest in selling General Motors, and if Insurance Company B called in and indicated a buying interest in GM, the Fourth Market broker would communicate with both A and B, see if they could agree on a price and number of shares, and if they did, arrange for the transaction to take place. The Fourth Market broker might charge a small fee to take care of clearing charges, handling fees, and so forth. Or he might not, taking his compensation instead from some fixed fee agreed to by his customers on an annual basis.

With set brokerage fees no longer the standard rule on the major exchanges, the competitive advantages of both Third and Fourth markets have diminished. Yet they still flourish—they actually handle a significant volume of trading every day. And they are tied in to the Central Market System, so that all transactions—whether they be on the exchanges, in the over-the-counter markets, or in the Third or Fourth markets—appear on the ticker tape that was once the exclusive domain of listed securities.

PART III
How to Judge the Stock Market and Gauge Where It Is Going

8

The Market and
How to Follow It

If nothing else is certain about stocks, one thing is: *The Market will fluctuate*. To be up or to be down, that is the question. While the stock market is looked upon by many as a *thermometer* of business conditions and the political climate, I view it more as a *crystal ball*. The stock market is always trying to forecast what will happen rather than reflect what has already occurred. That is why the axiom "Buy stocks when things look at their worst" is so important. When things seem to be at their worst, the public generally reflects pessimism by selling stocks on a wholesale basis. Smart investors buy these greatly depressed stocks on the theory that if things are at their worst, they can only get better. In the stock market, if you wait until things actually *are* better, you'll be late. By that time, stocks will have risen in value by a goodly amount.

People are always amazed when a company announces higher earnings, a raised dividend, or other good news—only to find its stock go *down* in price. Why does this happen? Because speculators anticipated the good news, bought the stock at low prices before the announcement was made, and then sold their stock when the news finally broke, forcing the stock down in price. Of course, many times a stock will rise on good news (in fact, this is usually the case), but this does not refute this theory. It only proves that the good news had not been anticipated by the majority of investors and speculators.

The stock market in general is subject to the same "anticipation of news." The market is always trying to *forecast* events. And that is why I say the market is more like a crystal ball than a thermometer. Now, many times the crystal ball is foggy—in fact, it can be as wrong as Madame Gadzooks, who tells you your future by reading the backs of tea leaves (or do they use tea bags now?). Sometimes people get optimistic about the near future (and the market goes high), only to be proved wrong. For example, the 1956 stock market was rising and anticipating continued good business for some time to come, only to find business slump very rapidly in mid-1957 and 1958. Sometimes the market will get worried about conditions, as it did in 1946–47, only to find that business was not bad when 1947–48/49 rolled around. The same thing happened with the 1962 and 1979 markets; no recessions developed. Many, many times, however, the market is correct in its forecasts of things to come. The main thing is that you, as a potential buyer of stocks, should always *look ahead* and attempt to forecast, too. Now you are probably asking how *you* can forecast complicated economic and political events so that you are just a little bit ahead of the next person. The following discussions should aid you in getting the jump. The necessary facts are available—it's only a matter of knowing where to find them and how to interpret them.

WHERE TO GET THE FACTS

Many local newspapers will give you most of the facts you need to know in judging business and the stock market. But the "bible" in our business is the *Wall Street Journal*. This daily (five days a week) publication will keep you current on economic statistics and reports by industries and individual companies. It also prints feature articles of interest. Countless other publications are valuable supplements to the *Journal*, namely *Barron's* (weekly), *Fortune* (biweekly), *Business Week* magazine (weekly—devoted to all aspects of business, including marketing, finance, labor, advertising), *Magazine of Wall Street* (strictly finance), *Forbes* (biweekly, exclusively devoted to the market and articles on stocks), *Financial World*, and many others.

In addition, there are some government publications that

will give you all the economic facts you can possibly digest, namely the Federal Reserve Board's monthly bulletin and two Department of Commerce publications—*Economic Indicators* (monthly business statistics in chart form) and the *Survey of Current Business.*

Furthermore, if you're willing to spend a few more dollars, there are many investment "services" that will boil down these facts for you and recommend individual issues as well as give advice on the market in general. *Standard and Poor's* and *Moody's* are perhaps the best known of these services, but there are countless others, such as *United Business Service, Value Line,* and *Babson's.*

Here I must point out one disadvantage to following the investment recommendations of these services. Many times a widely subscribed service will put out a buy or sell recommendation on a particular stock. When such recommendations are mailed throughout the country and arrive at different locations on different days, there may not be any concentrated orders coming from this recommendation on one day. Many such recommendations are mailed out, however, to arrive in the mail over the weekend. Hundreds of subscribers read their mail on Saturday or Sunday, call their broker and place an order for the opening on Monday morning, and what happens? The stock is subject to a sudden spurt! Perhaps it closed at $30 on Friday, but orders to buy a few thousand shares are placed "at the market" on Monday and it opens at $33, or the stock has a concentrated rise during the whole day because of this recommendation. You should beware of this, because chances are that when this concentrated buying from the recommendation subsides (which may be only a day or so later), the stock will drop back near its Friday's close. In other words, be discreet with your order—don't become "one of the mob" that rushes to buy the stock all at once. For example, a number of years ago a famed news commentator took to giving investment "tips" on his evening show (which would be in violation of FCC regulations today). These tips were followed by certain listeners and invariably a rash of buy orders would accumulate the next morning and cause the given stock to rise suddenly and sharply. In the great majority of cases these buyers paid inflated prices and it generally took them quite some time to get even on their purchases. Some of us in the securities business used to say, "Whatever Mr. _____ recommends on Sunday night, *don't buy, but instead sell short* on Monday morning." In practice, this was one of the most consistent theories ever in the stock market.

There are countless economic factors you should consider when reading the financial page of your newspaper. Like all statistics, these are only meaningful when compared with like figures for a previous period. Let's take a look at some indicators that tell you how *business in general* is at the moment. Naturally, it takes interpretation (and some guesswork) to shape these factors into a projection of what kind of business lies ahead.

Gross National Product

The GNP tells you the total goods and services produced in this country on an annual basis. Obviously the higher the GNP, the better business in general is. Inflated prices can fool you, however, so investors have learned to focus on *real* GNP— which subtracts inflation from the gross figures.

Employment

Employment figures are, of course, indicative of the state of business. You notice I stress *employment* rather than *unemployment* figures, mainly because the latter can be deceiving. For example, unemployment can rise even though business is booming if an exceptionally large group of eighteen-to-twenty-two-year-olds suddenly enters the labor force. In other words, a bumper baby crop eighteen to twenty years ago may be added to the employable list after their schooling—and unemployment figures might well indicate caution about business, whereas employment figures might remain high and be reassuring.

Disposable Personal Income

This figure tells you how much money people have to spend, which is basic to good business both currently and in the near future.

Index of Industrial Production

The IIP gives you the amount of general business volume, shown as a percentage of the average that existed in 1967 (given a base of 100). For example, an IIP of 150 means that business volume is 50% higher than the average of the base period.

Bank Deposits

It's always nice to see bank deposits rising along with higher consumer spending. Were deposits to drop substantially, it would be a sign for caution, because people can't draw down from savings forever. Savings provide future business. The burgeoning growth of money market funds has, however, made bank deposits a less reliable indicator of investor savings patterns.

Manufacturers' New Orders, Unfilled Orders, and Inventories

The importance of the first two of these three factors is obvious. *New orders* received by manufacturers build up the amount of *unfilled orders* they have on the books; the larger the unfilled orders, the more assurance you have that business will be good in the time ahead. Not quite so obvious, but of the very utmost importance, are *inventories*, which are the amount of goods already on the shelves of manufacturers.

Despite the old story "Salt," the more goods businessmen have on their shelves, the more cautious they are about buying.*

Businessmen are willing to buy more than they require when they sense booming conditions, but the minute business

---

*A customer entered a grocery store and asked, "Have you any salt?" "Salt" replied the grocer, "Have I got salt? Take a look!" Behind him were shelves filled with salt. Then he took the customer to the back of the store and showed him more rows of shelves filled with salt. "Have I got salt?" he repeated again and took the customer by the hand to the basement, where he had a roomful of salt. "Have I got salt!!" the grocer kept muttering.

The customer looked at him and said the obvious: "My, but you must sell a lot of salt every year!"

"Salt? Who sells salt?" cried the grocer. "Maybe three cases a year, I sell. But there's a salesman who comes here three times a year, and wow, can he sell salt!!!"

THIS IS DEFINITELY THE EXCEPTION TO OUR ECONOMIC REASONING ABOUT INVENTORIES.

starts to slip, they cut back on their buying of goods. And if they already have large supplies on hand, they delay buying altogether until their inventories go down to more manageable levels. *When inventories are rising from anything but depressed levels, it is a sign for caution.* At least two of our country's recessions since the end of World War II were the direct result of inventory cutbacks—businessmen ceased to buy because their inventories were too high.

Consumer Debt

This is another important indicator. People can only owe so much before they have to slow down their buying on credit. One of several causes of the 1957–1958 recession was the large amount of debt piled up by consumers during the bulging 1955–1956 automobile sales. The public simply saturated themselves and had to hold off purchases of goods—especially those usually sold "on time"—till their debt payment declined. A similar pattern (though more severe) existed in 1980. Consumer debt alone can be deceiving, however. Some effort should be made to relate it to personal income before reaching any conclusions about whether it is too high or too low.

Imports and Exports

Naturally these are important to the nation. While we encourage foreign trade and the building up of other nations, it is distressing to see an unfavorable balance of trade wherein the United States is importing more than we are selling to others.

Business Failures

A marked increase in failures is a credit caution signal.

Cost-of-Living Index

The cost-of-living index (CPI) and the producers price index (PPI) indicate how much inflation we are having. Inflation has become an ever more important consideration for investors, whether they be interested in bonds, stocks, real estate, gold, or whatever.

Money Supply

Money supply has become another important forecasting factor. Many investors have become "Fed watchers" (the Federal Reserve Board will be discussed later in this chapter), on the theory that the manipulation of the money supply has a significant bearing on future business conditions and inflation. Money supply is expressed in such terms as M1, M2, and M3, and a full explanation of its intricacies is beyond the scope of this book. Suffice it to say that the sharply rising money supply is stimulative to the economy *and* it is potentially inflationary (and vice versa).

"MORE SPECIALIZED" FACTORS TO WATCH FOR

The following are additional indicators, most of which have a double meaning to forecasters:

Paperboard Production

Certainly you should watch this statistic if you have an interest in paper stocks. In addition, this happens to be a very sensitive indicator of the trend of business. Why? Because everything that is produced has to be wrapped and shipped. And what is the most important material for this use? Paperboard, of course. Remember, most companies report their earnings every three months. You may not know how a company's business is going in between these quarterly statements. But the paperboard figures appear weekly and can be a good lead indicator of business in general, of an industry trend, or of the stock market in general.

Railroad Carloadings

A similar indicator is railroad carloadings, which is the number of railroad cars being loaded for shipment each week.

If you own railroad stocks, here is the best indicator of how the rail business is going. But these figures have added significance, for everything produced must eventually be shipped and railroads and trucks handle most of the manufactured goods in the United States. So when rail shipments decline, they show up *weekly* in the carloading figures. The carloadings are broken down for you by geographical location and by freight classification. A similar "Intercity Trucks Tonnage Index" exists for goods shipped by trucks. Here again, you can stay ahead of quarterly reports by following these important business indicators.

Electric Power Production

This is important for holders of utility stocks, but it also provides a check on overall business conditions. After all, when business is good, more power is used, so these weekly figures give a broad picture of activity.

Automobiles and Building

Figures from these two basic industries are very important. Aside from the huge sums of money paid out in wages to workers in these industries, think of the related industries that are so dependent on them. Auto-truck production has a great effect on steel, glass, chemicals, rubber, aluminum, and other metals, as well as on transportation. Building likewise involves steel, glass, and aluminum and has considerable effect on cement, gypsum, asphalt, lumber, plywood, and so on. Therefore both new car-truck sales and building activity give you insight into overall business conditions, especially into the major industries they involve. Auto-truck production figures are published weekly, while housing starts and other construction figures are generally published on a monthly basis.

London Metal Prices

If you're following nonferrous metal stocks (copper, zinc, lead, etc.), keep a close eye on London metal prices. Prices overseas eventually have an effect domestically. Incidentally, since nonferrous metal prices fluctuate more than steel, aluminum, and other ferrous metals, they are good indicators of business activity. When copper prices rise, for example, it is usually because of increased demand and this demand usually stems from higher production.

Steel Production, Store Sales, and Other Statistics

Steel production figures are released weekly by the American Iron and Steel Institute and, of course, give you early indication of what quarterly earnings of the steel companies will be.

Weekly department store sales not only tell how Macy's, Sears, and the other big stores are doing, but also give a clue as to how well the textiles and appliance makers are doing.

Then there are figures for *life insurance sales, crude and refined oil production,* and countless other industries.

One not-so-noticeable statistic involves *wholesale price levels.* Food chains and soap manufacturers can be expected to *increase* their profits in years when wholesale prices are low.

Needless to say, an owner of stocks or a potential investor should follow the *earnings* and *dividends* of companies. Later on, we'll explain how to use these figures in determining what price a stock should be selling for in the market.

FEDERAL RESERVE POLICY

No discussion of business forecasting would be complete without mention of the Federal Reserve Board. The importance of this governmental body cannot be overemphasized.

The Federal Reserve regulates the amount of money that flows through our economic system. Because money is the root of all business activity, the Fed has great power. Briefly, the Fed has the following tools:

1. It sets the *discount rate,* which is the rate of interest that the banks have to pay when they borrow money from the Federal Reserve. If the Fed raises the discount rate

from 9% to 9½%, banks have to pay more for some of the money they loan out. To compensate for this ½ of 1% increase, the banks will have to raise their interest charge by at least this amount. Theoretically, the higher interest charge should deter a certain amount of borrowing; thus the Fed can restrain lending by raising the discount rate. In contrast, lowering the rate has the effect of lowering interest rates throughout the country, which invites more borrowing. Borrowing does not always increase, however, because when people get cautious about borrowing, even abnormally low rates may not generate enthusiasm. "You can lead a horse to water, but you can't make him drink." Most economists agree that the discount rate is more powerful in restraining business than in stimulating it.

2. The Fed also sets the *reserve requirements* of banks. This has a direct effect on how much money the banks have available to lend and naturally it has an important effect on the economy. The lower the reserve requirements, the more money the banks have "free" for lending; the higher the requirements, the less money available for lending. In addition, the Fed can affect banks' reserve positions through purchases and sales of government securities in the open market.*

3. The Fed has direct control over the use of credit in the stock market through the establishment of *margin requirements*. Margin is the amount of cash one has to put up when purchasing listed securities (you must put up all cash when buying most unlisted stocks). When margin requirements are 70%, a buyer must put up at least $7,000 in cash for the purchase of $10,000 in securities; the remaining $3,000 may be borrowed from the broker at an interest rate set by the local stock exchange. By raising margins, the Fed requires higher down payments and thus restricts speculation. Incidentally, changes in margins are *not retroactive*. If you made a

---

*A detailed discussion of this complicated mechanism is unnecessary for our purposes. All you need to know is that the Fed decreases member bank reserve balances (restricts credit) when it sells government securities in the market, and vice versa.

$10,000 purchase with a down payment of $7,000 and the Fed raised margins to 90%, you would not be affected. You could keep that $3,000 loan for as long as you like. As a matter of fact, you can replace a security held in a margin account with an equivalent dollar purchase (and stay under the "old rules") as long as the switch is accomplished the same day. Any new purchases, however, would come under the new regulations.

4. The Fed can use *credit restrictions* (i.e., force car or appliance buyers to put up a given down payment). These have been employed only in rare circumstances such as war, but the early 1980 credit restraints indicated by the Fed had immediate impact on the economy.

The Federal Reserve Board has been criticized time and again for its policies. Tight money policies (higher discounts rates, reserve requirements, and margin requirements) are usually the brunt of attack by businessmen because they tend to hamper business. That's why it is especially important to understand the Fed's aims. In short, it tries to keep the economy on a steady rate of growth over the years and it wants to keep prices from skyrocketing. The Fed doesn't want a few years of boom and then a few years of recession—and it doesn't want rampant inflation. It estimates the country's average growth rate and tries to keep it on an even keel. I like to contrast the Fed's attitude with an experience I'm sure all of you have had as a driver or passenger of an automobile traveling along a boulevard that has stop signals set for a certain rate of speed. Perhaps you've seen drivers who insist on going 60 miles an hour for two blocks, only to have to screech to a halt at the next signal, while you make all the signals without stopping by driving 30 miles per hour. What happens to the 60 mph driver? He wastes gas by rapid acceleration, wears down his tires and brakes by quick stops, and ends up with constant aggravation. This is just what the Fed guards against. It wants the economy to go 30 mph and get to the destination with greatest ease.

The trouble is that the Federal Reserve Board cannot regulate the economy as you would the gas pedal of your car. Restraint may well choke business and create lower activity than originally planned (this was the complaint of many during 1956–1957). But a temporary dip in business is always better than a sharp depression that might last for a long, long time.

In recent years various moves have been made to reduce the independence of the Federal Reserve Board through legislation. Frankly, I consider this a mistake—one that would have serious consequences for the U.S. economy. This is not to imply that the Fed has always "behaved" as its role dictates; certainly its willingness to stimulate the economy in 1972, which "just happened" to be an election year, when the economy did not need such stimulation seemed strange (and inexcusable) to me. Its actions in 1978–1980 also left something to be desired—the Fed was more stimulative than those of us who feared inflation would have liked. But by and large, the Fed has tried to act in the best long-range interests of the country. If it were to lose its independence and become a political-type organization, its role as an economic "traffic controller" would be diminished. Monetary regulation is anything but an exact science, and thus the best efforts of the Fed have not always produced the desired results. Until human nature changes radically, however, every economy will need monetary regulation—and its chances for success are enhanced with an objective, independent body such as the Federal Reserve Board.

9
What's the Market Doing?

When people ask, "How's the market?", they want to know what the basic trend is. Many experts contend that there's no such thing as a "general stock market." Instead, they say there are separate markets for individual stocks and that an investor should be more concerned with what's going on in individual issues rather than the overall list. While I, too, prefer this approach, one has to be conscious of a trend and that's what we're going to touch on here.

Most investors judge "the market" by what is happening to the Dow Jones Industrial Average (DJIA). This average consists of an index of thirty stocks,* and measures their performance during the day. Actually, there are numerous disadvantages to this index. For one thing, it represents *only* thirty stocks and it doesn't seem fair to judge the whole market by just these thirty. Second, the thirty stocks are all recognized blue chip issues; there are no secondary stocks (since there are more secondary companies on the exchange than blue chips, the DJIA does not reflect the majority). Third, the stocks in the average are not all equally weighted. In 1928 Dow Jones revised its average in such a way that any stock that splits has—after the split—less

*The thirty include: Allied Chemical, Aluminum Co., Amer. Brands, Amer. Can, AT&T, Bethlehem Steel, duPont, Eastman Kodak, Exxon, General Electric, General Foods, General Motors, Goodyear, Inco, IBM, Inter. Harvester, Inter. Paper, Johns-Manville, Merck, Minnesota M&M, Owens-Illinois, Procter & Gamble, Sears Roebuck, Std. Oil of Calif., Texaco, Union Carbide, United Technologies, US Steel, Westinghouse Elec., and Woolworth.

influence on the index than those that leave their price high. Because of this, in any given day a large fluctuation in just one or two high-priced stocks like Proctor and Gamble or IBM can distort the average considerably. Thus, while the DJIA reflects the overall market trend *over the long run,* it is too often a very unreliable indicator of daily or weekly market action.

There are other averages one can follow. Perhaps the most inclusive are the Standard and Poor 500 Stock Index and the New York Stock Exchange Index. Because of their breadth, these do not have certain of the Dow Jones Industrial disadvantages. Actually, the S&P 500 has shortcomings, too, in that it is heavily weighted by a few dozen large capitalization (i.e., many shares outstanding) companies.

FACTORS TO CONSIDER IN JUDGING THE MARKET

There are countless factors to consider in judging what the market is doing. Here are some of the most important:

1. *Do* follow some of the averages (Dow Jones Industrials, Railroads and Utilities, and the S&P 500 or NYSE Stock Index), but remember that the most important consideration is the percentage change over one day or a long period of time. The newspaper headlines can be deceiving. "Stocks Drop Six Points" or "Market Declines Total $3 Billion." Remember that a 7-point drop in the Dow Jones Industrial Average, which is currently around 900, is less than 1%. And that the total value of listed securities runs into hundreds of billions of dollars.

2. Look for the ratio of *advances* to *declines* in the market on any particular day. If more stocks are advancing than declining, perhaps the market is really strong despite the fact that the averages showed a decline for the day.

3. Also useful in determining the breadth of the market on any given day is the number of individual stocks that made *new highs* versus the number that touched

new lows for the year. Obviously a market with a preponderance of stocks reaching new highs cannot be termed weak, even if the averages denote a decline.

4. What is the *volume of trading*? Like the preceding figure, this one appears every day in your local papers. The volume of trading is just another way of saying "the number of shares that were bought and sold." The reason this is important is that *volume usually moves with a trend.* That is, if the market is advancing on *low* volume and declining on *heavy* volume, most probably *the basic trend* is *down.* By the same token, if the number of shares traded is consistently higher on days when stocks are strong, then the overall trend is probably up.

5. How many shares have been sold short? The so-called short interest comes out once a month (the data are gathered on the 15th and published a few days later) and shows how many shares of each stock are held "short." The larger the number of shares sold short, the more pessimistic people are. Oddly enough, it is *not* a bad sign when the short interest is up. Why? Because the time to buy is usually when most investors *are* pessimistic, for that's when stock prices are low. And remember that a short seller must eventually buy back, so the more shares sold short, the more potential buyers there are "lying in the weeds."

6. *How do yields on stocks compare with yields on bonds?* This "spread between the yields" is important because bonds and stocks are in competition for the dollar. For many years stocks gave a higher return than bonds; this was natural, because there is more ordinary risk in stocks than in bonds. An investor would find the return on stocks anywhere from $\frac{1}{2}$ of 1% to $2\frac{1}{2}$% higher *than the yield on bonds.* As the 1958–1959 market boom progressed (stocks rose in value and bonds plunged), this situation changed to one in which a "minus spread between the yields" became standard. By this I mean that bonds have provided a higher return than stocks (in 1980 the return was as much as 5–8% higher for

bonds than for stocks). The fear of inflation is primarily responsible for this "minus spread" since, as we have seen, bonds do not provide the desired hedge against inflation, whereas many common stocks do. From a historical standpoint, however, a large minus spread is a sign for caution and investors should watch these figures (shown weekly in *Barron's*, among others).

7. *What is "the public" doing?* One of the old adages of Wall Street is "The public is always wrong." Who is "the public"? Usually the smaller investor, who buys in smaller amounts—in odd lots. Therefore we can gauge what he is doing by watching the summary of odd lot transactions, which shows how many shares in less than 100-share lots are bought, how many are sold, and how many are sold short. Also from a historical standpoint, it is time for suspicion when odd lot buys greatly overshadow the odd lot sells. Conversely, think about buying when the odd lot figures show heavy selling on balance.

8. *How much speculation is there in the market?* This can be judged by the types of securities that are most actively traded. One guide is the Standard and Poor 20 Low-Priced Stock Index. Another is the list of the most actively traded stocks on the exchange either daily or weekly. A predominance of speculative, low-priced, low-quality stocks indicates that the market has "poor leadership," whereas heavy trading in the blue chips gives the market stature—good leadership. For the most part, low-priced stocks are not purchased by institutional investors, but instead by the public or by speculators. Large activity in lower-quality issues happens occasionally, and it, too, presents a sign for heed.

Another reliable indicator of speculation is the relationship of trading on the American Stock Exchange to that on the Big Board (NYSE). Let's face it, the ASE is hardly the haven for quality issues—at least compared to the NYSE. Whenever the ASE is experiencing volume much above 50% of what is trading on the

NYSE for an extended period, it constitutes a strong sign for caution.

9. *How many "secondary offerings" and "new issues" are coming to market?* Secondary offerings (large blocks of stock being offered at a given price at one time) and new issues (shares of *privately* held companies being offered to public investors for the first time) have one thing in common: they both take investors' dollars that might instead have gone into stocks traded on the exchanges or over-the-counter. Too many of these "outside influences" must eventually drain investors' resources and reduce the demand for other securities. As with other commodities, a very sharp increase in supply of securities without a corresponding increase in demand will lead to lower prices—and that is why you must be conscious of the secondaries and the new issues coming to market.

10. *How high is the market in relation to earning power?* We will see later how to judge an *individual stock*'s merit on the basis of its earning power. The *market in general* should be judged the same way. Most statistical services show you how high the market is in relation to current earnings and in relation to projected profits—by figuring its "price-earnings ratio." This ratio is discussed fully in Chapter 22, but for now just remember that the lower the ratio, the better, and a higher ratio is a sign of warning. Over the past twenty years we have seen the market sell between the broad range of around 6 and 20 times earnings, with one year (1961) when the market sold well above 20 times earnings. Remember, however, that it is more important to determine how the market is selling in relation to *future earnings* (those of six to twelve months ahead) than to past or even present profits.

10
The Bulls Versus the Bears

As you gathered from the last chapter, it is important for investors to analyze what is happening in the stock market. Accomplishing this simply prepares you to *forecast* better what lies ahead.

Cycles of some kind are inevitable in the stock market, and you should be prepared to spot these cycles *before they arrive.*

The stock market is a place where many thousands of people "vote" every day. In the market, of course, there are only two ways to cast your ballot: you can vote that the market—or more specifically, a stock—will go up, in which case you buy; or you can vote your belief that it will go down—and you sell. As in political elections, a *trend* usually develops in favor of one party or another. If the trend is on the buy side, then the market goes up and we have what is called a "bull market." If, on the other hand, people are wholly pessimistic and are predominantly on the sell side, stocks go down and we have a "bear market."

Over the years, the stock market has experienced many bull and bear cycles. Fortunately, the bull trends have dominated, as evidenced by the fact that the present market is close to its all-time high point. Also, a study of stock markets in the United States shows that bull markets normally last twice as long as the declining bear trends.

As a potential investor, you certainly want to be aware of which trend you are in. Like a good fighter, you want to roll with the punches and be more fully invested in a bull phase than in either trendless or bear conditions.

SPOTTING (AND DISTINGUISHING) BULL MARKETS

Imploring you to recognize trend may sound silly; after all, if it's a bull market, stock prices are rising, and if it's a bear market, the reverse is true. But as I keep emphasizing, you want to be *ahead of the crowd*. You want to prepare for the rain and take your coat and umbrella with you—not be suddenly drenched and soaked, with no rain clothes at all.

So now I am going to show you how to forecast—how to know when the clouds will be moving in, despite the prevailing clear skies. To start with, let's consider the characteristics of the final stages of a bull market. First, business is usually very good near the top of a market; this may sound paradoxical, but remember that the wise investors are looking ahead and they know that booming business cannot last forever; it is normally followed by recession. Second, investors are enthusiastic and plum full of confidence; everywhere you go you hear talk of the "new and golden era." Even the stock market "experts" are exuding confidence and predicting higher markets ahead. In addition, the following factors generally exist:

1. The market has attracted wide public participation. The total number of stockholders in the country takes a sudden spurt. The odd lot figures mentioned in Chapter 4 show far more buyers than sellers.
2. Stock splits are commonplace; this is because stock prices have risen so high that there are many more high-priced issues (obvious split candidates).
3. These warning signals appear: bonds are yielding way more than stocks; the market is probably selling very high in relation to current and, most important, prospective earnings, and there is a rash of offerings and new issues for the public to absorb. (Watch out when the "hot" new issues suddenly turn cold and "sticky.")
4. Additional signs for caution:

A. Rallies, which used to carry a long way, don't carry as far.

B. Bond prices start to fall sharply, thereby offering much higher returns to investors (a lot of money is attracted away from inflated stocks into deflated bonds).

C. The key stocks in the market begin to fade and sell off (the leadership of the market is weakened).

D. The volume of trading on the advances slows down considerably (the tide of enthusiasm is ebbing).

E. The market does not react, as it used to, to good news (announcements that once created excitement and caused stocks to rise suddenly have no effect).

When you begin to spot these factors, it is time to switch from a heavily invested position in common stocks to a conservative approach. But don't expect your actions to prove correct overnight—the market won't plunge the day after you have lightened your holdings. There is little chance of your selling at the top, so expect to see the stocks you have sold go higher in price. In other words, don't be greedy and try to extract the last ounce of profit from a waning market. If the market continues to roll on, don't be deceived and buy back hastily.

It is equally important to be able to spot the end of a bear market so you know when to take a very aggressive position in the stock market. On a historical basis, bear markets last anywhere from one to four or five years, although overall downward trends have been much shorter in duration over the last twenty years (usually lasting little more than one year). In stark contrast to bull markets, bear trends produce a morguelike mood; everyone is in the dumps and interest in the stock market is apathetic. Oddly enough, a sharp decline in the blue chip issues is a sign that the end of the bear market is approaching (since investors hold on to these till the end). As the decline nears an end, an investor is able to find real bargains in the market; dividends are high and stocks sell very reasonably in relation to earning power. The market becomes resistant to bad news (announcements that used to cause stocks to sell off all of a sudden have little or no effect).

Once the market turns around and starts up, the volume increases, but gradually. You start witnessing more advances than declines, more new highs than new lows, and so on. In short, the storm has passed and it is time to look for the clearest of skies.

Let me emphasize here that, despite the analysis just presented, the stock market is seldom a feast-or-famine affair. There are stocks to buy in very bad markets, just as there are stocks to sell in a boom. The analysis is intended to make you aware of extreme danger signals and of exceedingly attractive opportunities that may present themselves sometime during your stock market life. "Everything is relative," and successful investing results from having as much knowledge, information, and insight as possible. In essence, this is but one girder in the bridge to success. The other girders will fall into place as we go along.

PART IV
Some Facts of Life for Stockholders

11

Getting More out of the Financial Page

Chapters 9 and 10 have pointed out that there's plenty to be gained from reading the financial pages. But there's still more! Now we'll take a look at the page that shows the daily performance of individual stocks.

DAILY PRICE MOVEMENTS

Common Stocks

Here are a few typical quotations from your daily paper.

Sls	Stock		High	Low	Close	N'Ch
266	GenMotors	4.30e	80	79½	80	+ ½
1520	Rohm & Haas	3bas	730½	724	726	−2

First of all, an explanation of the columns. Column 1, "Sls," means sales that took place in that stock on the particular day. These sales are in 100's; that is, you merely add two zeros to the figure under "Sls" to find out how many shares traded that day (in the case of General Motors above, 26,600 shares traded). The name of the stock follows—almost always abbreviated. Then comes the company's annual dividend rate, shown as 4.30e for GM, meaning GM pays $4.30 per share annually in dividends, including extras (which is what the "e" stands for). The "high" column signifies the highest price the stock reached during the day, and "low" signifies the lowest. "Close" indicates the very last sale that took place on the exchange that day. And "N'Ch means "net change," which is the change in market price of the stock between the previous day's close and this day's last sale price. In the GM example, the stock closed at 80 compared to yesterday's 79½ for a net gain of ½ point. Incidentally, stock prices are traded in fractions, with ⅛ of 1 point (12½ cents) being the smallest fraction for most issues (on lower-priced stocks a dollar price is sometimes broken down to 1/16's, and "stock rights" are often bought and sold in fractions as small as 1/64's).

Now let's take a more detailed look at the GM example. What can we learn from it, over and above the simple facts just presented? First of all, watch the volume figures ("Sls") because, like the market in general, individual stocks often show their *trend* by volume; that is, if GM consistently goes *up* on a large amount of "Sls" and shows consistently lower volume when it goes down in price, you might assume that the GM pattern is currently *up*. In stock market jargon such a pattern would "indicate a strong technical pattern" for GM stock. Second, notice that the stock closed at its high for the day—so enthusiasm for the stock was building up at the close, which hints that the stock might open at higher prices on tomorrow's market.

There are a few stocks on the exchange that do not sell in 100-share round lots. Certain high-priced issues like Rohm and Haas (shown above) used to be called "10-share traders," which means that 10 shares constituted a round lot (1 to 9 shares constitute an odd lot). I say "used to be," as most of these very high priced stocks have been split and their shares now trade in normal 100-share round lots. Rohm and Haas, for example, has been split and is a normal 100-share trading stock now. The only 10-share traders today are preferred stocks. In this case the explanation usually includes the letters "as," which means "actual sales." In such circumstances, you do *not* add two zeros to the volume figures at the left; in our Rohm and Haas example, 1520 shares were the total traded during that day.

You might also have noticed the letter "b" after the "3" in Rohm and Haas. It means the company paid out *stock* dividends in addition to the $3 annual *cash* payout. There are numerous other letters used to point out other information to the reader. Consult the small print either at the beginning or at the end of the price list to find out what the symbols mean.

Preferred Stocks

Sls	Stock	High	Low	Close	N'Ch
10	NiagMhk pf 4.10as				
		32	32	32	— 3
110	do pf 5.25as	41	41	41	+ ½
20	do pf 4.85as	37½	37½	37½	

Our preceding discussion explains most of this. Just a few additions: The company's name is Niagara Mohawk; the "pf" stands for "preferred stock," and "do" means "ditto"—the same company as above.

Here we have three Niagara Mohawk preferred stocks. You may wonder why there is a big fluctuation of 3 points in the $4.10 preferred, especially since preferreds don't ordinarily fluctuate as much as commons. The answer: This preferred had not sold for quite some time—perhaps a month or longer—and the "—3" means the stock closed 3 points lower than *the last time it sold* (not the previous day, because it didn't trade then). You will often find large pluses or minuses on preferred issues and the time lag is usually the reason.

These prices on the three Niagara Mohawk preferred stocks serve as an ideal illustration of what has happened to preferred stocks in general in recent years as well as explain how bonds and preferred stocks go up and down in price *with a change in money rates.*

Let's follow the history of these preferred issues. In 1954 Niagara Mohawk needed money and decided to sell some preferred stock to investors. The company determined that it would sell 210,000 shares at $100 per share. But what dividend would it pay on these shares? The decision was made by asking,

"What are comparable preferred stocks paying?" After looking over numerous other such stocks, the company determined that it could sell all these shares if it offered a rate of return just over 4%—4.10% to be exact. Thus a $4.10 dividend rate was set on the $100 stock to yield 4.10% yearly to its owners. The issue was sold on this basis. Incidentally, the company set a call price of 103¼ on this stock, which meant that the company could redeem all or part of the issue *at its discretion* at this price. *With such a call price, investors knew they couldn't expect the stock to rise very far in price, no matter how long it was held.*

As years went on, money rates changed in the United States. Whereas in 1954 investors were attracted by yields of 4.10%, by 1957 people were not willing to pay $100 for an annual $4.10 in dividends. Instead they were willing to pay only about 79 for the $4.10 payout. The Niagara Mohawk $4.10 preferred had gradually declined in price so that it, too, was selling at only 79.

Now Niagara Mohawk needed more money and decided to "float" a new preferred issue. It had only to look at its $4.10 preferred at 79 to know that a yield of around 5¼% ($4.10 divided by 79 gives you this yield of 5.25%) was "the going rate." So the company marketed 200,000 shares of a new $100 preferred with a $5.25 annual dividend rate, to yield this 5¼%. This time the company gave the buyers a little more upside potential by setting the call price at 107½.

Time marched on and once again money rates changed. Investors were getting lower returns on their money than in 1957 and were willing to pay more than $100 for Niagara Mohawk preferred with a $5.25 annual dividend rate. By the time 1958 rolled around, the $5.25 preferred had risen to 108 in the market price (pretty much a maximum price for the stock because of its 107½ call price) and the $4.10 preferred had come back to around 85. And once again Niagara Mohawk was looking for capital and decided to issue another preferred (the company had, over this history I'm referring to, sold considerable amounts of bonds and common stock, too). By looking at the $4.10 and $5.25 issues, the company could see that a rate of around 4.85% was now attractive to investors,* so it set a $4.85

---

*The $5.25 preferred selling at 108 was yielding 4.86% ($5.25 ÷$108 = 4.86%) and the $4.10 preferred was at a price that gave a 4.83% annual return ($4.10 ÷ 85 = 4.83%).

annual dividend rate on another $100 par issue. Call price this
time was 106.

By 1980 money rates had changed again, this time rather
drastically, and the example shown on page 77 shows all the
preferreds providing a return, or yield, of around 12¾%. Further changes in yield will continue to affect these preferreds on
the market. Niagara Mohawk's position as a company did not
change much over the years shown. Yet if investors get to a
point where they are attracted only by a return of 15%, we
would find the $4.85 preferred selling around 32, the $5.25
selling at 35, and the $4.10 around 27. Even without another
negative turn in prices, it is obvious how horribly the original
investors in these preferreds have fared. To watch an original
investment at $100 per share decline to levels in the $30–$40
range is a discouraging but vivid lesson in the lack of protection a preferred shareholder has in times of rising interest
rates. Bondholders likewise had a miserable experience under
these conditions, but bonds at least have a maturity date at
which the principal must be repaid; this limits losses compared
to those suffered by preferred holders. Of course, conditions
could reverse themselves—especially from the 1980 levels. If,
for example, interest rates trend *lower* (or if investor opinion
about either utilities in general or Niagara Mohawk in particular improves), the market prices of these preferreds—and other fixed-income securities—will rise, perhaps substantially,
from current depressed prices.

Convertible Preferred Stocks

Although the majority of preferred stocks and bonds fluctuate with money rates and do not provide a normal hedge
against inflation, some issues have a "kicker" in the form of a
conversion feature. When a preferred or bond has this feature, it
gives the owner the right to convert it into *common stock at a giv-
en price* under certain conditions at *the owner*'s option. For example, let's assume that back in 1960 you were considering the
purchase of the Pacific Coast Company's $25 par value convert-
ible preferred, which paid an annual dividend of $1.25 per
share. Were this a straight preferred, you could never expect
more than the $1.25 dividend each year and you couldn't ex-

pect the stock to sell much over its call price, which in this case was $25 per share. It so happens, however, that this preferred was *convertible* share for share into Pacific Coast Company *common* anytime until 1965. Thus if the *common* were to rise to $50 per share, your $25 preferred would be worth $50, because you could take the preferred and exchange it into one share of common (worth $50) whenever you wanted, up to 1965. The conversion feature gives you a chance to grow with the common.

It so happens that the 1960 market price of Pacific Coast common was only $15—not $50—and thus the conversion feature was not of any *present* value. You certainly wouldn't turn in a $25 preferred for one share of common worth $15, so you had to hope the common would eventually move up in price past the price of the preferred. Because the common was at $15 and the conversion feature was of no present value, the preferred sold pretty much like any *non*convertible preferred (on the basis of its yield alone) and thus traded around $20.

In contrast, let's see what happens to a convertible preferred when the common advances in price and makes the preferred valuable. In 1966, as a result of a merger with Thatcher Glass Company, Rexall Drug and Chemical (now known as Dart Industries) issued a preferred that carried a $2 annual dividend and was to be convertible at the owner's option into one share of Rexall common stock. Because of this conversion feature, the preferred should be expected to sell at least at the price of the common. Now let's see how both common and preferred showed in the newspaper in January 1969:

Sls.	Stock	High	Low	Close	N'Ch
286	Rexall .30b	45½	44½	45	+1
11	do pf 2	50½	50	50¼	+1

As you can see, the preferred sold for more than 5 points *more* than the common. This is because the former paid a healthy $2 per year to its owners in cash dividends, while the latter distributed a measly 30 cents. Thus, investors were willing to pay a premium of over 5 points for the privilege of receiving the larger cash return. Of real importance here is the existence of the conversion feature. When the merger with Thatcher took place, Rexall common was selling for around $35—and the preferred commanded a premium similar to that above and was trading slightly above $40. Subsequently, the common increased in value (from $35 to $45) and the preferred went right along with it. Thus *the preferred proved valuable because of the conversion feature and it could be expected to fluctuate up and down with the price of the common.*

Convertible Bonds

Conversion features have the same meaning for bonds as for preferred stocks—they give them added potential. Here are two examples of convertible bonds.

1. *When the conversion feature is of no present value.*

EXAMPLE: Douglas Aircraft 4% convertible debentures,* 1977 maturity date; each $100 debenture convertible into 1.08 shares of common stock until 1977. This debenture was originally issued when Douglas *common stock* was selling around $85 per share. (All of this, of course, took place before Douglas's merger with McDonnell Aircraft). The debenture might have looked attractive at that time; after all, if Douglas common rose to 100, the bond would have been worth at least 108 (1.08 shares of common selling at $100) and would no doubt sell well above 108 because of its interest rate and the prospect that the common would rise further.

Unfortunately, Douglas common went the other way—it declined to $35 per share in mid-1961. Was the conversion feature of this Douglas bond of any immediate value anymore? Certainly not! To convert a $100 bond into 1.08 shares of common now selling at $35 would give only $37.80 worth of common (1.08 × $35 = $37.80).

Where was our $100 bond selling in 1961? Around $80! The bond never skidded down to $37.80 because investors

---

*"Debentures" are bonds that have the general credit of the corporation behind them. No specific real estate, property, or securities are pledged directly to debentures. Naturally these bonds rank above preferred stock in every way, but they are inferior to secured bonds.

were attracted to it almost as a straight (*non*convertible) bond at $80. At $80, the $4 interest rate gave an annual return of 5% ($4 ÷ $80 = .05, or 5%), *and* the bondholder knew that Douglas would have to pay back the original $100 at maturity (1977). Thus the person who bought the bond at $80 in 1961 expected to realize a $20 gain by 1977—and this $20 plus the 5% yield attracted him.* For the conversion feature to be of any value, Douglas common had to climb back to about $75 ($80 bond price ÷ 1.08 = $74)—a long way from its then market price of $35. As it turned out, Douglas did stage a dramatic recovery. By the end of 1965 it was back to the $75–$80 level, which naturally brought recovery to the bond price, too.

2. *When the conversion feature is presently of value.*

EXAMPLE: R. H. Macy 5% convertible debenture, 1977 maturity date; each $100 debenture convertible into 12½ shares of common stock at $8.00 per share until maturity date. When this bond was first issued, Macy common stock was selling at a little under $7.50 per share. Thus the debenture gave the investor a 5% return, plus a long-term call on the common at $8.00.

Macy common rose from the approximate $7.50 figure to $37.50—up exactly five times since the 1957 issue date of the debentures. Obviously, the conversion feature of the bond was of considerable value. Since each $100 bond could be exchanged into 12½ shares of common, the debenture sold for 12½ times the price of the common. In this case, the common stock price of $37.50 made the debenture worth over $468 (12½ × $37.50 = $468.75).

---

*In determining bond yields it is important to figure both the current return of the bond *and* the increment in the bond's value to maturity (as a percentage rate of return). The combination of these two gives what is known as *yield to maturity*. In the case of this Douglas debenture, the $20 increment (the bond will be worth $100 at maturity compared to its present price of $80) amounts to a gain of almost 1½% a year over the fifteen years remaining to the 1977 maturity. This 1½% plus the 5% current return gives a yield to maturity of almost 6½%. In this way you can compare the Douglas bonds with any others on a realistic basis. If instead of selling below $100 (selling at a "discount" as we say), the bond sold over $100 (at a "premium"), then you would have to subtract the premium to arrive at the yield to maturity. For example, a 5% bond due in one year that sells at 101 will have a yield to maturity of 4% (5% current return minus the 1% loss in capital = 4%).

A FEW RULES ABOUT CONVERTIBLE PREFERRED STOCKS AND BONDS

Here are a few generalizations that I think will be helpful to prospective buyers of "convertibles":

1. Do *not* buy a convertible issue unless you think the outlook for the company's common stock is especially good.
2. Try to figure what your maximum downside risk is before buying. There are two considerations here:
   a. Ask: What is the investment value of the bond or preferred as a "straight" security—that is, what is its value without the conversion feature? Unless income demands by investors change generally, this investment value should constitute your downside risk. Then, even if the company's common stock market price declines substantially, the convertible should not be affected beyond this "yield value."
   b. Obviously, the investment value will fluctuate with the trend of interest rates. You may think a yield of, say, 10% is the highest return the bond (or preferred) should offer because 10% is pretty much rock bottom for comparable straight (nonconvertible) securities; but if rates are jumping and rise to 11% or 12%, your investment value changes accordingly.
3. Most often when you buy a convertible bond or preferred whose conversion feature is already of value, the bond or preferred *will fluctuate directly with the price of the common.* In the case of the Macy convertible, if the common declines from 37½ to 30, the debenture will fall from 468 to 375 (12½ × $30 = $375).
4. In many cases when you find a convertible issue selling way above 100, you are better off buying the common stock directly. This is especially true if the common stock provides a higher rate of return than the bond at these advanced prices. For example, if a 4% bond is selling at 200 (giving a yearly return of 2%) and the

common stock of the same company is yielding any-thing *above* 2%, you might as well buy the common di-rectly.

5. Whereas your borrowing power on a corporate *bond* through your broker is limited to the existing margin requirements at that time (1980: 50% borrowing al-lowed on listed convertible bonds and 70% on listed nonconvertible bonds), and whereas a broker cannot grant margin on all *un*listed securities, *banks can lend large amounts* (generally between 50% and 75%) on such *unlisted securities* under certain circumstances. For exam-ple, assume you are considering the purchase of a 8% convertible bond of the XYZ Company. Let's say that each $100 bond gives you the right to convert the bond into 2 shares of common stock. XYZ stock is selling for $47. On a straight conversion basis, the bond is worth 2 (the number of shares you get for each bond) × $47 (the price of each share on the market), or $94. The bond is certainly going to be worth more than this pure conversion value, however. For one thing, the interest rate on the bond (8%) is probably higher than the yield on its common stock, but even if it isn't, the bond no doubt carries less risk than the common, and with the conversion feature giving you a long-term call on the common, this minimized risk warrants your paying a premium.

Thus the bond may be selling for 105, 110, or even more. Let's say we buy it for 108, which means that the common has to rise to 54 for us to be even (2 × 54 = 108). Let's also assume that the stock goes a lot higher than 54—to 70! The bond will be worth 2 × 70, or 140, which is a 32-point profit on our $108 purchase, or an increase of almost 30%. But suppose we hadn't put up the full $108 purchase price. Suppose we had borrowed 70% of the $108 from the bank and invested only 30%, or $32 of our money. The 32-point profit on the bond is exactly the amount of our cash investment—and thus we actually doubled our money. Because of our borrow-ing, we turned a 30% gain into a 100% gain. By the same token, a 64-point rise in the bond would give us a 200% profit, a 96-point increase would mean a 300% advance, and so on.

Naturally the reverse is true if the bond declines—you will suffer a larger percentage loss on your investment dollars because of the borrowing. Needless to say, borrowing of any kind involves risk and you should be very cautious about it. Still, you can see the dramatic possibilities in borrowing on the right convertibles.

6. Convertible issues that provide more income than the common stock can be expected to sell at a premium over their conversion value (for instance, the Rexall preferred on p. 76.

7. Most convertibles are "protected against dilution" in that the conversion feature changes along with the issuance of stock dividends, splits, and so forth on the common stock. If XYZ convertible preferred, for example, is now convertible share for share into common and the common is split 3-for-1, the conversion privilege will change after the split. In this case, each preferred will become convertible into 3 shares of common, instead of 1. If you are considering the purchase of a convertible, make sure it is protected against dilution.

Also, *always find out if and when a conversion privilege expires or changes.* Not all convertibles give the owners the right to convert into common for the full life of the issue; and in many cases, the original provisions of the convertible provide for a change in the conversion feature as time goes on.

8. Well-chosen convertibles are an excellent investment medium. They can give you a high and stable return, a "senior" position above the common in the event things don't go too well for the company, and a chance to grow with the common stock over the years.*

---

*For more information on convertible securities, including a guide to "correct" pricing of them in the market, see Chapter 11 of *The Common Sense Way to Stock Market Profits*, (published by The World Publishing Company in 1968 and, in a revised edition, by New American Library in 1978), which was written by this author as a follow-up book to the first edition of *Stock Market Primer*.

12

More About That Financial Page

STOCK SPLITS

Perhaps at some time you've opened to the financial section of your paper to see headlines like "Minnesota Mining Splits 3-for-1." Stock splits always make news. And they capture the imagination of investors and speculators alike. *Yet stock splits are merely the breaking up of a large pie into smaller pieces.* When a stock is split 3-for-1, the company gives you two new shares for each one you already own, giving you a total of three shares (including your original) for each one you started with. This would be sensational if the market price of the stock remained the same after the new shares were mailed out to you. Unfortunately, this is *not* the case! Once the new shares are mailed, the stock will sell for about one-third its price before the mailing. In a way it's like a pack of gum. The pack of five pieces sells for 25 cents; **open the pack and you have five separate pieces—each worth** a nickel. After you've opened the pack and *split* the gum into five separate pieces, you have no more and no less than you had when you started.

Then why, you might ask, do people get excited and rush to buy a stock if they think a split is coming or after one has been announced? After all, aren't three shares of Minnesota Mining worth $60 each the same as one share at $180? Absolutely!

There are, however, many investors who won't buy a stock selling as high as $180 per share. "How much money can I make," they ask, "by owning only 10 shares?" Yet they'll not think twice about buying 30 shares of the same stock selling for $60. That's just human nature. And if more people are attracted to buying a stock at $60 than at $180, what does it mean? That the stock will *go up* in price after it is split and sells for $60. And this is the main reason investors are attracted to newly split issues.

There's another, and perhaps more basic, reason for being attracted to a company that has announced a split. *A well-managed company will not split its stock unless it is optimistic about its future and can foresee the prospect of raising its dividend or showing higher earnings in the immediate future.* You can be sure when Minnesota Mining splits its stock that management is reasonably certain business will be excellent in the current year. And chances are that the annual dividend rate will soon be raised.

Management usually states that it wants to improve its stock's "marketability" by splitting it. It hopes that fluctuations will be less (even on a percentage basis) if a person wants to buy or sell the $60 stock than they would be at the $180 rate. This improved marketability is encouraging to investors, and this, too, makes the split attractive.

All of this brings us to one or two little warnings. First, be skeptical of $10–$20 stocks that announce splits. A split in these instances smells of promotion because there is no real reason to bring a stock down in price from these levels—it's low enough already. Second, never buy a stock *only* because it's being split; be sure you want to own that company and look for good values rather than splits alone.

Here's how splits show in your daily stock prices.

After stockholders approve the split proposed by the company's board of directors, a stock is traded on the exchange in two ways—"regular" (the stock at its old price) and "when-issued" (the new split price). It may show as follows:

Sls	Stock	Div.	High	Low	Close	N'Ch
12	MinnMng&Mfg	1.60	183	179	180	$+1\frac{1}{2}$
45	do wi		61	$59\frac{3}{4}$	60	$+\frac{1}{2}$

Trading will continue this way until the new stock is actually mailed out. The first day after the official mailing the stock will show with the word "New" after it, meaning that from here on it will only be traded at the lower split price. The exchange allows the two-way trading as shown above as a convenience to buyers and sellers. Say, for example, you want to buy $6,000 worth of MMM stock. If there is no "wi" (when-issued) trading, you have to buy 33 shares of the $180 stock; in this case, you may have to pay some premium for the odd lot and you end up with 99 shares after the split and will then have to transact a one-share buy order to round out your shares to 100. Both these disadvantages are overcome by buying 100 shares of the $60 stock. You don't have to fuss with odd lots and you end up with the exact number of shares you want, without making another purchase. The term "when-issued" means you cannot take physical delivery of the certificate until the new stock is mailed out, but still it's your stock, and if you turn around the next day and decide to sell it, you can do it (on the "wi" basis).

Splits provide some extra speculative prospects because margin regulations require that you put up only 30% of the money to buy "wi" stock (you can buy your $6,000 worth of MMM wi and put up only $1,800). Remember, though, that you have to put up the other 70% the day the stock trades "new." (After putting up the 70%, you can later convert the transaction to margin and thus withdraw in cash whatever amount existing market regulations allow.)

MERGERS AND "ARBITRAGE"

Every so often two companies will announce they are merging, which is the corporate way of getting married. For example, in March 1958 Texaco and Seaboard Oil announced that the board of directors of both companies had agreed to a plan whereby the two companies would merge. In this case, they had agreed that each share of Seaboard would be exchanged into an equal share of Texaco (and that Texaco would be the surviving company). They announced that the stockholders of both companies would vote on the merger proposal and that the results of their voting would be ascertained at a special meeting on May 23. Here is the way the stocks of Texaco and Seaboard traded on the stock exchange between the time of the merger announcement and the day the merger became official:

| | Market Price on | | | |
	Mar. 13	Apr. 10	May 5	May 23
Seaboard Oil	58	60⅝	66¾	66
Texaco	61⅛	62⅜	67⅜	66
Difference in market price between the two	3⅛	1¾	⅝	—

Even though the two companies' directors had agreed to the terms of the merger, there was a difference of 3⅛ points between the two stocks on March 13. Why shouldn't they sell at the exact *same* price? Simply because the merger was not yet *official;* many things could happen between March 13 and May 23 (the directors might change their minds for many reasons or the stockholders might fail to approve the plan or the government's antitrust forces might object to the merger). Thus the market reflected this element of uncertainty, with Seaboard selling 3⅛ points lower than Texaco.

As the approval date grew closer, however, the spread in price between the two narrowed: by April there was only a 1¾-point differential; in early May there was only ⅝ spread; and finally they sold at the same price after the approval. This is an illustration of a typical merger and respective market prices, but in most cases, the spread will be far wider than 3⅛ points (just 5% away from Texaco's $61 market price). Usually you will see a 10–15% disparity if the approval date is as much as a few months away, and an even wider discount when additional elements of uncertainty are involved.

Now let me show you a *guaranteed* way to make a profit *if you believe the merger* is going to be approved. If you buy the Seaboard Oil in March at 58 and at the same time sell the same amount of Texaco stock *short* at 61, you will give yourself a 3-point gain (you eventually cover your short sale of Texaco by delivering your Seaboard stock—remember, the Seaboard actually becomes Texaco stock after the approval). The transaction would look something like this:

Sell 100 shares of Texaco short and receive approximately	$6,100
Buy 100 shares of Seaboard and pay approximately	5,800
Your profit	$300

You have effected what is known as *arbitrage,* which is the buying and selling of similar securities for profit. Of course you have no guarantee of profit, because the merger could be broken off and you'd own 100 shares of Seaboard Oil that you could no longer use to cover your Texaco short sale. Chances are that Seaboard would fall in price if the merger talks were terminated, and you would stand to take a loss on your purchase. At the same time, Texaco would no doubt go up in price because short sellers would be rushing to cover—and thus you would lose on your short, too.

There are some types of arbitrage, however, that do *not* carry such risks and that do guarantee a profit, albeit a small one. Unfortunately, because of brokerage commissions, these profits are usually too small to warrant wasting one's time on them. Brokers and members of the exchange, however, who do not have to pay commissions (they would only be paying themselves), can make a nice living on arbitrage. One way to do this involves buying a convertible bond or preferred stock and selling the common of the same company short if it temporarily sells a little higher than the convertible issue. For example, let's assume that ABC Company stock sells at 101 today and the company's convertible bond (which is exchangeable share for share into common) is selling at 100. You have a guaranteed profit if you buy the bond at 100 and immediately sell the common short at 101, and then march to the bank and exchange the bond into the stock and deliver this stock to cover your short sale. In this case, you make a 1-point profit with no risk whatsoever. The drawback is that you have to put up a lot of capital to do the buying and selling, and thus the return on your money is small—perhaps only a profit of ½ of 1% on all your capital. But if you can get a guaranteed profit of ½ of 1% on your money 200 times a year, you end up with a 100% profit yearly, and that isn't bad.

There is one thing to keep in mind here. Whenever a company has a convertible issue outstanding, it *may* be subject to this arbitrage, which means that there may be constant short selling in its common stock. This constant selling may put temporary pressure on the stock and hamper its upward movement somewhat. If and when this convertible issue is called for redemption by the company, this short selling will cease and the stock will have an easier road.* Many of our country's very good growth stocks, however, do have convertible issues outstanding, so don't let that fact alone be a deterrent to buying an issue. As we'll see later, buy good value and the rest will take care of itself.

---

*Of course, the sudden conversion of bonds or preferred stock into a large amount of common means the company will have many more common shares outstanding, which tends to dilute earnings *per share*. By itself, this should hamper the stock. Absence of the short selling—as described above—is usually a stronger factor than the dilution of earnings, however, which is why the stock can be expected to do better after the conversion.

13

About Those Dividends

IMPORTANT DATES TO KNOW

Ah, those lovely dividend checks! How important they are to so many millions of Americans. Unfortunately, some essential facts about dividends are understood by only a small percentage of stockholders.

I'm referring mainly to the term "ex-dividend date" and its importance in determining just who is entitled to dividends.

There are four dates to consider when a company is paying a dividend to its owners:

> Declaration date
> Payment date
> Record date
> Ex-dividend date

The declaration and payment dates are simple: the former is merely the day the board of directors meets to consider paying a dividend; the latter is the date they set to *mail out the checks* for whatever amount of money is declared as a dividend.

Think how many stocks change hands daily and you can imagine the problem of deciding who is entitled to which dividend. The directors have to draw a line somewhere, so they set a record date, which is the date you have to have your name *on the corporation's books* to be paid that particular dividend.

The trouble is that the corporation (or the transfer agent bank that generally handles dividend payments for the company) is not informed the very day a stock changes hands. As a matter of fact, a seller has *five business days* (excluding weekends and holidays) to deliver his stock certificate to his broker; a buyer doesn't have to pay for his purchase for the same five-day period. In other words, the company doesn't know for five days who sold and who bought its stock. Thus, if Friday is the established record date for a certain dividend, you have to buy it *five days* before—on the preceding Friday—to have your name on the company's books and be entitled to the payment. If you buy the stock *four days* before the record date (in this case, on Monday), your name will *not* be on the books and you will miss the dividend. You can see, therefore, that there is a big difference between owning a stock four days before and five days before its record date. For this reason, the stock exchanges (and the OTC market) inform investors that they must buy a stock five days before record date to be entitled to a dividend, and if they buy it four days before, they are out of luck—they are not entitled to the dividend. To simplify the situation for investors (to save them from having to count back the days), the dividend declarations signify which day is *four (business) days before record date*—and they call this "*ex-dividend date*" ("ex-dividend" means "without dividend"). *Anyone buying the stock on or after the ex-dividend date is not entitled to that payment.* In other words, you have to buy before the ex-dividend date to get that dividend.

Obviously, the reverse is true if you already own the stock. If you sell before ex-dividend, you miss the upcoming payment; if you sell on or after ex-dividend, the dividend check is yours (even though you will receive the check a number of weeks after you have sold the stock).

Let's trace a theoretical 75-cent quarterly dividend by General Motors:

Declaration Date	Ex-Dividend Date	Record Date	Payment Date
April 10	April 19	April 23	May 30

If you already own GM, you need to hold it *through* April 18 to be entitled to this May 30 payment. If you sell it on April 19 or after, the dividend is still yours. As a new buyer of GM, you must buy the stock *before* April 19. The new owners on April 19 will not get the dividend. So someone who buys on April 20 is getting 75 cents less value than he would have gotten had he bought on April 19. *For this reason, a stock should be expected to decline by the amount of the dividend on the ex-dividend date.* As a matter of fact, all open-limit buy orders are automatically reduced on the specialist's book by the amount of the dividend each time a stock goes ex-dividend (the 75-cent dividend is equal to ¾ point, so all such orders on GM stock are lowered in limit price by ¾ point).

The stock exchanges designate that a stock has gone ex-dividend by putting the letters "xd" after the dividend figure in the daily quotations. General Motors, which in 1968 distributed a total of $4.30 including extras, would show "GenMtrs 4.30xd." If the stock closed at 80 the day *before* ex-dividend and closed at the same price *on* ex-dividend date, the stock actually rose *in value* by the ¾ point dividend, so the paper will show the net change as +¾. In other words, the stock was expected to drop by that ¾, and because it didn't it was actually up ¾. If GM stock closed at 81—a 1-point gain over the previous day's close—the net change would be +1¾.

One general rule comes to mind here in answer to the obvious question: Should I wait to buy a stock on its "xd" date when it's lower in price, or buy it the day before and get the dividend? *Given a static market,* I would always advise you to buy before "xd" (so you will be entitled to the dividend), because chances are the stock will come back up by the amount of the dividend not too long after "xd."* In the same vein, if you're going to sell a stock and it's the day before "xd," wait till the "xd" date or after because odds are that the stock will recover whatever amount it declined due to the "xd" and you will still be entitled to the dividend check when it comes a month or so later.

*Investors in extremely high tax brackets would be the exception here. They would prefer to buy the stock at the lower "xd" price rather than buy it before "xd" and have to pay a heavy tax on the dividend.

STOCK DIVIDENDS

So far I have been discussing dividends paid out in the form of cash to stockholders. This is not the only type of payment made by corporations, however. Many firms either supplement cash distributions or substitute for cash with payments of additional stock; these stock payments are called *stock dividends*.

Let's see the benefit of stock dividends both when they supplement cash payments and when they are a substitute for cash. As a supplement, stock dividends can be interesting. Suppose, for example, that Company A—whose stock sells for $100 per share and pays an annual *cash* dividend of $3 per share—declares an additional 10% stock dividend. This 10% distribution means that existing stockholders will get 1 share free from the company for every 10 shares they own. This sounds like a bonanza and would be except that once the stock goes "ex" this distribution, it will drop in price by the amount of the stock dividend. Just as with cash dividends, there is an "ex-dividend" date on stock dividends and all open-buy limit orders on the specialist's book are reduced by the amount of the dividend. In the case of Company A, its stock will drop by about 10% on the "ex" date—from $100 per share to about $91.* With this in mind, you might then ask what is so valuable about a stock dividend. What's the difference whether you own 10 shares of a stock at $100 per share or 11 shares (1 extra share from the 10% stock dividend) of the same stock worth $91 apiece? Actually you are correct in your reasoning that there is no difference. Remember, however, that Company A is also paying a $3 per share *cash* dividend, and *if no change is made in this payout, the stock dividend has the effect of increasing the stockholder's cash dividend income.* In our example, an owner of 10 shares of A stock was receiving $3 per share yearly in cash, for a total of $30 income. After the 10% distribution, ownership increased to 11 shares—and these 11 shares with the same cash payout of $3 provide income from then on out of *$33* a year. Therefore the real advantage of the 10% stock dividend was that it increased the stockholder's cash dividends. If instead of

*100 ÷ 1.10 (the 10% stock dividend) = $90.9, to be exact.

retaining the $3 cash rate after the distribution, the cash rate was reduced by 10%, the stockholder would have had no material benefit at all. *In the vast majority of cases, companies do retain their present cash rate after a small stock dividend, and the increased income resulting is the main reason for viewing small stock dividends optimistically.* Incidentally, *large* stock dividends (50%, 100%, 200%, etc.) *are stock splits* and therefore fall under the discussion in Chapter 12.

After this conclusion you have probably gathered that *there is really no benefit to be had from stock dividends that are a substitute for cash.* If, in the example of A, the company is *not* paying out any cash dividends at all, what good is the 10% stock payout? In effect, the company is simply giving you more stock certificates, but with these extra certificates your holdings are worth no more and no less than they were before the stock distribution. Many investors argue that the stock dividend without a cash rate gives the stockholder a tax advantage; that is, the stockholder is not forced into reporting cash income, on which he will have to pay income tax; if he wants cash income, he only has to sell off whatever stock dividends he gets and these sales will be taxable at the lower capital gain tax rates (Chapter 30) rather than at the high ordinary income tax rates. This tax benefit is valid. The trouble is that—*by selling the stock dividend— the investor has reduced his actual ownership in the company.*

Another argument for stock dividends without corresponding cash payouts is that after the stock goes "ex" and is reduced in price by the amount of the distribution, it will go back up in price to where it was before. In theory, this should *not* be the case, because the company's earnings per share, book value per share, and so on are also reduced by the amount of the stock dividend. In practice, stocks often do recoup the stock dividend amount not too long after "ex." When this happens, we should assume that the subsequent rise in price is not due to the stock dividend. Instead, it is due to the more important factors we will soon learn about, i.e., attractive industry and company, increasing net income, and the like.

14

Stock Rights

When a publicly held company needs money, it can resort to numerous channels. It can sell bonds, in which case it is *borrowing* money for a specified period of time. It can sell preferred stock, which gives it permanent capital (unlike bonds, there is no money to repay). Or the company may choose to sell more of its common stock.*

Assuming that it is decided to market more common stock, there are basically two ways this can be done:

1. Through sale *to the public* of an agreed number of shares.
2. Through the offering of stock to *existing stockholders*.

The first method may be the simplest, cheapest, and speediest way to raise the money. The company looks at the present market price of its stock, sets the number of shares it will have to sell to get the needed money, and then "hires" a group of brokers (called "underwriters") to sell those shares to the public at the existing market price. One of the difficulties of this plan is that it does *not* guarantee existing stockholders that they will be able to buy some of this additional stock if they choose. In other words, a stockholder's current ownership position is not protected. For example, if you currently own 10% of the XYZ Company and the company sells new stock—of

*Chapter 18 on *leverage* explains the pros and cons of issuing different securities.

which you buy none—you no longer own 10%. Assume the company has 100,000 shares outstanding, of which you own 10,000 or 10%; if an additional 100,000 shares are sold and you buy none, your ownership has been decreased to 5% of the new total shares—200,000—company.

For this reason, many companies prefer to offer new stock to *existing stockholders first* and always provide an incentive for the stockholders by giving them the right to buy the stock *at a reduced price*. But what happens if the stockholder has no more money to invest or simply chooses not to buy any more of the company's stock? Remember, he has been given the option to buy the stock "wholesale" and this option to buy at a cheaper price than the prevailing market should be valuable to someone. It is! And the company allows its stockholders to sell this option if they want.

The option to buy stock at a price below the market is called a stock "right." Let's trace through an example of these rights, how they work, and how you compute their value.

Assume the ABC Company has 1 million shares of common stock outstanding and its stock is selling for $50 per share on the market. The company has expansion plans and needs new money in the amount of about $4 million. It decides that it will offer new stock to existing owners at a discount of $10 per share from the present $50 price—or at $40 per share. At $40 per share, the company will have to sell 100,000 shares to raise the $4 million. Since 100,000 shares constitute one-tenth of the 1 million shares outstanding, you can see that the company plans to sell 1 new share (at $40) for each 10 outstanding. In giving written evidence of this right to buy, the company *issues 1 "right" for each share outstanding and then explains that it will take 10 of these rights to buy one share at $40.*

Thus, if you own 100 shares of ABC Company stock, you will receive 100 rights from the company. Your 100 rights entitle you to buy 10 shares at $40, and if this is what you want, you merely mail in your $400 to the company and wait for your new share certificate.

If, however, you decide *not* to buy more stock you can sell your option to buy at $40 per share to somebody else. Because many people choose to sell their rights, the stock exchanges (or the over-the-counter market) set up trading in these rights just as they do in stocks. For the few weeks that the option is open to buy at $40, "do rts" will appear under the name of the stock ("do" means "ditto" and "rts" means "rights"). For example, the financial page might show the following for ABC Company:

Sls	Stock	Div	High	Low	Close	N'Ch
52	ABC Co	1	50	49	50	
150	do rts			1	⅞	1

Notice that the rights have a value of $1 when the stock is $50. This is because it will take 10 rights to get the $10 discount (to buy one share at $40) and thus each right is worth $1. The formula for figuring how much rights will be worth is:

$$\frac{\text{Stock's current market price} - \text{Subscription price to stockholders}}{\text{No. of rights needed to buy 1 share at subscription price}}$$

In the case of ABC, the formula would work like this:

$$\frac{\$50 - \$40}{10} = \frac{\$10}{10} = \$1 \text{ (the value of each right)}*$$

Naturally, as the current market price of ABC stock goes up, the right to buy the stock at $40 has more value (and vice

---

*This is the formula for determining the value of rights *after* the stock has gone "ex-rights." As with regular dividends, you have to own a stock before it goes "ex" to be entitled to the rights. Also, you should expect a stock to decline on "ex-rights" day by the amount the right is worth, since the buyer on "ex-rights" day gets less in value than the person who bought the stock the day before.

Because there is the value of 1 right in each share before it goes "ex-rights," a different formula is used in computing how much each right is worth *before* the ex-rights date. This formula is:

$$\frac{\text{Stock's current market price} - \text{Subscription price to stockholders}}{\text{No. of rights needed to buy 1 share at subscription price} + 1}$$

In our ABC example, the value of each right would be:

$$\frac{\$50 - \$40}{10 + 1} = \frac{\$10}{11} = .91 \text{ or 91 cents}$$

versa). If ABC common rises from $50 to $55, the rights will rise from $1.00 to $1.50:

$$\frac{\$55 - \$40}{10} = \frac{\$15}{10} = \$1.50$$

Notice here the speculative possibilities in buying rights. In this case, we're assuming the common goes up $5, which is a 10% rise on a $50 stock; yet the rights went up 50 cents each—a 50% increase on a $1.00 original price. By the same token, you can take a large percentage loss if you buy rights and the stock declines very sharply during the rights period.

Now to some generalizations about rights that should be helpful to you in the future:

1. Under normal conditions, a stock will be somewhat depressed in price during a rights offering. This is because numerous stockholders will decide to sell their option, and since the stock and the rights will fluctuate together during the offering period, any heavy sales of rights will not only force the rights lower in price, but will also force the stock lower.

2. If you own stock in a company that is issuing rights, your decision to buy more stock at the option price or to sell the rights should depend strictly on how you feel about the stock as an investment. Many people will argue: How can I turn down the chance to buy the stock at $40 when it's selling at $50? The answer is: If you decide to sell the rights instead of subscribing at $40, you will realize the $10 from the sale of your rights, so it's six-of-one, half-dozen of the other as to which you should do.

3. Remember, you lose your proportional interest in a company by selling the rights. If you own 10% of a company and subscribe to the new stock, you will still own 10%; if you sell your rights and do not add to your

holdings, you will own less than 10%. This is not of great consequence to the average stockholder who owns only a small fractional interest in the company.

4. Any company issuing rights is adding to the number of common shares outstanding; thus it will have to increase profits to keep the net income *per share* at least equal to that of the previous year. In many cases, the new money received from the offering goes for new production facilities, introduction of new products, or other elements that should increase the company's long-range potential. Profits from these additions, however, will usually not show up for a year or more, and thus stockholders often see earnings *per share* temporarily reduced. In times of very high interest rates such as the present, however, common stock financing may actually produce an immediate *increase* in earnings. If, for example, a company has been borrowing money at 10% or 12%—which amounts to a net charge to income of 5% or 6% after an approximate 50% tax rate—*and* if its price-earnings multiple (see pp. 162–165) is above approximately 20, the company's earnings per share may rise as the proceeds from the stock sale are used to reduce its borrowings. At early-1981 interest rates of around 20%, money is costing the short-term corporate borrower about 10% after taxes; common stock sold at a P/E multiple of $12\frac{1}{2}$ or above to reduce these borrowings will actually increase net income after taxes.

5. Rights have a normal life of only a few weeks. Therefore, as a stockholder in a company such as ABC, be sure you either exercise the rights (buy the stock at the discount price) or sell them before their expiration date. If you don't, you have just thrown money away.

6. Rights do hold attractive speculative possibilities, but you have to consider point 5 when you buy them with the idea of making money on them. Since the rights are worth zero at their expiration, you have either to sell them before that date or be in a position to subscribe (by putting up $40 per share, in the case of ABC) before that date.

7. Since stocks are normally slightly lower in price during their rights offering period, this period can create attractive buying opportunities. A stock usually recovers in price shortly after the expiration date of the rights.

15

Warrants

"Make 1,000% on your money through warrants."
"A chance to make a fortune through warrants."

Perhaps you've seen advertisements like this in the financial pages of your newspaper or in finance magazines. These ads are not pure hokum—people have made fortunes by buying warrants and have done far better than 1,000% on their money through their purchases. As you can well imagine, these are very exceptional cases, but let's examine this explosive area and see what makes it tick.

In the previous chapter I explained how stockholders are sometimes given "rights" to buy more stock at a reduced price for a specified period of time. Warrants are just like rights. They, too, give their owners the privilege to buy stock at a set price. The differences are that warrants may be perpetual or have a life of *at least a few years* (remember, rights last only a few weeks), and the option price of a *warrant* is usually set *above the stock's market price at the time it is issued* (rights give you the option to buy stock at a discount).

Warrants are born differently than rights. Whereas the latter are born to raise money immediately for the issuing company, warrants are brought into the world as a "financing gimmick" and a method of possibly raising money for the company in the future. Warrants usually start out as a way of "sweetening up" a company's proposed new issue of either preferred stock or bonds.

Let's say that ABC Company needs more money and decides to float a bond issue. Let's assume that to sell an ABC bond today, the company would have to offer a 10% interest rate. This is a high rate for ABC to pay for its money, especially since the bond is going to have a twenty-year life. If ABC were to throw in a "kicker," however, it could probably get away with offering a 6% or 7% bond, or even one at 5½%.

The "kicker" in this case might be a warrant. Each $1,000 6% ABC bond might carry with it one warrant that entitles the holder to buy 100 shares of ABC common stock any time over the next ten years for $12 per share. The present market price of ABC common is $10 per share, but you can see that this warrant could become extremely valuable to its owner over the years if ABC does well and its stock rises above $12 per share. If this happens, the warrant owner can turn in his warrant and $1,200 (for 100 shares at $12 per share) to ABC and receive the 100 shares that have been set aside for him. If ABC common is now at $20 per share, these 100 shares are actually worth $2,000 in the open market, and he can turn right around and sell the same 100 shares that cost him $1,200 for $2,000 and make himself an $800 profit. And remember he still has his $1,000 6% ABC bond.

Thus, by using warrants, the ABC Company accomplished two objectives: (1) it sold its bond issue successfully and with a lower interest cost; (2) it received an additional $1,200 for each $1,000 bond, and this solved a future financing problem, because this money provided new cash that the company needed.

HOW TO EVALUATE WARRANTS

Shortly after the 6% ABC bond was sold, the bondholders were advised that they could detach the warrants from the bond if they desired. In other words, they had the choice of keeping the bond and the warrant or selling either one separately. Then, instead of there being just one market for the bond *with* warrants, there commenced a market for the bonds themselves and the warrants by themselves.

In figuring how much the warrants should be worth, you should ask: What is the worth of a piece of paper that entitles you to buy ABC common at $12 per share anytime in the next ten years, when the stock is now selling at $10?

You might answer by saying that this piece of paper—this warrant—isn't really worth anything. Why should you pay anything for this warrant to buy the stock at $12 per share when you can buy the stock itself right now for $2 less, for $10 per share? Right you are in your reasoning. But you've forgotten one thing. If you buy the stock right now you have to put up the $10 per share. But if you only have to pay, say, $2 for the warrant, you can get the option on five times as much ABC stock through the purchase of the warrants as opposed to buying the common stock outright.

For example, assume you have $1,000 to invest in ABC. You can buy 100 shares of the common at $10 per share. But if you buy the warrants at $2, you can buy 500 warrants, which in turn gives you the option to buy 500 shares of ABC at $12 per share over the next ten years. Assume that a few years from now ABC is selling at $20 per share. Had you bought the 100 shares outright at $10, your $1,000 investment would be worth $2,000. You would have doubled your money!

How did your 500 warrants come out? Assuming you sold your warrants instead of exceeding the option—because you didn't want to put up any more money—here's how you would have ended up:

Each warrant would be worth a minimum of $8 ($20 current market price of ABC − $12 option price) and thus your 500 warrants would be worth at least $4,000—you would have quadrupled your $1,000 original investment.

If ABC common had gone to $40 per share over this period, the comparison is even more startling. You would have quadrupled your money by buying the common outright ($10 stock advancing to $40). This is fine, but let's see how much the warrants would be worth now:

Market price of the common stock	$40
Less option price of the warrant	12
Minimum worth of the warrant	$28

Thus the warrant you paid $2 for is now worth at least $28—your investment has appreciated at least 14 times.

You can see the possibilities that exist in warrants. You get a tremendous play for the money invested. For this reason, you will usually find warrants selling much higher than this ABC example. Instead of paying $2 for the ABC warrant, you might find the market $4–$7, depending on how optimistic people are about the future of ABC Company.

From a near-term standpoint, once the warrants have established a base, you will often find the common stock and the warrant fluctuating by the same amount. In other words, once the ABC warrants are traded separately and the market is established at, say, $4, you will probably find the warrant going up 1 point to $5 if the common rises 1 point to $11. Of course a 1-point rise in a $4 warrant is a 25% advance, while the 1-point increment in the $10 common is only 10%. By the same token, declines in the common would bring about much more severe declines in the warrants on a percentage basis.

Remember, too, that warrants never pay dividends—you must depend solely on the warrants' going up in price to make your money. As I have shown, they can provide terrific gains for you, but they are highly speculative. If you find a stock you like very much and it has warrants outstanding, you should consider this medium for investing in the company. But do not buy warrants unless you are really enchanted by the stock's growth promise.

16
Puts and Calls (Options)

The two preceding chapters were devoted to forms of *options* to purchase stocks, namely:

1. *Rights*, which provide stockholders with the *temporary* option to buy more stock at prices lower than the existing market price.
2. *Warrants*, which are originally issued as a financing "sweetener" and serve as an option to buy stock at a set price for a longer period of time.

Both rights and warrants are issued by a company primarily for its own selfish purpose—to raise capital; the fact that these options are bought and sold after their issuance and that profits and losses result from their existence is incidental to their purpose. *As we have seen, rights and warrants are popular profit-making vehicles because they provide their owners with great leverage—with the opportunity to control a maximum amount of ownership for a minimum amount of invested capital.*

Another type of option—and one that provides even greater leverage than rights and warrants—exists in the form of *puts* and *calls*. In a book such as this, which is intended to give you A to Z coverage and instruction in the stock market, some discussion of puts and calls is essential.

Let me point out at the beginning that these somewhat mysterious options differ from rights and warrants in that they are *not* issued by operating companies. These options are not corporate securities and have no place or effect on a company's capitalization, balance sheet, or income statement. Instead, puts and calls come into being through a group of brokers and dealers who arrange for the buying and selling of these option contracts and who collect a fee for their work.

Now let's look at these unusual instruments and see what makes them tick. First of all, we'll answer the question: What is a call?

A *call* is a contract that gives its owner *the option to buy a specified number of shares of a stock* (usually 100 shares) *at a set price for a stated period of time* (anywhere from 30 days to over one year). When you buy a call, you are buying a privilege to purchase the stock anytime during the agreed period at an agreed price. Naturally you don't have to exercise the option, you don't have to buy the stock; but if the stock rises appreciably anytime within the contract period, you can direct the maker (of the contract) to sell you the stock at the guaranteed lower price and make a nice profit.

A put is just the opposite of a call. A *put* is a contract that gives its owner the *option to sell a specified number of shares at a set price for a stated period of time.* In this case, you are purchasing the privilege to *sell* the stock anytime during the agreed period at the agreed price. You will, of course, profit if the stock declines substantially during the contract period, because you can buy the stock on the open market at the low price and direct the maker to purchase it from you at the guaranteed higher price.

You buy a call if you think a stock is going up in price, and you buy a put if you think it is going down.

Basically, puts and calls are bought (instead of buying and selling the equivalent number of shares in the marketplace) for the reason mentioned earlier—you are able to control a lot of stock for a small amount of money. Assume, for example, that you wish to purchase ABC stock, which is presently selling for $50 a share. If you buy 100 shares, you will have to put up $5,000, or at least $2,500 if you are operating under 50% margin requirements. If ABC rises 12 points to $62, the resulting $1,200 gain amounts to a 24% profit on a $5,000 cash outlay, and almost a 50% gain if you margined your purchase and put up only $2,500. Assume that, instead of buying the stock itself, you purchase a six-month call on 100 shares of ABC stock at $50 per share for a cost to you of $600. The $1,200 appreciation in this case is reduced to $600 (since the $600 outlay is gone—it has been paid to the put and call dealer), but this gain amounts to a 100% increase on your cash outlay of $600.

The same thing goes for the purchase of puts. Suppose you believe XYZ stock is overpriced at $60 per share, where it is now selling. You decide you want to speculate that the stock will go down in price from these levels. To do this, you have to sell XYZ short, and if you engage in a 100-share transation, this will mean an outlay of $6,000 in cash, or $3,000 on 50% margin. To control the same number of shares through a put might cost you only $600, however, so you can imagine the prospect for greater return on invested capital from buying the put. For the sake of example, let's assume that your judgment proves correct and that XYZ does decline from $60 to $45 and that an approximate profit of $1,500 results. Here's how you will come out under the three possibilities mentioned:

1. Short sale of 100 shares at $60 with full cash outlay of $6,000: a $1,500 profit amounts to a 25% increase on invested capital ($1,500 ÷ $6,000 = .25 or 25%).
2. Short sale of 100 shares at $60 with 50% margin cash outlay of $3,000: a $1,500 profit amounts to a 50% enhancement ($1,500 ÷ $3,000 = .50 or 50%.)
3. Purchase of a six-months' put on 100 shares at $60 for a $600 cash outlay: the $1,500 profit is reduced to $900, since the $600 cash outlay is gone (it has been paid out to the put-and-call dealer); the net profit of $900 amounts to a 150% increase on invested capital ($900 ÷ $600 = 1.50 or 150%).

Thus you can see how puts and calls offer money-making possibilities. In addition, I should point out that puts and calls have the advantage of *limited risk in dollars* for their owners. *The person buying either the call on ABC or the put on XYZ knows from the start that the very most that can be lost is the original $600 invest-*

ment, regardless of what happens to the respective stocks. You can't make this statement about the person buying or selling short on a regular basis. Of course, if the person loses the full $600 on the put or call, he is losing 100% of his invested capital, so you can see that there are two sides to the coin. There are other disadvantages to put and call options, and I'll cover these a little later. In the meantime, let's explore other motives for putting money into these contracts.

One such motive involves using puts and calls as a hedge while buying or selling stocks in the normal manner. Assume that you are interested in ABC stock at $50 per share. You think it will go higher in the next six months, but you want to protect yourself and limit your loss in case you are wrong. In this case, you might buy 100 shares of ABC on the market, and at the same time purchase a six-month put on ABC at $50 per share for, say, $600. Now you can relax a little, knowing that no matter how low ABC goes in price—you can always exercise your put and sell your stock to the put dealer at $50. Therefore the most you can lose is the cost of your put, or $600 (plus commissions, taxes, etc.). Naturally, if ABC goes above $50, you will let your option lapse and sell the stock itself in the open market. Since whatever profit you make on the transaction will have to be reduced by the $600 cost of the put, you can see that both your upside and downside potential have been tempered by this hedging. Certainly a hedge such as this is unsuitable for the vast majority of stocks. It only makes sense if you are buying the type of stock that might fluctuate widely either up or down. The trouble is that with such volatile stocks, the cost of the put might be higher than the $600 example. Incidentally, the reverse of this illustration can be accomplished by the investor who is selling short and wants to hedge with the use of a call option.

Another reason for buying puts and calls might be to protect a profit on a stock owned or on one sold short. Suppose you bought a stock some time ago and now have a sizable gain on it—to the point where you are worried about it declining sharply. Uncertain about the future, you can purchase a put on the stock. Then, if the stock continues to rise, you can eventually sell at a larger profit and disregard the option. If, instead, the stock plummets, you can fall back on your put and sell the stock to the maker at the agreed price. By the same token, you can protect a profit on a short sale by the use of a call option.

A third motive for using options is to turn a short-term gain into a long-term gain. Twelve months is the dividing time between a short-term and the highly advantageous long-term capital gain. Sometimes a person has a short-term profit on a stock and is very uncertain about the stock's immediate future; he wants to sell the stock, but he also wants to avoid the excessive taxation of a short-term gain. In other words, he wants to hold the stock for more than one year, but he is afraid his profit will be reduced substantially by that time. He can solve this problem by buying a put on the stock—one that will expire after the twelve-month period following the original purchase of the stock. If the issue holds its gain beyond this twelve-month date, there is no need to exercise the put; he can sell the stock in the open market. But if the stock does fall sharply over this period, he can exercise his put and sell the stock at the option price to the maker. By doing this, he will preserve his profit (less the cost of option contract) on the favorable long-term tax basis.

The mechanism for handling puts and calls has changed drastically in the past decade with the formation of Options markets (the major one is located in Chicago), which are central marketplaces where options can be easily bought and sold. Thus a market now exists for these option contracts, providing investors with greater flexibility (and lower costs) than was previously possible. So many changes are taking place in this area that I advise anyone contemplating the option vehicle to obtain a copy of rules and regulations from either their normal brokerage affiliation or from a specialized option broker.

A great deal has been written of late about the burgeoning new options markets. I direct your attention to some interesting facts uncovered by a thorough study of puts and calls made by the SEC in the years 1959 and 1979. Here are some of the pertinent findings, including my interpretations:

Option buyers in the earlier study paid an average of 14% of the value of the stock optioned for most six-month calls.

Excluding the very low priced and very high priced stocks, six-month calls were priced at an average of 12% of their existing market price at the time. As mentioned, the new options markets have lowered costs for put-and-call buyers and sellers. Both the costs and the relative prices for various contracts, as explained below, are very much different from the 1959 study conclusions.

The premium paid to buy six-month options was about double the amount paid for *thirty-day* contracts (this means that the average fee for thirty-day options was 6–7% of the stock's market price).

The premium paid to buy six-month options was about 1½ times the amount paid for *ninety-day* contracts (the average fee for ninety-day options was 8–10% of the particular stock's market value).

Calls are slightly more expensive to purchase than comparable puts.

Premiums charged on puts and calls depend not only on the market price of the stock involved but also on the volatility of the stock. The stock that has a record of erratic price behavior in the market will cost more on an option than the relatively stable performer.

The SEC completed a special survey of six-month calls bought in June 1959. Despite the fact that the stock market in general (as measured by the Standard & Poor 425 Stock Index) increased slightly over the six months from June 1959 to January 1960, the experience of call buyers was most disappointing. *Overall the public lost about 43% of its investment on these calls. Over half (54%) of the call money invested turned out to be completely worthless. Another 28% of the money wound up with losses amounting to an average of 60% of invested capital. Only 18% of the call money ended up with a profit—although this select group did reap a return of about 150% on investment.*

Before going into the disadvantages of puts and calls and some conclusions, I should point up two unusual contracts, namely "straddles" and "spreads." Both straddles and spreads are "double options" in that both a put and a call are written simultaneously on the stock involved. In the case of a straddle, the put and call options are written on the basis of the current market price of the stock. For a lower cost, an investor can buy a spread, in which the call will be a point or two above the stock's market price and the put will be a point or two below the market. These double options give their owners flexibility; they provide the opportunity to make money on both up- and downswings in the market. Obviously, someone who makes a profit on both sides of a stock is extremely lucky. Straddles and spreads are expensive to buy and a person has to count on wide price fluctuations in the stock to make them at all profitable.

SOME CRUCIAL WARNINGS

Time now for a magnifying-glass look at puts and calls and some conclusions about them:

1. You receive no return on invested capital from dividends when you place money in puts and calls.
2. Puts and calls now have marketability; in some cases, trading volume of option contracts exceeds that of the underlying securities. Options are, however, available on only a limited number of securities—thus you may not be able to use the vehicle for the stock of your choice.
3. You are limited by the time element of options. Good investments often take time—generally more time than thirty days, 90 days, or even six months or a year. Your idea may be completely right, but still you could be thwarted by the restriction of a short period of time in controlling stock through options.
4. The high cost of puts and calls burdens you right from the start. You start out with a high break-even point when you purchase option contracts. For example, a six-month call on ABC at $50 per share for $600 means that the stock has to advance to at least $57 ($600 option cost plus about $100 in commissions) for you to break even.

5. A new and interesting field has evolved for those who are willing to "write" options on stocks they own or contemplate owning. Option writers are the source of puts and calls, and they receive a part of the premiums (described earlier) that are charged to the put and call buyers and sellers. Some high rates of return have been earned by those who have written options. And some investors have insisted that option writing equates to "riskless" returns. Such is not really the case; just because you own XYZ stock and write an option for a fee against this holding does not mean that your return is guaranteed or that you incur no risk. Market moves in the stock you have written an option against may be so volatile that you cannot protect yourself as you would like; and the ability to manage your investments might be hampered by certain stock movements. Lastly, more and more investors (including certain institutional portfolios) are becoming involved in writing options, which signifies to me that the margins will be lowered substantially over time.

My conclusion is that *puts and calls should be used on only isolated occasions.* If you happen to come across a stock that greatly excites you, one for which you can visualize a very large advance in the market, then a call might be useful in your planning. Or you might consider the use of puts and calls for their tax utility (but this is a complicated matter and requires professional tax advice). Or if you are dealing in securities for truly speculative purposes, then options certainly give you an outlet.

If you do invest in options, I have one bit of advice: *Do not buy them with a time fixation in your mind.* Too many people purchase options with the fixed idea (either conscious or subconscious) that they will do nothing with them until the expiration date. Too often they see their price objectives on a stock reached before the option's expiration, only to procrastinate on exercising the option till the very end. Invariably the stock will retreat in the interim and these option holders see that their profit has faded away. So set some kind of price objective when you purchase the option and do not let the expiration date of the option interfere with your investment judgment.

I caution you against active participation in the put-and-call market. It is my contention that the percentages will "eat you up" in time. The statistics (you are working against a high break-even point and a time element) are against you from the start, so you will have to choose unusually good stocks to make consistent profits in puts and calls over the years.

PART V
Security Analysis Made Easy

17

Tools to Build Your Road to Success

One of the basic rules of investing is "Get the facts before you invest," or "Investigate before you invest." Fortunately in stock market investing the facts are available to you in research bulletins from brokerage firms, annual reports from individual companies, statistical services, and other publications. It's up to you to use these facts correctly, and if you do, your successes will be greater.

Some of these facts involve fundamentals, such as understanding a little something about a company's financial position and earning power. The basic aim of this book is to show you how to make money—big money—in the stock market. To understand what is to come, I ask you to start by building the foundation for your success. After all, no builder starts with the roof.

THE BALANCE SHEET

Have you ever known a fellow who lives as if he's earning $100,000 a year, but who doesn't have the price of a cup of coffee in the bank? Chances are he's up to his ears in debt and would be a very poor risk for a $20 loan. Your good heartedness in lending him anything might be termed a poor investment.

The same thing goes for certain companies that lack a strong financial position—if you buy their stock, you are taking a substantial risk. That's why it's important to know something about a company's financial status before you invest in its stock. This kind of knowledge is available to you from a quick glance at its *balance sheet. The balance sheet tells you in detail a company's financial condition at one particular date.*

Perhaps the simplest way to familiarize you with this first tool is to compare it with the balance sheet of a typical American family.

The left-hand column is concerned with "assets," which is just a fancy way of saying "these are the things we *own.*" First of all, we have "*current* assets," which are those that are *easily converted into cash.*

JONES FAMILY BALANCE SHEET
AS OF DECEMBER 31, 1980

Current Assets			Current Liabilities	
Cash		$ 5,000	Accounts payable	$ 1,000
Savings bonds		1,000	Balance due on car	2,000
Common stocks		20,000	Notes payable	2,000
Total current assets		26,000	Total current liabilities	5,000
Other investments		10,000	Mortgage on home	25,000
Fixed Assets				
Automobile				
Cost	$ 9,000		TOTAL LIABILITIES	$30,000
Less reserve for			NET WORTH	67,000
depreciation	3,000			
		6,000		
Home		50,000		
Home furnishings				
Cost	10,000			
Less reserve for				
depreciation	5,000			
		5,000		
Total fixed assets		$61,000		
			TOTAL LIABILITIES	
TOTAL ASSETS		$97,000	AND NET WORTH	$97,000

Then we show "other investments," which could be anything, but in this case probably represent a small business thought to be worth $10,000.

Then we have "fixed assets," which are tangible items that are not as easily converted into cash as the current assets. Under fixed assets we have an automobile, home, and home furnishings. Notice that the auto and the furnishings have a "reserve for depreciation," which has reduced their carrying value on the balance sheet. Why? Because these items depreciate, or are worth less, as time wears them out. The minute you drive a new car out of the showroom window it becomes a "used" car and is worth less on resale than you paid for it. The same thing goes for furniture and other home furnishings. You might make the greatest buy of the century on a new sofa, but get it home and try to resell it and you'll know that it has already "depreciated."

Because of depreciation, you would only be deceiving yourself if you valued your car and furniture at their original retail price. To know what your assets are truly worth, you should subtract this depreciation from their original price. In our family balance sheet you can see that the $9,000 original cost of the auto has been reduced by $3,000 of depreciation, for a more realistic net value of $6,000.

But, you might ask, how much depreciation should one account for? The correct way to figure this is to *estimate the life of the asset itself.* In the case of the car, assume it has a useful life of five years, or sixty months. After that time, you figure it'll be ready for the junk heap. If you take the original cost of $9,000 and divide it by this sixty-month "life," you'll come up with $150 a month depreciation to subtract from the $9,000 cost. At this rate, the care will be worth $8,850 after the first month,* $8,700 after the second, and so on until, at the end of sixty months, it will show on the balance sheet as having no value. Actually, the car will have some small value at the end of this period, so you can see that depreciation is seldom exact, but it

*This is an example of "straight line" depreciation in which an even amount is deducted each month. Many companies use more realistic depreciation methods where higher depreciation is taken in the early stages of an asset's life. Such "accelerated" depreciation should be used by individuals, too, because for most assets, the resale value drops very sharply right after purchase.

is realistic and does give you a good idea of the worth of what you own as time goes on.

Notice that I did *not* set up a reserve for depreciation for the Jones home. In this day and age of rising real estate values, chances are 10 to 1 that the home has *ap*preciated, not *de*preciated, in value over the years. You should set up a reserve for appreciation by the amount you estimate your home is worth.

Adding all these things the Jones family owns gives us "total assets" of $97,000. Is this what the Joneses are really worth? No! They *owe* something to somebody, and naturally we have to deduct this from what they *own* to find out what they're really worth. Now we come to the right-hand side of this balance sheet, the column "liabilities" (amounts *owed*). The first item shown is "current liabilities," which states the debts the Jones family has to pay *within one year* (here are charge account bills and any other obligations that must be met within the year).

Next we have to show the other debts due over a longer period of time than one year. When the Jones family bought the $50,000 home shown under assets, they borrowed $35,000 from their bank, which was to be paid off over a period of twenty years (and which has been paid down to $25,000 in our example). We have to show this *long-term debt* separately from the current liabilities. Now we've listed all the debts and have totaled them under "total liabilities": $30,000.

At last we can tell the real worth of the Jones family:

Total value of what they *own* ("Total Assets")	$97,000
Less total amounts they *owe* ("Total Liabilities")	30,000
Total amount they are worth ("Net Worth")	$67,000

The balance sheet has served its purpose—it tells the world the Jones family's current financial position and it determines what the family would be worth if they cashed in all their chips on the date this statement was compiled.

THE CORPORATION'S BALANCE SHEET

A company sets up its balance sheet just as a family does. Below is a typical corporate balance sheet (of the Ichabod Crane Company).

ICHABOD CRANE COMPANY BALANCE SHEET AS OF DECEMBER 31, 1980

Current Assets		Current Liabilities	
Cash	$ 2,000,000	Accounts payable	$ 1,000,000
Marketable securities	1,000,000	Notes payable	1,000,000
Accounts receivable	2,000,000	Accrued wages, taxes,	
Inventories	3,000,000	expenses	2,000,000
Total current assets	8,000,000	Total current liabilities	4,000,000
Other investments	2,000,000	Long-term debt	4,000,000
		Total Liabilities	8,000,000
Fixed Assets		Net worth	
Property plant and equipment		Common stock	
Cost	$10,000,000	(1,000,000	
Less reserve for depreciation	5,000,000	shares)	$1,000,000
Total fixed assets	5,000,000	Capital	
Prepaid expenses	200,000	surplus	1,000,000
Deferred charges	500,000	Earned	
Patents and goodwill	300,000	surplus	6,000,000
		Total net worth	$ 8,000,000
		TOTAL LIABILITIES	
TOTAL ASSETS	$16,000,000	AND NET WORTH	$16,000,000

The "current assets" contain the very liquid items the company owns, but there are two items here that would not usually be found in the family's balance sheet. A company in business has large sums owed to it by those who have bought its goods, and these are shown as "accounts receivable." Then, a company has a supply of its own products on its shelves waiting for sale (in this case, cranes), and these "inventories" are also a part of the current assets. In analyzing the current assets, we would prefer to see more cash items (cash, marketable securities, accounts receivable) than inventories because the latter are less certain of being converted into cash.

There's no telling what you will find in a corporate balance sheet under "other investments." Most often you have to read some small print shown as "notes to the financial statement" to determine what these other investments include. Some interesting facts can be learned from digging into these footnotes. For example, the Matson Navigation Company owned 500,000 shares of Honolulu Oil for years and always showed this holding under "other investments"—valued at Matson's original cost, which happened to be *50 cents per share*. In case you weren't aware of the real market value for Honolulu Oil (then listed on the New York Stock Exchange), the footnote explained that this value as of the balance sheet date was *not 50 cents a share but closer to $50 per share.* Thus instead of Matson's 500,000 shares being worth $250,000, as shown, the holding was worth about $25 million. Quite a difference! Many balance sheets are like this (management is being conservative by not writing up these hidden values) and the investor should be conscious of this "carry-all" category, which can lead to profits for those who are alert. Incidentally, some large profits were made on Matson stock—the company partially liquidated in 1959 and stockholders realized how valuable Honolulu Oil stock was (its actual liquidation price was $100.85 per share).

Next under the asset column of the corporation come "fixed assets." Rather than show these fixed assets separately, most companies lump them into one category "property, plant, and equipment." Like the Jones family's automobile and home furnishings, Ichabod is realistic and depreciates this carry-all asset—thus the "reserve for depreciation." Deducting this reserve from the original cost of the property, plant, and equipment give a more realistic appraisal of the fixed assets.

The last asset items on Ichabod's balance sheet are termed "intangible assets." They include prepaid expenses, deferred charges, patents, and goodwill. Whereas the "prepaid expenses" item is generally legitimate, the "deferred charges" can be a "hideout" for expenses that really should be charged currently. This is an area open to considerable interpretation. For example, let's assume that the $500,000 on the Ichabod Crane balance sheet is explained in the footnotes (all balance sheets have explanatory footnotes to certain assets and liabilities) as "deferred research and development expenses."

The company will no doubt explain that it has poured excessive efforts into one or more programs from which it does not expect sales for some time in the future. In essence, management is claiming that it should not be penalized currently for something that appears certain to provide revenues (and profits) in the future.

Legitimate though this reasoning is, the bugaboo question is whether the products being developed will be as successful as projected. If they are, then the deferrals can ultimately be written off against the revenues and a profit may still be forthcoming from them. If the products are ultimately *unsuccessful*, however, the company has nothing to write deferrals off against—*and the deferrals have to be charged off*. Thus some unpleasant surprises may be forthcoming.

Frankly, I am extremely skeptical of large deferrals. Management can always rationalize their existence, but I prefer owning companies that charge off everything currently.

Incidentally, one of the beautiful elements of most large high-quality companies such as IBM, MMM, and GE is that they charge off all they can. Not only does this practice eliminate sudden writeoff surprises but it lowers the company's present tax bill as well (since lower profits mean lower taxes) and thus the company has the use of money that a deferring company must pay in taxes.

Investors who ignored the deferred balance sheet items of Cordura, Memorex, and countless other companies lost huge sums of money.

A word about "patents and goodwill." Even though a company's patents have large value and its name and reputation (goodwill) are also extremely valuable, it is conservative accounting practice to carry patents and goodwill on the balance sheet at the nominal figure of $1. This is because there is no way of evaluating what they are worth. Beware when you find patents and goodwill carried for huge amounts on the balance sheet—management may well be deceiving you!*

*An exception is when one company has recently purchased another, in which case it may have paid for patents, goodwill, and so on, and these will be written off (amortized) over the years.

When we total all the assets in this case, they add up to $16,000,000. But, like our Jones family, Ichabod has some bills to pay, too.

First of all, we find "current liabilities"—those have to be paid within one year. Here we have "accounts payable" (current bills) "notes payable" (possibly to the bank), "accrued wages, taxes, and expenses" (all of which are to be paid out in cash shortly), and so on.

Just as the Jones family took out a mortgage on their home to be paid over twenty years, Ichabod needed some money for a long period of time, too. This borrowed money is termed "long-term debt" when it has *more* than one year to run.

Now we total the current liabilities and the long-term debt and come up with "total liabilities" of $8,000,000. Finally we can gauge approximately what Ichabod is worth if it goes out of business tomorrow:

Total assets	$16,000,000
Less total liabilities	8,000,000
Total net worth	$ 8,000,000

The total net worth of $8,000,000 is divided between "common stock," "capital surplus," and "earned surplus" on the balance sheet. It's not necessary to our discussion to distinguish between these terms. All three represent values to the common stockholder, and the main thing to consider is the total of the three.

We're through now with the fundamentals of the balance sheet. The next step is to put these fundamentals to work and learn how to judge whether a company is financially strong or not.

18

Some Simple Surgery on the Balance Sheet

BALANCE SHEET ANALYSIS

Analyzing a balance sheet can become highly complicated. Ordinarily, however, only a few simple tests are necessary to determine whether the stock of your dreams is financially sound.

You want answers to the following questions:

1. Can the company pay its bills?
2. What is the company worth in the event it goes out of business?
3. Has the company gotten itself too deeply in debt?

It may come as a surprise to you, but a very cursory glance at the balance sheet will answer these questions for you. Here's how.

1. *Can the company pay its bills?*

You pay your bills out of your checking account, savings account, or the money you have stored in the sugar bowl. You depend on your cash items. You do not depend on your auto, home, home furnishings, and so forth to do this. In other words, you depend on your current assets (readily convertible into cash)—not your fixed assets—to pay your current liabilities (which have to be paid within one year).

Thus it's easy to see whether you can pay your bills by comparing your current assets with your current liabilities.

The same thing goes for a company. You can determine its ability to pay bills by comparing its current assets with its current liabilities. To compare companies of all sizes, you simply divide current liabilities into current assets and arrive at what security analysts call the *current ratio*. For example, Ichabod's balance sheet showed:

Current assets of	$8,000,000
Current liabilities of	4,000,000

By dividing current liabilities of $4,000,000 into current assets of $8,000,000, you obviously arrive at a current ratio of 2 to 1. In other words, there are twice as many current assets as current liabilities. The more assets, the better; thus the higher the current ratio, the better.

What Is a "Normal" Current Ratio?

A company is obviously in bad shape if its current assets are less than its current liabilities. By the same token, a company with a current ratio of 1 to 1 (current assets the same as current liabilities) can't keep living from hand to mouth forever. *As a general rule, we like to see a company have a current ratio of 2 to 1 or better. But the ratio will vary from industry to industry.* For example, your gas and electric company will no doubt have a current ratio of only a little over 1 to 1. It doesn't need a ratio higher than this because its revenues are steady and are all paid in cash monthly and it does not have the problem of carrying inventories on its shelves. In contrast, companies that have to build up inventories for seasonal sales will need a higher current ratio.

Two words of caution here! First, always look to see what portion of a company's current assets consist of immediate cash items. A company can have a high current ratio and have almost no cash in the till. A large portion of inventories is not as reliable because you can't be sure when and at what price these inventories will be sold and converted into cash.*

---

*To measure real liquidity, compare cash and marketable securities alone (omit accounts receivable and inventories) to current liabilities and get the company's "quick ratio." A quick ratio of 1 to 1 is exceptionally good.

Second, don't buy a stock only because of a high current ratio. We'll see later just what to consider in buying and selling stocks, but remember that one of the most disappointing stocks in the 1950–1960 decade—Texas Gulf Sulphur—had one of the highest current ratios—about 11 to 1. Still, you should look at the current ratio for background because it's reassuring to know the company of your choice has the ability to pay its bills.

2. *What is the company worth in the event it goes out of business?*

Recall how we determined what an individual or a corporation is really worth. A balance sheet will usually set this out with the words "net worth." Then all the investor has to do is to add to this any understatements of value (such as the Honolulu Oil–Matson situation discussed previously) and arrive at a true net worth.* Then divide this by the number of common shares outstanding and you get net worth, or "book value" as it is usually called, per share. This will usually be done for you by management in its annual report, but just in case it isn't, here's how Ichabod Crane book value would be figured:

Total net worth of $8 million ÷ 1 million shares = $8 per share.

In other words, this company would be worth $8 per share were it to liquidate tomorrow.

How important is it to know a company's liquidating value? I contend that it can be very important, but only in a limited number of cases. After all, who cares about the liquidating value of General Electric, International Business Machines, General Foods, and a host of large companies *when they will never liquidate?*

Therefore I suggest that you *deemphasize book value unless:*

1. There is a chance that the company will liquidate its business (this is a rare occurrence).
2. There is a chance that it will merge with another company in the future (in such a merger book value would be given some weight in arriving at a price).

---

*Preferred stock usually appears under "net worth," but it should be deducted, since we are interested in what the *common* stockholders would get in liquidation.

3. There is some likelihood of tender offer (attempt at control of the corporation) by outside investors. With the languishing of stocks over the inflationary decade of 1970–1980, the appetite for companies with understated realistic book value has increased enormously.

If you believe one of these three possibilities may occur, you can make fine returns over time in those investments that go one of the routes. The undervaluation of asset-type companies in the late 1970s produced some real bonanzas for "book value investors." So long as it is cheaper to buy whole companies through the marketplace (at premiums to quoted market prices) than it is to build new plants or establish businesses, the "buying assets" philosophy can bring excellent returns for investors.

If, however, you see little chance for the three prospects listed, ignore book value in your appraisal of the stock. Incidentally, let me point out that the term "par value" has no significance whatsoever in the appraisal of a stock, even though it appears on a balance sheet. Since it bears no relationship to book value, earnings, market price, simply ignore it.

3. *Has the company gotten itself too deeply in debt?*

Have you ever considered how much money to put up in cash to buy a home or another piece of property? If you can put up all cash—and thus avoid taking out a mortgage—you will have no monthly payments to make (except for taxes and insurance). Your worries will be small. You can even lose your job and still know you'll have the roof over your head.

Assume that instead of paying all cash for this house, you are forced to take a large mortgage from the bank. You borrow $50,000 or $75,000 and have to make payments of $600 or $1,000 per month. Now what happens if you lose your job and the income isn't rolling in? You're in trouble.

The same principle applies to companies that have to borrow to conduct their business. The more they borrow, the higher the "monthly payments" they have to make and the greater the risk they take. This is because the interest becomes a *fixed* charge that must be paid through thick and thin.

I'm sure you remember the song "What a Difference a Day Makes." Following is a song you should get to know—let's call it "What a Difference a *Debt* Makes."

Assume you're looking to buy the business of the Hotentot Pot Company. Last year Hotentot earned $20,000 before taxes, or $10,000 after taxes.* You and the present Hotentot owners agree on a selling price of $100,000 for the business and now it's yours.

You shell out $100,000 *in cash.* This year the business once again earns $10,000 after taxes, and thus you are realizing a 10% return on your cash investment.

Then you think: Why should I tie up my cash in Hotentot? I can use some of that cash to buy some more businesses. And the interest rate from the bank is only 6%. So you arrange with your banker to borrow $70,000 of the $100,000 purchase price—and to pay the bank 6% on the $70,000, or $4,200 per year interest. Now you only have $30,000 cash invested in Hotentot.

The next year Hotentot once again earns $20,000 before taxes. Of course, now you have an expense of $4,200 for interest and you have to deduct this from the $20,000. Here's how you'll come out:

Net income before interest and taxes	$20,000
Less interest expense	4,200
Net before taxes	$15,800
Less income taxes (50%)	7,900
Net income	$ 7,900

Your net income shows at $7,900 instead of $10,000, but now you have only a $30,000 investment in the business. But look what has happened to the return on your money:

Before: $10,000 net income ÷ $100,000 investment = 10%
Now: $ 7,900 net income ÷ $ 30,000 investment = 26.3%

*Actually the corporate income tax is only 22% on income under $25,000, but I have used 50% for the sake of simplicity.

What a genius you are! Merely by borrowing the bulk of the purchase price, you have increased your rate of return from 10% to 26.3%.

Next year Hotentot has a booming year—net income before interest and taxes advances to $40,000. Let's see what this means to profits under both conditions (full $100,000 in cash and borrowing $70,000):

	All Cash Purchase	Borrowing $70,000
Net income before interest and taxes	$ 40,000	$40,000
Less interest expense	None	4,200
Net income before taxes	$ 40,000	$35,800
Less income taxes (50%)	20,000	17,900
Net income	$ 20,000	$17,900
Cash investment made	$100,000	$30,000
Return on original cash investment	20%	59½%

Fantastic! You have tripled the return of your money by going into debt (by "leveraging" your investment as they say in investment circles). Of course, you know that there are two sides to this coin. So now we have to ask: What happens if Hotentot's business slides off? Assume the net before interest and taxes declines to $4,000:

	All Cash Purchase	Borrowing $70,000
Net income before interest and taxes	$ 4,000	$ 4,000
Less interest expense	None	4,200
Net income before taxes	$ 4,000	$ (200) Loss
Less income taxes (50%)	2,000	——
Net income	$ 2,000	$ (200) Loss
Cash investment made	$100,000	$30,000
Return on original cash investment	20%	Minus return

The fixed interest charge of $4,200 looms big when business falls off and, because of this expense, you have a loss instead of a profit. The risk of borrowing has reared its ugly head.

I hope this discussion is helpful to you in deciding how much borrowing you should do if you buy a business, invest in real estate, or undertake some other venture. Actually, with 1981 interest rates running two to three times the mythical 6% used in our examples, leverage (borrowing) is even riskier. But back to stocks!

One of the things you should look for before buying a stock is the amount of borrowed money a company is using. Since heavy borrowing entails risk and corresponding rewards, you ought to check what kind of leverage exists before buying.

Naturally we can't arbitrarily set a limit as to how many millions of dollars a company can soundly borrow because we will be looking at companies of all sizes. The debt figure means something only if we relate it to the amount of total capital the company has. A $5 million debt to a $100 million company is nothing, but to a $10 million company it constitutes half the capital. Here's how to determine how heavily leveraged a company is:

1. Total all the invested capital in the business by combining these figures:
   a. All the *long-term debt* shown on the balance sheet (this may include bank loans, notes, bonds, debentures).
   b. All the *preferred stock* (if any exists), also as it is shown on the balance sheet.
   c. All the *common stock money that is invested in the company.* Rather than use the common stock and surplus figures as they show on the balance sheet (we have just seen how this net worth, or book value, has little significance in appraising a stock's real value in the marketplace), it may be more realistic to use *the market value of all the common stock outstanding.* In other words, *multiply the number of common shares outstanding by the stock's current market price.*

2. See what percentage of total invested capital (a + b + c) is represented by the securities that have fixed charges on the company—i.e., by long-term debt (a) and preferred stock (b).

On Ichabod Crane's balance sheet you would figure leverage as follows:

1. Total all invested capital by combining:
   a. Long-term debt, which in this case is . . . . . $ 4,000,000
   b. Preferred stock, which in this case is . . . . .   None
   c. Common stock
      Instead of using the $8,000,000 book value figure shown on the balance sheet, multiply the company's 1,000,000 outstanding common shares times the present market price on the stock (assume it to be $16 per share), for a total of 16,000,000
      Total Capital $20,000,000
2. See what percentage of total capital ($20,000,000) is represented by long-term debt and preferred stock ($4,000,000):
      $4,000,000 ÷ $20,000,000 = .20 or 20%

Thus Ichabod has 20% of its capital in debt. Naturally, the higher this figure, the more risk the investor takes. Like the current ratio, the "proper" amount of borrowed capital will vary according to the industry and the individual company. Once again, your gas and electric company can afford considerable borrowing because of its stability—it may have as much as two-thirds of its capital in debt and preferred stocks. But this kind of leverage might be suicide for industrial companies. In fact, any time the leverage is over 25% you have to be very conscious of the possible risks.

In a growing and profitable industry some amount of debt shows management aggressiveness. As in our example, some borrowing can greatly enhance the return on your money. As a matter of fact, management may well leave itself open to criticism if it fails to take advantage of "cheap" borrowed money. After all, a company that consistently earns 10–20% on its invested capital may have acted foolishly in not expanding when borrowed money cost only 5% or 6% after taxes. Perhaps management was overly conservative; on the other hand, the business may simply not have possessed opportunities that warranted further capital investment.

I must mention that some companies are in the fortunate position of having ample cash to handle their business and take care of expansion as well. Thus they need no debt or preferred stocks. They have what we call a *clean capitalization—free of debt and preferred charges.* The stockholders of these companies can relax, knowing that there are no fixed interest charges to cause extraordinary swings in their profits. Companies such as CBI Industries, A. T. Cross, Pinkerton's, Intel, Hewlett-Packard have had clean capitalizations, with no debt, and yet have been able to show sufficient growth (in some cases, quite spectacular growth) to provide their owners with both a feeling of security and very attractive capital appreciation over the years.

The prospective investor should consider a company's leverage in order to know what risks investment in that company entails. It's another "background" fact to know about a stock before making the plunge.

Other Balance Sheet Ratios

Other clues to a company's health—and to future prospects—are also available through balance sheet analysis. I do not want to turn this chapter into an accounting course, but a lot can be learned from considering:

a. The sales/inventory ratio—i.e., are inventories building up in relation to sales (if inventories are rising too fast, it may indicate "stale merchandise")?

b. Sales/accounts receivables—i.e., are the company's collections lagging?

c. Depreciation (see p. 117)—if it is declining, management may not be realistic in assessing replacement needs of the corporation in years ahead.

Finally, a study of notes to the financial statements is a must. Explanations of deferred charges (p. 120), unfunded pension liabilities, pending legal matters, stock options, company investments, inventory evaluation, and so forth can all give a clue to the future. Therefore my advice to you is similar to good legal advice: Read the small print!

CONCLUSION

The *current ratio*—easily figured and usually computed by management in its report to stockholders—shows you a company's current financial position and tells you whether the money is there to pay the bills.

Leverage tells you whether the company is too heavily laden with debt and gives you a hint of certain risks that may exist.

Book value is useful only in specialized instances.

These are by no means the only yardsticks for balance sheet analysis, but when you understand the relative importance of these, you will have the background necessary to back up your decisions. I emphasize that they give *only background* because, as we shall see very shortly, your decisions will stem from other considerations.

19

More Road-Building Tools

We now know how to judge the solidity of a company by whether it can pay its bills, by determining whether it is too much in debt, and by knowing how much it would be worth if it were to go out of business tomorrow or possibly be bought as a whole by another company (or outside investor).

So far we've overlooked one all-important consideration: *How much money is the company earning?*

As we'll see a little later, it is present and potential earning power that makes a stock a buy or a sell candidate. I would be remiss if I didn't discuss the accounting statement that tells the world about a company's earnings—the so-called *income statement* (also called the *statement of profit and loss* and/or the *statement of earnings*). The income statement tells *how much money has been earned over a given period of time.*

Despite the importance of the income statement, its analysis is relatively simple. I'm sure that you will understand immediately most of the sample income statement that follows. There are, however, a few pointers I'd like to pass on to you to prepare you to judge which stocks to buy and when to buy them.

HOW EFFICIENT IS THE COMPANY?

You've no doubt had contact with inefficient people. You wouldn't invest a plug nickel in them, I'm sure. Nor would you be eager to invest in inefficient companies.

RUM DUMB RUM CORPORATION

INCOME STATEMENT
FOR THE YEAR ENDED DECEMBER 31, 1980

Net sales		$100,000,000
Less:		
Cost of goods sold	$70,000,000	
Selling, general & administrative expenses	10,000,000	
Depreciation	5,000,000	85,000,000
Profit from operations		$ 15,000,000
Less interest charges		1,000,000
Net profit before taxes		$ 14,000,000
Add nonrecurring income		4,000,000
Total profit before taxes		$ 18,000,000
Less income taxes		8,000,000
Net profit		$ 10,000,000

Many investors have asked me how they can determine whether a company is efficient when they are so far away from it and have no personal contacts. One answer: by looking at its *margin of profit.*

The margin of profit tells you how much gross profit the company is getting from each dollar of sales and is arrived at by relating the "profit from operations" on the income statement to "net sales." In the case of Rum Dumb, the margin of profit would be:

Profit from operations ÷ Net sales = Margin of profit
$15,000,000 ÷ $100,000,000 = 15%

In other words, on every $1 sale, Rum Dumb makes 15%, or 15 cents (before interest, taxes, etc.).

Obviously a company that makes 15 cents on every $1 of sales must be far more efficient than one that makes only 10 cents on the same $1. Thus, *in the same industry,* you can compare the efficiency of any number of companies merely by comparing their margins of profit. Notice I have stressed comparison *in the same industry*. This is because every industry has its own profit structure and mode of doing business.

The food chain industry, for example, is a high-volume business and the margin of profit on each $1 of sales is very low. You can't compare the margin of profit of Safeway—the world's largest food chain—with that of Caterpillar Tractor, for example. The latter sells high-priced tractors, crawlers, and other construction equipment, and by necessity there is a larger profit in each $1 of sales than there is in the stable, high-turnover food business.

Assuming that you are comparing companies in the same line of business, you can conclude that *the higher the margin of profit, the more effective management is in getting profit for the stockholders*. It is the *trend* of margins that is most important. Rising margins are very healthy, so look for that trend when you are evaluating management's recent success.

BUYING "INEFFICIENCY"

Now that we've decided it is better to buy the *most* efficient companies, I have to turn around and say that *sometimes it can be very profitable to buy companies that have been plagued with inefficiency*. Of course, this only holds if there is some definite change in philosophy or personnel that makes a sudden endeavor to improve efficiency and the margin of profit.

Take the case of Safeway Stores! The years 1949–1955 were spent building up sales. But it is not volume of sales that pays off for stockholders, it is profits—and here is where Safeway had fallen down. Here's the company's record over this seven-year span:

Despite the increase in sales, Safeway's profits per share

had declined (the company had added to its common stock out-standing and this dilution forced earnings *per share* down over this period). As a result, Safeway common stock was a dull performer. Something was obviously wrong because the company was operating at a margin of profit *about half of what the average company in the industry was doing.*

Year	Sales (Billion)	Margin of Profit (%)	Earnings per Share
1949	$1.1	2.7	$1.68
1950	1.2	3.2	1.61
1951	1.4	2.1	.75
1952	1.6	2.3	.67
1953	1.7	3.0	1.36
1954	1.8	2.8	1.16
1955	1.9	2.8	1.08

New management took over in 1955 and it was their announced intention to improve the efficiency—the margin of profit—of Safeway. This change of philosophy offered some real money-making opportunities to stock buyers. All you had to say was: "I believe that new management at Safeway will be able to reach industry averages of efficiency" (no more) and you could have bought the stock with assurance. After all, if Safeway doubled its margin of profit, its earnings would at least double and the stock would be a good investment.

Here's what happened at Safeway in the ensuing four years:

Year	Sales (Billion)	Margin of Profit (%)	Earnings per Share	Market Price of Safeway Stock
1955	$1.9	2.8	$1.08	19⅜–14
1956	2.0	4.1	2.04	23⅞–16⅞
1957	2.1	4.3	2.43	27½–20⅛
1958	2.2	4.4	2.60	41¾–24½
1959	2.3	4.5	2.82	42¼–34⅝

You can see the importance of efficiency here. Earnings went from $1.08 per share to $2.82 and the stock rose from a low of 14 to a high of 42¼. There are countless examples of constructive management changes that have achieved similar results. Over the past five years, from 1975 to 1980, Amcord, Boise Cascade, General Dynamics, General Instruments, Litton Industries, and Rohm and Haas are just a half dozen of hundreds of companies in which successes have been made by "investing in inefficiency." Remember, however, that improving margins is not an easy task, so do not assume that it will be accomplished overnight.

IS ANY PART OF NET PROFIT "UNUSUAL"?

Naturally you want to know whether a company's reported profits will continue at the same levels in the future. You certainly want to know if one year's profits have been "bloated" by some nonrecurring gain. Say, for example, a company sells a plant or some real estate in one year. It will have a gain to report, and since it may be many years before it sells off another large asset such as this (perhaps it never will), you should not be deceived by this gain.

Therefore I caution you to look at a company's income statement to see if there are any large "nonrecurring profits." Rum Dumb had just such an addition to its profits—in the amount of $4 million. You should deduct this $4 million (approximately $3 million after capital gain tax) from Rum Dumb's net profit to arrive at the company's "true" earnings for the year.

Usually management will do this for you: it will separate the nonrecurring income from the normal income and tell you what the company actually earned on an operating basis. *If it does not do this, it is to be criticized.* To my way of thinking, it's a sign of weakness if management doesn't advertise the truth, rather than deceive the public. Look for this, too, in assessing management.

Likewise, a company may have some nonrecurring *expenses* or *writeoffs* that *reduce* normal profits. Writeoffs will usually show separately on the income statement, but nonrecurring expenses (such as the opening of new facilities or moving to a new plant) will usually be lumped together with normal expenses rather than shown separately. In either case, you can count on management to explain these nonrecurring items and tell you how much they reduced profits. Naturally you'll want to allow for these items when you appraise the company's efficiency.

WHAT IS THE NET INCOME PER SHARE?

When you buy a stock on the market, you pay for it on a *per share basis.* Whether you buy 10, 20, or 100 shares, the important thing is what price you pay for each share. Thus it makes sense to know how much money the company is earning on a per share basis.

Almost all companies report their earnings in both total dollars and on a per share basis. Just in case you're wondering how the latter is figured, it is done as follows:

Net income (after taxes and after preferred dividends, if any) ÷ number of common shares outstanding.

In the case of Rum Dumb—which had 1 million shares outstanding—net income per share would be:

Net income of $10 million ÷ 1 million shares = $10 per share.

Rum Dumb management would no doubt deduct the nonrecurring income for you and show you that net income from operations is $7 million after taxes, or $7 per share.

As we'll see later, the relationship of a company's net income per share to its market price per share tells us a great deal about whether or not its stock should be bought.

WHAT IS THE "CASH FLOW" PER SHARE?

In Chapter 17 we discussed "reserve for depreciation," which is an accumulation of the periodic adjustments companies (or individuals) make in writing down their assets to realistic figures. There are various methods of computing depreciation: some companies use accelerated depreciation and write down their assets just as rapidly as possible, whereas others use the straight line method. A company that uses the former method is going to have *higher current depreciation expense and correspondingly lower reported earnings* than the company that uses the latter. Take Companies A and B, both of which just completed new plants costing $50 million. Company A decides to depreciate this plant very fast, and in the first year charges off depreciation expense of $5 million; Company B uses a slower method and incurs a depreciation expense of only $3 million for the same year. Because of this accounting decision, Company A is deducting $2 million more than B from its sales, and solely for this reason, A will have to report lower net income than B. But A is not really any less profitable than B, and therefore it should be obvious that an investor has to be conscious of depreciation expense in an income statement.

In order to compare companies like A and B more fairly, analysts use what is known as *cash flow—the total of net income after taxes plus depreciation.* As in the case of net income, it is important to compute this figure on a *per share basis.* In the case of Rum Dumb, cash flow per share would be:

Net profit (after deducting nonrecurring income)	$7,000,000
Add depreciation	5,000,000
Total cash flow	$12,000,000

Per share ($12 million ÷ 1 million shares) = $12 per share

In the same industry, it is often very important to compare companies on the basis of *cash flow per share.* In extreme cases like that of A and B, cash flow per share can be the most realistic measure of comparison.

CONCLUSION

You can easily learn what you need to know from a company's income statement. You now know how to judge a company's efficiency and how—in rare cases—you can profit from spotting inefficiency (accompanied by a change in management or a change in philosophy). You also know how to uncover some hidden items and how to arrive at the all-important net income and cash flow per share. All of these are valuable tools for your future investing.

PART VI

How to Buy
the Right Stocks
at the Right Prices

20
What to Buy—Part One

Studies have shown that workers are happier when they have soothing background music while they work. Not only are they happier, they also get more work done, and this increased productivity leads to higher wages for themselves and higher profits for their employers.

In a way, the last few chapters have provided you with the "background music" for investing in the stock market. Your "productivity" should improve by knowing the few important facts I've emphasized.

But background music isn't enough. If workers haven't been properly instructed in how to assemble the product they're working on, the music will do them little good. In fact, it might just put them to sleep.

The same thing goes for investing. We've turned on the background music—now let's see how to assemble the product so you know *what to buy* in the market.

Knowing what to buy involves using a fairly simple and very logical procedure. Actually, it's just like buying a house. When you shop for a house, you're most interested in its location. Regardless of how beautiful a house may be, you're not going to buy it if it's located next to the city dump. The most logical approach to house hunting is to determine *where* you want to live and then find the house you want for the right price in this approximate location.

Buying stocks involves the same approach. The first thing to do is to find the best location for your money—that is, the *best industry*.

MY INDUSTRY APPROACH THEORY

Most of the mistakes made by investors stem from not giving proper weight to the industry in which a company is engaged. People get excited about certain companies for a variety of reasons, but in so many cases they could save themselves a lot of time, bother, and money by sitting down and putting a magnifying glass on the industry involved. After all, even the very best company in a poor industry will generally be only a mediocre investment. And a mediocre company in a poor industry will be a very poor investment.

My industry approach theory involves only one basic rule: *Before you invest a penny, be satisfied that the industry is attractive.*

The industry approach theory is not a new one. All security analysts are trained to use it. My theory involves asking a few important questions about the industry you are considering. Here they are:

1. *Is the industry growing?*

This is so obvious I'm almost ashamed to list it. The person considering putting his dollars into International Buggywhip in the early 1900s—just when the automobile was going into mass production—should have known enough to ask this, too. His answer would certainly have been: No, this industry is not growing—it has reached maturity and will eventually be replaced by the advent of the automobile. Yet I'm sure there were many people who lost Buggywhip money at that time because they failed to ask themselves whether the industry was in its early stages of growth or had reached maturity. You must ask the same question today about steel (aluminum, plastics, and glass all aim at markets that now belong to steel), glass (plastics are penetrating more and more markets), rayon (newer synthetic fibers are making sharp inroads into rayon usage), and so on. Don't *ever* forget to ask this first important question about the industry you are investigating.

2. *How important are labor costs?*

It is said that there is nothing certain in life but death and taxes. Add "and higher labor costs" to this and you have a broader truism. The job of union leaders is to improve working conditions and wages for their members. They have done this in the past and I'm certain that they will fight to expand such benefits for their members in the future. Companies with high labor charges have to depend on either (a) corresponding increased productivity from their workers, or (b) increased selling prices of their products, or they will see their profits squeezed in the future. Naturally there is no guarantee that they will be able to accomplish either of these remedies over the years. Therefore it is important to recognize the importance of labor costs in the industry you are considering.

3. *What is the pricing structure of the industry?*

Certain industries compete solely on the basis of the selling price of their products and are always fighting "price wars" among themselves. Other industries are not subject to these wars because they have disciplined themselves (I am talking about firm price-policy groups that do *not* resort to collusion or price fixing), realizing that price wars are injurious to everyone involved.

Asphalt, plumbing fixtures, and plywood come immediately to mind when discussing industries that often engage in price wars. The record shows that most companies in these industries have lacked the consistent year-by-year increases in profits to be found in certain other industries.

In contrast, consider Bristol-Myers at the time it brought Bufferin to the market. Here was a product that was intended to penetrate the aspirin market, so you might think that Bufferin was brought out at a price either under aspirin or at the same level. If it had sold *under* aspirin's price, then the aspirin producers might have been forced to cut their prices and down would go profits for all the companies involved.

Instead, Bufferin was brought out to sell *much higher* than aspirin. Bufferin, as we all know, was a success. It did penetrate the aspirin market and it became a profitable item for Bristol-Myers. What happened to the aspirin producers? They subsequently *raised* the price of their branded aspirin and are probably making as much money—or more—on this product than they did before the advent of Bufferin.

Proprietary drugmakers (proprietary drugs are those that can be purchased without prescription) have found that price is *not* the important thing in marketing their products. If the public thinks Bufferin or Pepto Bismol or XYZ formula will accomplish the job in mind, the public will pay the price. For example, right now test your own "knowledge" of prices of nonprescription drugs that you might buy to relieve yourself of some discomfort. Think of products like cold pills, laxatives, pain relievers, cough medicines. Then see if you can pinpoint the selling prices of these products. Chances are that you won't be too accurate. Of even greater importance, however, ask yourself whether an extra dime or 20 cents added to these product prices would cause you to switch to something else. If the products are any good at all, you'll stick with them *despite the slight increase in price.* Of course, this type of loyalty is of great benefit to the manufacturers.

The earnings record of companies such as American Home Products, Bristol-Myers, and Schering-Plough all bear this out; each of the three has shown steadily rising profits in every year as far back as 1953.

One of the fine examples of what makes a good investment and what makes a poor one emanates from a former "member of the club" of firm-price-structure industries. Norwich Pharmacal, though never the most dynamic proprietary drug merchandiser, had compiled a record of consistent growth over many years—and I used it (and its key product, Pepto-Bismol) as an example in lectures for many years. In contrast to the Pepto-Bismol, I would point to a carton of salt—which, of course, is a nondifferentiated product that lacks the characteristics emphasized above.

Lo and behold, one day in 1969 Norwich announced its intention to merge with Morton International—the makers of—guess what?—Morton's salt (among other products).

I wrote the management of Norwich and told them I felt they were making a mistake, sold all the Norwich stock I had outstanding, and placed the money in "pure" companies that would not have to struggle with saltlike products.

Since 1969, Morton-Norwich has had four "down years"— and its stock has fallen from the $50 level to around $25.

'Nuff said?

Other industries that have at least a fairly "disciplined" price structure are cosmetics, soft drinks, tobacco, automobiles, dress patterns, and selective "service" areas. In 1980, certain resource-type industries showed signs of firmness in pricing policies not experienced before, namely iron ore, industrial gases, certain forest-related products, and specialized chemicals.

4. *How easily can new competition come on the scene?*

A famous American industrialist made an extremely sage and interesting statement some years ago: *It is easier to make a million dollars than to make ten thousand.* The comment was shocking to many people, but actually it made a great deal of sense. Why? Simply because there are relatively few people in the world who have the capital, the know-how, and/or the fortitude to engage in million-dollar deals, whereas the world is full of individuals who are trying to make $10,000. How very true this is. And how valuable this lesson can be to investors—so valuable that I insist you keep it in mind at all times when considering an industry for investment.

Naturally you don't want to invest in an industry in which new competition can easily set up business and cut into your market. Don't invest in what I call "garage" industries—ones in which persons can set up similar operations to yours in their garages. Invest instead in industries that require some real know-how, heavy capital, or control of important resources. In short, invest in industries where new competition is going to be scarce.

Some years ago there was a wild flurry for boat stocks in the market. As sure as night follows day, I was convinced that this flurry would end in partial disaster for most investors. The reason: Small boats can be made locally for competitive prices by small operators and it was obvious that most glamour boat companies would soon fall by the wayside—which, in fact, they did.

5. *Is the industry cyclical? (Does it fluctuate with the business cycle?)*

I mentioned earlier that the Federal Reserve Board and other monetary authorities endeavor to keep business on an even keel—going gradually upward. Despite this, fluctuations are inevitable. Business is bound to have its ups and downs over the years.

Certain industries are very sensitive to changes in business conditions. When business in general is good, they thrive. When business turns bad, they show rather drastic declines. I will discuss later how money can be made from buying and selling so-called cyclical stocks (those that are very sensitive to the general economy). I don't recommend that the average investor buy many cyclicals because investing in cyclical stocks requires great flexibility, which most investors lack. From a mathematical standpoint, it doesn't make sense, either. *Buying cyclical stocks entails making frequent decisions,* which are both difficult to time and hard to handle emotionally. When you buy cyclicals, you are competing with owners who for the most part are conditioned to selling and know that they must anticipate the proper cycle in order to maximize their returns. They are tough competition. Because of this, and because you, too, know that cycles cause volatility, you are less apt to be relaxed with your investment (and don't think that this is unimportant—after all, investing should bring you peace of mind along with a good rate of return).

This is not to imply that you can take a Rip Van Winkle approach to noncyclical growth-type stocks. However, the proper growth companies do allow you more time as a holder (i.e., less frequent buys and sells are necessary). Besides, their growth should bring steadily increasing dividends and less-nervous fellow shareholders.

Therefore, in determining whether an industry is for you, take a good look at its past record to determine whether it has been subject to ups and downs. If it has, then you need only ask one question: Has anything in the industry changed to eliminate this fluctuation?

If not, then you should beware!

6. *What is the overall outlook for the industry?*

The answer to this question involves a summation of what we have just discussed plus many other factors that have to do with the future. Here is where you have to let your imagination run wild in deciding what the future has in store. Here is where I recommend my "vacuum approach" in reaching a conclusion. Put yourself in a vacuum! Tear down all those emotional ideas you have with some negative thinking. In other words, become completely objective about the plus and minus factors and decide what the overall outlook is for the industry you are considering. Later on—in Chapter 27—I will do some of this vacuum thinking for you.

CONCLUSION

By now you should be able to make a decision about investing in an industry. If your feeling toward an industry is negative, then do not consider buying stock in a company in that industry. Look elsewhere for your success. I can't stress the importance of this industry approach enough.

21
What to Buy—Part Two

MY COMPANY APPROACH

After you've decided that a certain industry is attractive for investment, the next step is to rate the company you are considering. I have compiled a few questions you should ask of every company you consider for investment.

1. *How good is management?*

Obviously management is all-important. A company is no better than the people who make its major decisions and form its backbone. There are countless examples of the difference good and bad management can make in an organization.

Perhaps the classic example is Montgomery Ward and Sears, Roebuck. In 1947 sales of Montgomery Ward were $1.1 billion and those of Sears amounted to $1.9 billion. Both companies had been battling for the consumers' business and both had achieved considerable success. Following the war, however, the two companies differed enormously in their attitudes about the future:

Montgomery Ward was pessimistic about the future of the United States. Management felt a depression was right around the corner and therefore it was necessary to conserve cash and reduce operations so that overhead and expenses would be at a minimum.

Sears envisioned the opposite. It saw startling prospects.

The buying of almost all items had been curtailed during the war, so there was a pent-up demand for good merchandise. Now was the time to modernize existing stores, build new ones, go into suburban shopping centers.

The results are startling. Here's what happened to Sears and Montgomery Ward from 1947 to 1967:

| | Sales | | Per | |
| | 1947 | 1967 | Share Earnings | |
	(Billions)		1947	1967
Sears, Roebuck	$1.9	$7.3	$0.75	$2.51
Montgomery Ward	1.1	1.9	4.43	1.31

And here's how the stockholders of these two companies fared over the same period:

| | MARKET PRICE OF STOCK Mean Price | | Percent Increase over | Dividends per Share | | Percent Increase over |
	1947	1967	20 Years	1947	1967	20 Years
Sears	5⅞	52½	793%	$0.29	$1.20	314%
MW	28½	26	decrease	1.50	1.00	decrease

What a contrast—and it was due to a difference in management philosophy and know-how. There are countless other illustrations of companies engaged in identical fields whose sales performance, earnings, and dividends are as different as day and night. In the vast majority of cases, the difference between success and failure is attributable to management and management alone.

Perhaps you're wondering how you can judge management from your living room chair. Well, there are many ways of doing this. First of all, your broker can help you. His research people call on various companies throughout the year and they give you a first-hand "feel" about management through the research reports they publish. Second, I always recommend reading the annual report of a company you are analyzing, so you can get your own "feel" of management and its ideas and their planning. There are many other management guideposts, among them stress on research, ability to bring out new products, efficiency of marketing and distribution of products, trend of profit margins, and trend of sales and profits.

A word of caution: Remember that management is inclined to be prejudiced; it is bound to be optimistic about how the company is managed, how it can market products, and so on. Research reports, annual reports and the like should all be read with this prejudice in mind.

2. *How good is the company's research?*

As you know, research is the backbone for the future. Top companies all possess strong research teams and put a strong emphasis on R&D. Here are a few hints in analyzing a company's research:

    A. Is the company spending a higher or lower *percentage of sales* on research and development than other companies in the same industry?

    B. How many new products has the company developed successfully in the past few years?

    C. What percentage of last year's sales came from products recently introduced?

Don't think research is important only to glamorous industries like electronics and chemicals. It's equally important in even the most conservative food company. What has made Procter & Gamble outperform its competitors? Strong research and new product development, for one thing.

The future lies with those who prepare for it. The efficient research companies will continue to outstrip their competitors, so give this element strong consideration when you are considering a company for investment.

3. *Is the company diversified?*

As you know, it's dangerous to put all your eggs in one basket. Likewise, it's dangerous to own companies that have only one product. Someone comes up with a better mousetrap and you're out of business.

One interesting example of a company that was one-product for many years is Clorox. Here was a well-managed business making a product that had become a household word. Yet Clorox Chemical lived under a "one-product black cloud." If someone developed a capsule that when dropped into a gallon of water made a bleach like Clorox, the latter's extensive bottling facilities would become relatively obsolete. Here was a risk that Clorox stockholders faced every day of their lives—whether they knew it or not. Like most one-product companies, Clorox eventually merged with another company (in this case, Procter & Gamble) and stockholders finally could breathe easily with good diversification. (Later P&G was forced to divest itself of Clorox and thus the latter became an independent entity again—after which management moved into numerous areas to diversify.).

Most companies have sought diversification in recent years. But some have overdiversified, entering a variety of industries on a helter-skelter basis—i.e., the so-called conglomerates. It's a difficult job indeed for management to become familiar with the ins and outs of many businesses and be able to make correct decisions for all. Some companies have been able to succeed in a multitude of businesses and have built admirable records. For the most part, however, the burden of proof rests with the optimist. There are many obstacles to overcome, and failure and mediocrity are far more common than dramatic success among conglomerates.

To my way of thinking, proper diversification should fit a pattern: it should be done in related businesses. American Home Products is a good example. This fine company diversified from drugs into foods and related household products. This makes sense, because drugs and foods go to similar markets, take similar merchandising, distribution, production, and so forth. Success is not so difficult to achieve when diversification is in a related field.

4. *What new products does the company have?*

It's probably unnecessary for me to tell you to watch for new products that might suddenly increase a company's sales and profits sharply. Yet I would be remiss if I didn't list this as a factor to consider.

Some new products are easy to observe. In the 1960s the smoker shift to Kent cigarettes provided an obvious boom for Lorillard. In the 1970s the same kind of enthusiasm for Marlboro hyped the earnings of Philip Morris. Polaroid's Land Camera had the market all to itself until Kodak entered it in 1978. The automatic pinspotters produced by AMF and Brunswick pretty much revolutionalized bowling—and created burgeoning profits for these two companies for half a decade.

Other new products are not quite so obvious, but can be equally important. Ages ago (in the late 1950s) a company considered to be dull and suitable mainly for income (not growth of capital)—Otis Elevator—had a bonanza from the conversion of manual to automatic elevators. Hewlett-Packard's sophisticated calculators, introduced in the mid-1970s, may have been too complicated for most people—but they created huge profits for the company. All types of computer products provided investment opportunities in both the manufacturing companies and those supplying the components (semiconductors) throughout the past decade.

5. *What kind of patent protection or specific know-how "protects" the company from outside competition?*

This is just as apparent as the preceding point, but has to be mentioned. DuPont had the synthetic fiber market to itself for many years, until other companies developed their own processes. Minnesota Mining's Scotch Tape patent protected it for many years. Kimberly Clark's "pop-up" Kleenex patent allowed it to get a hold on the tissue market. Owens-Corning was one of the few companies in the country that had the know-how in production and fabrication of fiberglass. Polaroid had instant photography to itself for years (as mentioned, Eastman has now successfully entered this field). Xerox's advanced office copying literally destroyed companies that offered only wet-process machines. Now that dry-process is used by other manufacturers, Xerox's domination has been diminished.

These few examples point out the importance of patent protection and know-how in analyzing a company's strength.

6. *How well does the company control its costs?*

As we saw in the discussion of profit margins, some companies operate far more efficiently than their competitors. It goes without saying that an investor will fare much better with an efficient company than with one that is a bit sloppy in controling the costs of doing business. Some companies have better manufacturing plants, some have better labor, some boast more efficient distribution of their products, and some know how to control their inventories better. These factors should be prime considerations in analyzing an individual company and I urge you to consider them. In addition, there is one important factor that has much to do with the answer to the original question and that is: *How dependent is the company upon others for raw materials, etc.?*

Confucius might well have said: "Housewife who depends on neighbor for sugar three times a week will eventually drink unsweetened coffee." Just as a person will be happier if he doesn't have to go through life depending on other people for everything, a business that is less dependent on others is better off.

Thus, in looking at prospective investments, give more consideration to self-sufficient companies than to those that must depend on everyone else for their existence. These self-sufficient ("fully integrated") companies have the following advantages:

A. They have control over their resources.
B. They are not as vulnerable to shortages. Example: Chrysler, after some very lean years, finally came up with a model car in 1959 that was slated to be successful. But then its glass supplier got involved in a drastic strike. Result: Chrysler had another bad year.
C. From the standpoint of reported profits, certain companies with their own resources can choose which re-

sources to use at what time and thereby "fix" their reported profits. Example: Numerous forest products companies, which have huge timber holdings. When plywood prices are low, they can cut low-cost timber and thus show good profits even though their final selling price of plywood is below last year's levels.

D. If inflation is here to stay, natural resource companies (such as those owning timber) should see their reserves worth more and more over a long period of time.

E. Companies that have to buy from others have to pay their suppliers a profit—a profit that would be their own if they did the work themselves.

Naturally there are notable exceptions to this reasoning. A company such as Bristol-Myers, for example, does not want to tie up its capital and management in the production of containers for its product. For one thing, it prefers the flexibility of being able to switch to whatever container it desires—which it could not do if it were tied to its own manufacturing output. In other words, management concentrates on producing the right products and putting the most efficient merchandising behind these. The small profit paid to someone else for the right container is insignificant in relation to the central goal.

7. *What is the company's past record and future outlook?*

In many cases, a company's past record will give you a good clue to its future outlook. Therefore, just as when you analyze the overall outlook for a specific industry, you should start out by looking at a company's past record and ask: "What, if anything, makes this company's outlook any different today from what it has been over the past three or five or ten years?"

If the answer is, "Nothing is any different," then you may be able to project the future. Usually, however, it is not that simple because things are seldom static in this world. Thus you have to consider all the previously mentioned factors to arrive at a conclusion as to whether the company's rate of growth will be faster or slower than its recent past.

CONCLUSION

Now we have satisfied ourselves that the *industry* we are considering is attractive and that the *company* within this industry is for us. Does this guarantee us a successful investment? No. Because our timing in buying the stock may be wrong.

Our next step, therefore, is to determine when a stock should be bought and when it is overpriced and should be sold.

22
What Tools to Use

Earlier I discussed some yardsticks you should apply in analyzing the stock market in general. I hope you will use these yardsticks, but I feel it is even more important for you to learn when
individual stocks are too high or too low. I emphasize this because there are times when individual stocks will rise sharply
while the general stock market is declining—and just as many
times when individual stocks will fall while the market in general is rising.

You're probably aware that there are a multitude of yardsticks and ratios that can be used in analyzing stocks. Actually
I don't think it necessary that you bother yourself with most of
these.

We've already discussed balance sheet analysis and decided that the various yardsticks given can be used to bolster your
confidence in a company or to warn you of certain dangers. We
concluded that the balance sheet can be the determining factor
mainly when market price is below either stated book value or
what might be termed "going concern value" (i.e., what the
company might be worth to a potential buyer). All of this is important, as mentioned in Chapter 18, only in companies small
enough to be acquired by others.

One problem for the book-value stock buyer is that most
companies that sell at big discounts from liquidating value do
so for a reason; oftentimes they are not particularly well situated competitively, or they are very cyclical. So, in many cases,
it is like buying property that is not in the very best location.

Still, buying assets "cheap" is one legitimate strategy and it should not be overlooked.

Most common stock purchasing, however, is done on the basis we have already described—the desire to own sound businesses that seem to have attractive future prospects. Here, there are two major yardsticks to consider, namely *yield* and *market price in relation to earnings*. Let's look at these separately.

YIELD

"Yield" is just another way of saying "annual rate of income return on your investment." This is figured by *dividing the yearly dividend rate of a stock by its present market price*. Thus a stock paying $4 per year in dividends and selling at $100 gives an annual rate of return (yield) of 4% ($4 ÷ $100 = .04 or 4%).

This is just like figuring the return you get when you put money in the bank in your savings account. If you deposit $100 and keep it there a year, the bank will pay you $7.50 interest, for a yield of 7½% on your money.*

Many people give great weight to yield in figuring whether a stock should be bought or not. This is fine if current return is your investment objective. If you have to depend on dividends from your stocks for your everyday living or for necessary "luxuries," then yield should be your consideration in buying stocks.

Oddly enough, most investors don't really need the dividends right now. Most people are looking to the future. They are more interested in building up capital and in building up *future* income than in present yield.

If growth of capital is your objective, *give only limited consideration to yield*. If you have invested your money in a growing company, it may be better that they do *not* pay out high dividends now. Here's why:

1. If dividends are paid to you, you will have to pay income tax on them. Under the present tax structure, this

---

*Actually you will get slightly more than 7½% if the interest is computed more than once a year.

could amount to as much as 70% of the dividend income.

2. You may spend the dividends and not "let them ride" and compound for you.

3. If you don't spend them, you may not be able to reinvest the dividends at the same high rate that the company could invest them for you. Most growth companies earn 10–20% (and some considerably higher) return on their invested capital. I ask you: Where could you invest your money and achieve such a high rate of return, especially since you will have to pay income tax on these dividends? Furthermore, you would probably put your after-tax income from dividends into some sort of savings account which pays a lower return than the company might earn.

If it's growth you want and you're looking to the future, deemphasize dividends and yield now. Most important, consider annual growth of your capital as the major part of your "annual return" equation.

I should point out that yield can be important in a declining stock market. It can provide a "floor" for your stock and limit your downside risk. Take a stock paying a $1 annual dividend and selling for $16 on the market, for a yield of over 6% ($1 ÷ $16 = .0625 or $6\frac{1}{4}$%). If that $1 dividend is safe, what is the lowest you figure that stock can go? If it declines to $10, the $1 dividend gives a 10% yield and this is awfully high for other than very mature industry groups such as utilities and steel. Perhaps the lowest the stock would go is $12\frac{1}{2}$ or so, because the yield there would be 8%—and this is high, too. In other words, because of the $1 dividend, you can feel secure your stock will not go much below $12\frac{1}{2}$. If there is no dividend on the stock, you cannot say this. Who knows, maybe the stock will go to 10 or 8. Thus yield should be a consideration if you cannot afford much risk in your investments.

The above illustration does point up, however, how yield *can* provide some *temporary* appreciation in stocks. The example of the stock that declines to $12\frac{1}{2}$ (with a secure $1 dividend) is a case in point: the very high yield of 8% attracts considerable interest from investors, and before long this "bargain" stimulates buying and the stock recovers—perhaps back to the 16 level or higher. The rise from 12½ to 16 (a gain of almost 30%) is due to yield and yield alone. The trouble is that this rise will probably constitute the major part of the stock's appreciation potential, *unless the company's earnings are growing.*

As you can see, I contend that *the best defense is a good offense.* Buy a stock that you think is a good value and that you feel confident will go up in price. If you're right and the stock goes from $16 to $20, $25, or $30, then your worries about it going down to $12 or even $16 should diminish.

It is difficult, of course, to have your cake and eat it. High-yielding stocks generally lack significant growth potential. As a matter of fact, they *generally indicate weakness.* I have heard so many people say about a given stock that "it looks attractive because it's paying X% yield." Nine times out of ten there is good reason for the stock to be selling so low on the market that it provides a very high yield. Usually:

1. The outlook for the industry or the company is very poor and investors have no reason to buy the stock.
2. Or the dividend is *not* adequately covered by the company's earnings—to the point where the present dividend rate is *not safe.*

A number of years ago a friend called me and asked about Waldorf System common stock (then listed on the New York exchange). He was interested because Waldorf stock was selling at 16½ and paying $1 annual dividend, for a yield of over 6%. I took a look at this company and found that it was in the restaurant business, which at that time was not a popular industry with security analysts and/or stock buyers. I went over Waldorf's record of earnings for the preceding five years, which were as follows:

1955	$1.01 per share
1956	.90 per share
1957	.98 per share
1958	.91 per share
1959	1.08 per share

The company had exhibited little growth over this period; unless there were some new developments on the Waldorf scene, one wouldn't get excited over this stock for growth. The stock's major attraction was its $1 dividend, which, as my friend pointed out, gave a yield of over 6%. But was the $1 dividend secure? Definitely not! First of all, Waldorf was paying out $1 in dividends out of a bare $1.08 in profits. Only a minor decline in Waldorf's business would put earnings *below* the $1 dividend and the dividend would no doubt have to be reduced.

Furthermore, a check of Waldorf's earnings for the first few months of 1960 indicated that profits were running below the 1959 levels. Now it was doubtful that there was *any* coverage of the $1 rate.

After appraising Waldorf's business and discovering that the dividend was not well protected, I advised my friend against investing in the stock. Only a few months later Waldorf was forced to reduce its quarterly dividend from 25 cents to 15 cents; the $1 rate had suddenly become only 60 cents, and that 6% yield had faded to 3.6%. It wasn't long before Waldorf stock reflected the new unattractive yield and fell to 11½.

Remember, then, that there is usually a good reason for a stock offering an exceptionally high yield—and it is a real mistake to reach for high yields. Experience has proved this. I have a motto that sums it all up: If growth of capital is your goal, concentrate on *outcome*, not income.

WHAT YARDSTICK SHOULD YOU USE?

If you were to buy a business or a piece of real estate, what would determine the price you would be willing to pay? Answer: *The present and potential earning power* of the business or property.

Common stocks should be bought the same way. You should buy them according to their present earning power and according to what you believe they should earn in the future.

To do this, you should emphasize one ratio—the price-earnings ratio (or price-earnings multiple, as it is most often called). This is not a new yardstick; in fact, it has been the backbone of security analysis for years. But the applications of this multiple have changed considerably over the years.

My application of this yardstick is somewhat different, and it will help you decide when a stock is good value and when it is overpriced in the market.

The Price-Earnings Multiple

First of all, let's see exactly what the price-earnings multiple is. It is simply the relationship between a *stock's market price and its earnings per share.* It is arrived at by *dividing a company's earnings per share into the market price of its stock.* For example, suppose Company A earned $1 per share last year and Company A stock is selling for $10 per share. The price-earnings multiple is 10:

$$\$10 \text{ Market price} \div \$1 \text{ Earnings per share} = 10$$

Let's suppose that Company A had earned $2 per share instead of $1. What would the price-earnings multiple (let's call it P/E multiple from now on) be?

$$\$10 \text{ Market price} \div \$2 \text{ Earnings per share} = 5$$

Naturally you'd rather buy Company A stock at $10 with $2 earnings (P/E of 5) than with $1 earnings (P/E of 10). Thus you can see that the *lower the P/E multiple, the more value you are getting.*

Another way of looking at this is to say that the P/E multiple tells you how many years you will have to wait to recoup your investment *if earnings remain the same in the future.* In Company A's case, if it continues to earn $1 per share each year, it will have earned your $10 market price back in ten years (remember, 10 was the P/E multiple, or as we say in our business, "the stock is selling at 10 times earnings"). If Company A earns $2 per share every year, you will only have to wait five years to have your $10 market price earned for you.

Naturally the quicker your investment is earned back, the better for you—which is another way of saying that the *lower* the P/E, the better.

If companies earned the same amount of money every year, it would be easy to decide which stocks were the best buys: all you would have to do would be to compute the P/E multiple and buy the stock that had the lowest figure. The trouble is that companies do *not* earn the same amount of money year after year. There are always fluctuations, either up or down. Thus *you can't buy stocks on the basis of P/E multiple alone.*

Instead, *the price you pay for a stock should depend on what you expect the company's profits to be in the future.* Let me show the vast difference between four theoretical companies, all of which are now earning the same $1 per share—but which are going to grow very differently over the next ten years. The first of these is a *supreme growth company*, with an expected 30% annual compounded growth rate over the next ten years; the second is a *normal growth company*, with a 10% annual growth rate; then come *stable company* (no change in earnings expected at all), and the *stagnant company*, which is going downhill.

Here's how these four will change in this ten-year period:

Year	Supreme Growth (30%)	Normal Growth (10%)	Stable (no change)	Stagnant (declining)
Base Year	$ 1.00	$ 1.00	$ 1.00	$1.00
First	1.30	1.10	1.00	.95
Second	1.69	1.21	1.00	.91
Third	2.20	1.33	1.00	.87
Fourth	2.86	1.46	1.00	.83
Fifth	3.72	1.60	1.00	.80
Sixth	4.83	1.76	1.00	.76
Seventh	6.28	1.94	1.00	.73
Eighth	8.16	2.13	1.00	.70
Ninth	10.61	2.34	1.00	.67
Tenth	13.79	2.57	1.00	.64
TOTAL EARNINGS FOR THE TEN YEARS	$55.44	$17.44	$10.00	$7.86

What amazing differences among these four companies. *Supreme* earned a total of $55.44 over the ten years, which is more than 3 times what *normal* earned ($17.44), about 5½ times what *stable* earned ($10.00), and over 7 times what *stagnant* reported ($7.86).

In addition, take a look at the difference in earnings per share *in the tenth year*. *Supreme* is earning $13.79 per share in this year, which is over 5 times *normal*'s $2.57, almost 14 times *stable*'s $1.00, and over 21 times *stagnant*'s 64 cents.

It is obvious that you should be willing to pay a far higher market price for the *supreme growth company* than for the others; by the same token, you should pay more for the *normal growth company* than for the other two; and you shouldn't be interested in buying either of the latter two, *if growth is your objective.* Note that you could have paid $50 or even $100 per share for the *supreme growth* stock in the first year and only $10 for the *stable company* (5 or 10 times as much for *supreme* as for *stable*) and still had a far better investment from the growing company. So it is obvious that *you should be willing to pay a premium in the marketplace for growing companies.*

But just how much? How does one know whether one should pay 15, 20, 40, 80, or 100 times earnings for a growing company?

One answer lies in my *compounding growth theory.*

A COMPOUNDING GROWTH THEORY

Guesswork will always have a lot to do with the stock market, but it is amazing how stock prices *eventually* revolve around their basic values. Said another way: Both the general market and the evaluation of individual securities seem to adjust (in time) to what kind of growth is in store. Low P/E multiples evolve when growth rates are falling, and high P/E's result from an acceleration of profits.

For example, at the time of *Primer*'s first edition, I computed the growth in profits in the United States over the fifteen years that followed World War II—and then became more specific and did the same for the companies constituting the Standard & Poor 425 Stock Industrial Index. I found that the figures coincided at about 4% (growth) per year. Then I looked at the stock market itself over the previous decade and found that its average multiple of earnings was around 14½ times. Thus investors had been willing to pay around this multiple for an average of 4% growth.

A few years later I recomputed the growth in profits, this time using the 1951–1965 span. I found that earnings were going up approximately 6% per annum and that the market had adjusted to this acceleration and had averaged around 16 times earnings over the period.

Let's see whether there is a common thread running through all this. To make it simple, let's substitute an individual company for the whole market and see what five years of growth at various rates do when we start with a base year's profits of $1 per share—and then apply the kind of average multiples described above both to the base year's earnings and to those five years hence. Here is the way 4%, 6%, and 7% growth companies would look:

Annual Growth	Base Year	Fifth Year	Market Price Paid for Base Year	Market Price Paid for Fifth Year
4%	$1.00	$1.22	$14.50	$11.88
6%	1.00	1.34	16.00	11.90
7%	1.00	1.40	17.50	12.50

The interesting statistic here is contained in the last column on the right, where all the figures are around $12. Thus, whereas the price of $14.50 was paid for $1.00 earnings for the 4% growth company in the base year, that $14.50 amounts to a price of $11.88 for the $1.22 earnings in the fifth year ($14.50 ÷ $1.22 = $11.88). The same thing goes for the 6% and 7% companies. *The purchase price amounts to approximately 12 times earnings at the end of the fifth year.*

According to this formula, let's see what market price an investor should pay for a company growing at a 10% compounded rate. Here's the way a 10% growth company's record will look over five years:

Earnings per Share	
Now	$1.00
First year	1.10
Second year	1.21
Third year	1.33
Fourth year	1.46
Fifth year	1.60

Earnings per share will be $1.60 in five years. The investor should be willing to pay now a market price equal to about 12 times this $1.60 figure, or $19.20 per share (12 × $1.60 = $19.20). Thus, whereas we paid $14.50 for the 4% growth company, we should pay around $19 for this 10% growth stock.

Now let's look back at our *supreme growth company*—with a 30% rate:

Earnings per Share	
Now	$1.00
First year	1.30
Second year	1.69
Third year	2.20
Fourth year	2.86
Fifth year	3.72

Multiply 12 times the $3.72 earnings (12 × $3.72 = $44.64) and we find that we should be willing to pay almost $45 for this stock compared with $19 for the 10% company and $14.50 for the 4% stock.

Setting this up mathematically, here is what we should be willing to pay for stocks according to their projected rate of growth over a five-year period:

Company's Expected Annual Rate of Growth (%) in Earnings per Share over Next Five Years	Multiple You Should Be Willing to Pay
5	15.4
10	19.2
15	24.0
20	29.7
25	36.6
30	44.5
35	53.7
40	64.3
45	76.7
50	91.0

There is one glaring problem with accepting the mathematics and the conclusions on price-earnings multiples just shown: *Competitive interest rates from bonds may be (and usually are) very much different at any point in time from the long twenty-year period used as the basis for the formula.* Whereas, for example, interest rates through most of the 1950s and the early 1960s were in a range of 3½ to 5%, we found ourselves in 1980 with the competition of 11–15% high-grade bond interest rates. On *this basis alone, the multiples shown should be cut by about two-thirds.* Therefore, any any point in time, the investor has to make adjustments to our mathematical table depending on competitive rates from bonds.

There are other factors to consider in this or any other evaluation table. One is the assumption that one can project a company's growth rate over, in this case, a five-year period—something that is difficult to do indeed. Because of this, I insist that other changes be made to the pure mathematical formula.

First of all, I vigorously warn you not to assume companies will grow at such rates as 20–50% a year indefinitely. After all, *the areas that promise such growth invite competition* and this competition will no doubt cause a reduction in the growth rate of almost all individual companies in the field.

Second, many companies that are growing at a 20–50% rate are smaller companies that don't have to show a very large increase in their business *at the beginning* to achieve such large percentage increases. For example, a company with $20 million in sales need add only $10 million the next year to show a 50% increase, and perhaps just one or two new products will add this $10 million. As the company becomes larger, however, it takes larger increases in volume to continue this growth rate. Once this same company reaches $100 million in sales, it has to add a whopping $50 million the next year to keep up the 50% growth rate, and this may necessitate bringing out more new products than it is capable of doing.

Third, the industries that are showing the fastest growth rates are generally in some phase of technological advancement and are dependent on new discoveries to realize their growth. The industries that are advancing at slower rates may be depending mainly on population increases or gradually changing habits of consumers—and these are more reliable than technological breakthroughs. The spending on health and beauty aids is an illustration of a dependable growth pattern, which is why you can project with more assurance the growth rate of American Home Products, Johnson and Johnson, and similar companies than those that are now *apparently* in this 20–50% growth class.

For these reasons, I insist the pure mathematical table on p. 168 be changed. (A new table is presented to you in Chapter 24.) The P/E multiples for companies projecting unusually rapid growth should be lowered. And the multiples should be altered on the basis of the afore-mentioned competitive interest rates from high-grade bonds. Each case has to be considered on its own merits, of course, but you have to be pretty positive of your growth projections to pay more than 12 or 15 times earnings for a stock.

But there's another reason why you can't rely on a mathematical table alone. Investors, being human, may appraise two companies with identical growth patterns in entirely different ways. Take Company A and Company B, both earning $1 per share and both expecting to grow 10% a year. You may find Company A stock at $6 per share, while Company B stock is selling at $10. The reason for this discrepancy may be that Company B simply has more glamour in the eyes of the public.

My method for making maximum gains in the stock market combines mathematical and emotional elements. Before I give you this method, however, let's explore the emotional aspects of buying stocks a little further.

23
Sex Appeal in Stocks

The past few chapters have taught us how to judge what to buy and what price to pay. It's simply a matter of:

1. Choosing the right industry.
2. Selecting a good company in this industry.
3. Paying a price that is reasonable in relation to the company's present earning power and, most important, its potential profits.

All of this assumes that investors are completely objective in buying and selling stocks. Nothing could be further from the truth! Human beings live by their emotions, and it's tough to shut them off suddenly when investing.

Have you ever seen a movie and "fallen in love" for ninety minutes with the glamorous, curvaceous leading lady (or if you're a female, with the strapping, handsome leading man)? Psychiatrists tell us it's not abnormal to do this, but I ask you: Did you, during the whole ninety-minute movie, even once consider whether your love of the moment could cook, raise a family, or provide any of the countless characteristics necessary for a life of more than ninety minutes?

Stock buyers fall in love with stocks, too (though the love lasts more than ninety minutes—sometimes it lasts a lifetime). But the analogy doesn't stop there. Just as you'd gladly pay $5 to see Cheryl Tiegs exhibit her wares, you might feel cheated paying $1 to see Hilda Duffledinker. Because of *glamour*, investors are willing to pay a premium for some stocks while others remain in the "$1" category.

Because of emotional influences, stock prices often get out of line with their growth rate. Why, for example, did Minnesota Mining and Manufacturing sell, in 1973, at around 35 times earnings (which, according even to the mathematical table that has not been adjusted for higher interest rates, meant the company should have been growing at a 25% yearly rate) when MMM's growth rate over the five-year period 1967–1972 averaged only 10%?

There were then, just as there have been historically and just as there were in 1980, many recognized blue chips like MMM that sold (sell) at higher P/E ratios than their recent growth rates would seem to dictate. Going back to 1973, let me show you the astronomical premiums paid by investors for MMM and five other "thought-to-be-blue-chip" companies, adjusting the mathematical table for interest rates at that time (these were about double the levels at which the computations were made—hence, P/E ratios should have about half the figures shown on p. 168):

Stock	Annual Compounded Growth Rate over Five Years 1967–1972	P/E Ratio They Should Sell at Based on Growth over These Five Years on a Pure Mathematical Basis	Approximate P/E Ratio at Which They Were Selling in 1972
Corning Glass	1%	?	30
Eastman Kodak	9%	9	35
International Business Machines	14%	11½	35
Minnesota Mining and Mfg.	10%	9½	35
Avon	14%	11½	55
Sears Roebuck	9%	6½	27

All these stocks were selling at higher prices than their actual growth rate dictates. The reasons for this were:

1. Their names alone indicated strength in the minds of investors.
2. They were recognized leaders in their respective fields—all of which were glamorous at that time.
3. They had shown growth over a long period of time, and they had proved their ability to make money "through thick and thin." In most cases, heavy depreciation charges were causing earnings to be understated (but certainly not so understated as to narrow the gap between the "mathematical P/E" and the existing P/E significantly.
4. They were recognized as well-managed enterprises.
5. Their outlook seemed to be for continued success in the future.
6. They were on approved investment lists of banks, insurance companies, pension funds, and other large institutional investors. They were consistently purchased by these investors for their long-term benefits and this constant demand kept their market prices higher than "normal."

Because of these six points, investors felt more confident owning these stocks than other not-so-well-known companies. Buying them seemed like buying a home with an underground bomb shelter. These stocks provided—*in the minds of their owners*—a shelter against attack from outside competition, from recessions and depressions, from all sorts of catastrophes. Buying these stocks had always proved profitable, so why not keep betting on a winning horse!

Results from these six stocks in the 1973–1980 period were, frankly, terrible. They experienced a real comeuppance because they had been overpopularized and expectations of growth had been far too ebullient (as a matter of fact, both Avon and Sears had real interruptions in their growth and their fundamental outlooks are being questioned today).

These examples typify both the success and the failure that can emanate from glamour. On the success side, these six stocks—and many others—went through long periods in which they were upgraded; and this glamour produced significant gains for their holders. Failure came when the glamorization process simply went too far and/or when fundamentals deteriorated.

A sensible philosophy emerges from these examples: Avoid paying large premiums for glamour, but do not neglect it entirely. Very well situated companies, especially those in fields with bright futures, will indeed command higher P/E's than mathematical computations might suggest. In the next chapter we will discuss just how much investors might rationally expect from glamour. Now let's discuss a bit further the overall philosophy.

To begin with, there are many non–blue chip stocks that have also sold way out of proportion to their growth in earnings over the last three to five years. In these cases, the premiums paid by investors emanated, not from a sense of stability, but mainly from an expectation that future growth will be faster than recent growth. This projection of accelerated growth may or may not be a figment of the imagination of the investor. Only time will tell. In the meantime, such stocks sell way above what one might expect because of their glamour status. Needless to say, overpriced stocks such as these carry substantial risks; if projections fail to materialize, these stocks, which generally lack any consistent institutional buying, can "fall out of bed" sharply and the sellers' exit can get mighty crowded.

At any rate you can see the importance of judging what kind of glamour status a stock might take on. The human mind can do strange and interesting things; it can place rockets *and* stocks into orbit.

Look, for instance, at the common stocks of Automatic Canteen (the vending machine company now known as Canteen Corp.) and Merchants Fast Motor Lines (a trucking company operating almost exclusively in the state of Texas) as they appeared in early 1961. I choose these two because five years earlier their per share earnings were almost identical. Here's how they grew from 1956 through 1960:

Year	Automatic Canteen	Merchants Fast Motor Lines
1956	$ .67	$ .61 .
1957	.72	.64
1958	.76	.80
1959	.91	1.18
1960	.73	1.40

Perhaps you'll be amazed to learn that—even though Merchants grew more consistently and twice as fast, Automatic was selling in early 1961 for 3 times the market price of Merchants. At $45 per share, Automatic commanded a P/E multiple of about 60; while Merchants ($15 per share) sold at little more than 10 times earnings. The reason, of course, is accounted for mainly by sex appeal. Automatic's vending machine business had captured the imagination of the public (whose judgment, incidentally, is most often wrong), while the trucking business had no such glamour, hence the very wide disparity in price between the two stocks. This happens to be an extreme example—a case where one stock was simply *over*glamorized and the other *under*glamorized. As a matter of fact, Automatic subsequently dropped in half from 1961 to 1965, while Merchants increased some in value. Extreme as these two illustrations may seem, I could cite scores and scores more—and provide many more exciting reevaluation-upward situations than Merchants'. What the Automatic versus Merchants comparison shows, of course, is what glamour, or lack of same, can do to a stock.

A more mundane but worthwhile comparison is of two fine companies, Emerson Electric and Philip Morris. Here are the earnings and P/E multiples for the two over the 1970–1980 decade:

	Emerson Electric		Phillip Morris	
Year	Earnings per Share	Mean P/E Multiple	Earnings per Share	Mean P/E Multiple
1970	$1.15	24	$ .80	12
1971	1.19	32	1.01	15
1972	1.32	33	1.17	20
1973	1.54	29	1.36	22
1974	1.66	20	1.58	15
1975	1.74	19	1.81	14
1976	2.05	18	2.24	13
1977	2.47	13	2.80	10
1978	2.93	12	3.39	10
1979	3.37	10	4.09	8
1980 (est.)	3.60	10	4.80	6½

You can see that Emerson sold at a higher P/E in each and every year, despite the fact that Philip Morris's profit growth was vastly superior (the latter's earnings grew from 80 cents per share to an estimated $4.80, or up 6 times, while Emerson's $1.15 in 1970 about tripled to $3.60 in 1980). The reason: Cigarettes and beer (Phillip Morris) have far less glamour than the image of electrical equipment (Emerson).

It must be obvious by now that investors have to assess a *stock's potential glamour appeal as well as its expected growth rate* in determining what P/E multiple it should (or might) command in the market. By combining what we have learned in the last two chapters, we are now ready to lay out a guide for selecting the all-important "proper P/E."

24

My Compounding Growth Guide

Since the stock market first began, investors have been seeking a guide that will tell them when a stock should *definitely* be bought and when it is too high and should definitely be sold. Unfortunately there will never be such a *guaranteed* system! If there were, the stock market would almost cease to exist, because those stocks that showed as buy candidates by the infallible system would be bought by everyone and sold by no one—and no market would be needed. By the same token, those stocks the system signaled as sell candidates would find few buyers.

Still, investors have to rely on some methodology to determine value. To help you here, I have developed a guide that I believe will be extremely useful to you in making buy and sell decisions. I call it my Compounding Growth Guide.

My Compounding Growth Guide combines the elements described in the last few chapters. Your judgment is, of course, needed. You have to decide the approximate rate of growth expected for the company you have in mind over the next three to five years, and you have to determine whether the company's glamour appeal is *super, above average,* or only *average.* Once you have determined these, then all you have to do is consult my guide and see what P/E multiple the stock might reasonably be expected to sell for.

Let me emphasize again that this is *only a guide.* It is not a formula for guaranteed profits. The market is too fickle for such a thing. The guide makes no representation that a stock that looks too high will not go a lot higher in price. Even if you're dead right in your assessment of a glamour status and annual growth rate, you can still be wrong. Look at Studebaker stock in 1959. No line of reasoning would have prompted a sensible investor to buy that stock anywhere along the line on its rise from 10 to 29¼. And yet that's where the stock went. (Of course, it reversed itself sharply and dropped back to 8 within the next year.) The same thing can be said of innumerable other stocks. (Using another auto industry example, it's hard to understand Chrysler's selling at $22 in 1977 when the company was "on its way" to bankruptcy.)

The guide is not all-inclusive. It is based on growth in earnings, competitive interest rates, and market psychology, but an investor has to use it with some flexibility. The guide will help you to conclude what market price range is warranted for a stock, but you must remember that the market for stocks can fluctuate substantially—sometimes to the extreme of great optimism or great pessimism. In other words, the guide provides the market prices that investors should be willing to pay for the various growth rates *as an average*. As I pointed out in Chapter 10 ("The Bulls versus the Bears"), investors in some years will pay only very low multiples for stocks, whereas in other years they will pay very high P/E's for the same stocks. Naturally one has to roll with the punches and attempt to judge the market's overall tone.

The main value of this guide is that it *will force you into organized thinking and into judgment based on value.* As I will repeat again and again in this book, buying *value* is the best guarantee for success in the stock market.

Now let's look at the guide—and then at some examples of its usefulness.

There are bound to be innumerable elements that have to be considered in arriving at the "proper P/E," but let me talk about three that should be coordinated with the guide.

The first is obvious: *risk.* It stands to reason that two companies with basically similar past and future projections should sell at vastly different valuations if they carry divergent risks.

Because of this, investors are constantly assessing the potential dangers that lurk in every stock. As you can imagine, this assessment is far from exact. The fortunes of industries and individual companies are bound to change—some positively and some negatively—and as they do, so should the prices of their securities. Our glamour-status approach is a constant reflection of this. Inherent in our Emerson Electric/Phillip Morris example is the fact that investors are more apprehensive about cigarettes and the health issue than they are about electrical equipment; so the lower P/E on Phillip Morris is really based on a combination of little glamour (from cigarettes) *and* the risk that the smoking hazard will curtail usage much further.

A list of risk elements to be considered would include:

1. Industry cyclicality (the more stability, the better).
2. Company stability (including management capabilities).
3. Financial structure (cash position, debt burden, amount of leverage).
4. Accounting conservatism.
5. Dividend-paying ability, cash-generating nature of the business.
6. Price volatility of the stock itself. (In recent years academicians and investors have emphasized what is known as Modern Capital Theory—part of which included a judgment of risk by what is termed "Beta," a statistical measure of a stock's volatility in price relative to the general market. Betas on individual stocks can be very deceptive, however, and the subject is too involved for discussion here. Suffice it to say that past relative market action is not necessarily indicative of the future. On the other hand, investors should include in their assessment of risk some conviction of the kind of volatility that it is practical to expect. Obviously, the more volatility there is, the more one has to weight higher risk. Let me repeat, however, that this is just *one* consideration in risk assessment—and the more "fundamental" factors, such as points 1–5 above, demand greater emphasis.)

A second consideration that should be factored into our guide is *trend of institutional ownership*. A stock that is widely held by pension funds, insurance companies, banks, and investment trusts already has attracted a lot of the demand side of the supply/demand balance that determines market price. And while such institutional support may be no more than an indication of attractive prospects for the security in mind, an investor has to play devil's advocate and query. If the stock has already attracted this large demand, what can we expect for an encore? What happens if these large holders lose enthusiasm? Wouldn't that create a huge amount of stock for sale and lead to sharply lower prices?

The answer is, of course, that a diminution of demand should indeed lead to lower prices. Hence we have to exercise some caution whenever we note broad institutional ownership. The corollary is that if we find what we believe is a very attractive stock and discover it is "underowned" by large holders, we can "dream a little" and postulate the positive effects on the stock if it suddenly attracts this kind of buying.

To conclude, "overownership" raises the fear of potential liquidation and a resulting lower P/E; and vice versa. Once again, high-quality companies deserve premium multiples and it would be surprising if they did not attract ownership by large investors. But you should be aware of the consequence—the unraveling of demand—should the recognized qualities come into question. All of which means that you should try to make some sort of adjustment in your P/E figuring for the under-ownership/overownership situation as you perceive it.

The same sort of adjustment has to be made for our first consideration—risk. If obsolescence is a possibility, if the industry is cyclical, if the financial position of the company is weak—if there is simply a greater-than-average risk involved—then adjust the P/E downward, maybe only 5% or 10% for a slightly risky company to perhaps 50% for a very speculative venture.

Back to the institutional support overlay. You are probably wondering how you can get the proper inputs. The Standard & Poor Stock Guide tells you how many institutions own each security and in what amounts, as does the William O'Neill service (Los Angeles, California).

Our third responsibility is to determine whether or not the competition against common stocks is radically changed, with either higher or lower bond interest rates. For example, 1969 and most particularly 1970 brought sharply higher interest rates on fixed-income securities. Whereas a few short years before an investor could get only 5% or 6% on bond investments or from similar nonequity securities, rates of 9–10% suddenly became plentiful. This posed severe competition for common stocks. Investors had to have confidence that 12% or higher could be achieved through stocks in order to consider them attractive relative to the 9–10% "riskless" yields available from bonds. This, in turn, meant that price-earnings multiples deserved to be lower than normal—something that obviously deserved some downward reevaluation of the Compounding Growth Guide. The competitive situation worsened further by 1980, with interest rates skyrocketing to almost 15%. Because of the importance of competitive interest rates, the following Compounding Growth Guide shows different "deserved" P/E multiples for three sets of interest rates: the $3\frac{1}{2}$–5% area that prevailed through most of the post–World War II era; the 8–9% that prevailed from 1969 to 1975; and the 11–15% rates prevalent from 1975–1980. The range between the three (that is between 5% and 8%, or between 9% and 11%) can be extrapolated easily by you. At any rate, here is our guide:

MY COMPOUNDING GROWTH GUIDE

THE P/E MULTIPLE YOU SHOULD PAY FOR A

Company's Expected Annual Rate of Growth in Earnings per Share over Next 3-5 Years	Super Glamour Company			Above-Average Glamour Company			Average Glamour Company		
	When bonds yield			When bonds yield			When bonds yield		
	3½-5%	8-9%	11-15%	3½-5%	8-9%	11-15%	3½-5%	8-9%	11-15%
5%	18-20	9-10	6-7	15-18	8-9	5-6	10-15	5-7	3-5
10%	20-25	16-18	8-9	18-20	13-15	7-8	16-18	9-12	6-7
15%	25-30	21-24	10-12	20-25	17-20	9-11	19-20	13-16	8-9
20%	30-35	24-30	13-15	25-30	21-23	12-14	20-25	16-20	10-12
25%	35-40	30-35	16-19	30-35	25-30	15-18	25-30	20-25	13-15
30%	40-45	35-40	20-23	35-40	30-35	19-21	30-35	25-30	16-18
35%	45-50	40-45	24-26	40-45	35-40	22-24	35-40	30-35	19-21
40%	50-55	45-50	27-30	45-50	40-45	25-28	40-45	35-40	22-24
45%	55-60	50-55	31-33	50-55	45-50	29-31	45-50	40-45	25-28
50%	60-65	55-60	34-36	55-60	50-55	32-35	50-55	45-50	29-31

HOW TO USE THE COMPOUNDING GROWTH GUIDE

The guide is simple to use.

1. Look at the past record of the company you are considering and approximate its rate of growth in earnings per share over the past three to five years. (I show you how to arrive at a company's annual compound growth rate in the Appendix. I suggest you familiarize yourself with the method now. Naturally you will want to check the growth rate over the most recent year or two, to see whether the trend is increasing or tapering off.)
2. Determine if there is any reason for the company's basic trend to change.
3. Consider any new elements in the company's outlook (new products, larger production facilities, added competition in its field, etc.).
4. Decide whether these new elements will increase or decrease the company's previous rate of growth.
5. Arrive at a reasonable growth rate for the next three to five years (barring any drastic recessions in the economy).
6. Decide which glamour category the company deserves.
7. Consult the Compounding Growth Guide and see, according to its expected growth rate, competitive bond interest rates, and glamour status, what P/E multiple is suitable for the stock.
8. Assess the company's approximate risk along with the stock's institutional ownership. Substract for high risk and overownership.
9. See what P/E multiple the stock is now selling for.
10. Conclude whether the stock should be bought or not. If the present P/E is lower than the guide indicates it should be, the stock is undervalued and should be bought. If, on the other hand, the stock is selling at a higher P/E than the guide indicates, the stock is overvalued and should not be purchased.

Now let's see how effective the guide can be and go through some examples of its use.

EXAMPLE I. A. Let's look at General Foods stock as it appeared in 1960—and then in a number of years thereafter. In 1960, the company's most recent six years looked like this:

Year	Earnings per Share
1959	$2.48
1958	2.21
1957	1.99
1956	1.81
1955	1.66
1954	1.33

Following the steps outlined, here is the way General Foods could have been analyzed in 1960.

1. General Foods has shown a 13% annual compounded growth rate since 1954. The Appendix shows you how to compute a company's annual compounded growth rate. In this case, it is figured as follows:

   A. General Foods has shown an increase in earnings per share of 86% over this five-year period ($2.48 − $1.33 = $1.15; the $1.15 increase ÷ the $1.33 base year figure = 86%).
   B. In the Appendix glance across column A of the table till you come to "5 years."
   C. Look down the "5 years" column until you come to 84% (the nearest figure to 86%).
   D. Glance to the far-left B column and you will conclude that an 85% growth over five years amounts to a 13% annual compounded growth rate.
2. There is no reason for any change in the company's basic trend (population is still increasing, consumers are eating better and spending more on convenience foods, etc.).

3. Just as in the past, the company will introduce new products, and General Foods' established lines (Postum, Post Cereals, Jell-O, Maxwell House Coffee, Baker's Chocolate, Calumet Baking Powder, Minute Rice and Tapioca, Birds Eye Frozen Foods, etc.) will provide consistently growing volume.

4. The rate of growth may decrease slightly because it is reasonable to assume that other food companies will enter the "convenience" market. Also, GF's heavy dependence on coffee makes it vulnerable to commodity fluctuations; and competition is building up in this area.

5. A 10% rate of growth seems reasonable for the company.

6. GF should probably command a glamour status of Above Average. While foods in general do not generally create great excitement in the minds of investors, GF's stress on convenience products, its well-regarded management, and its consistent record over the years warrant its receiving something of a premium. Result: A stature of Above Average (not as high as Super Glamour).

7. The Compounding Growth Guide shows that the high P/E for Above-Average Glamour is 20 for a 10% growth company under the 3½–5% interest rate competition that existed at that time. Therefore you will use 20 as a P/E starting point.

8. GF qualifies as a low-risk company because of its noncyclical business—so this is a plus for our table. The stock had decent, but not excessive, institutional support, with about 300 institutions then owning about 8% of its stock. This should lead to a higher multiple—by about a 2–5 increment. Thus GF stock "deserves" to sell at about 22–25 times earnings.

9. GF stock was selling around $50 per share. In 1959 the company earned $2.48 per share; therefore the stock was selling for just over 20 times earnings ($50 ÷ $2.48 = 20.2).

10. GF is selling at 20 times earnings, whereas our conclu-

sion in point 8 was that it should sell at 22–25 times earnings. Since the stock was selling below what we deemed it should, it qualified as a slightly undervalued situation and thus we conclude that it could be purchased.

RESULT: Over the next year and a half, GF stock rose steadily. It went to 25 times 1961 results of $2.90 per share, or up to around $75. Then it proceeded to go way beyond these figures—up to the 30–35 times multiple range.

B. Now look at GF stock as it appeared in the five years following 1960:

Year	Earnings per Share	Market Prices of Stock
1965	$3.73	89⅞–77½
1964	3.44	93¼–78¼
1963	3.34	90½–77⅝
1962	3.14	96–57¾
1961	2.90	107¾–68⅝
1960	2.69	75½–61½

Without going through all the details as shown above, the record of General Foods through this period is indicative both of how value rules out in the long run and how our guide can be useful in both the purchase and sale of stocks. In 1962 the median price of GF was $78; for 1963–1965 the median was $84, $86, and $84, respectively. In other words, each time the stock rose past 25 times earnings, it ran into selling pressure. As a matter of fact, the stock's median P/E for the years 1962–1965 was as follows: 24.5, 25.2, 24.9, and 23.3.

C. And here is how GF stock looked in 1965:

Once again shortening the procedure used in A we should start with the company's growth for the latest five-year period. GF showed profits of $2.69 per share in 1960 and $3.73 in 1965. This amounted to a 39% advance or, according to our Appendix, a 7% growth rate. This diminution in growth had relegated the stock to no more than Above Average status; a look at our guide indicates that 7% growth for such a company,

nder the 3½–5% interest rate column, is only worth a P/E of
bout 18 times. The company still appeared to be low risk,
hich would have added to the 18 P/E. Institutional support,
owever, had increased some, raising fears of overownership.
hus we should cut back the 2–5 increment to around 2, giving
s a P/E target of about 20 times. Multiplying this by the $3.73
arned for 1965 gives a price of only $75 (20 × $3.73 = $75).
he stock looked to be overpriced in the $80 range, unless
ere were new developments to alter the future outlook.

RESULT: GF stock ran into considerable selling pressure
through the 1965–1968 period as its growth rate diminished. The year 1966 showed only a 5½% increase over
1965; the 1967 increase was only 3½%; and 1968's was
just 2%. As you can imagine, the P/E slipped along with
the growth rate. Furthermore, interest rate changes would
have forced an investor to shift his P/E to the 8–9% column in our guide. Even if one believed GF could grow 5–
10% per year, the maximum P/E for an Above-Average
Glamour company would have been 15 times—and the
range would have indicated a possible multiple as low as
8 times if growth rate were deemed to be more like 5%.
So, whether it be a diminution of the growth rate or an increase in competitive interest rates from bonds, GF common was obviously slated to become a disappointing
investment—which is just what occurred in the 1965–1980
period.

KAMPLE II. A. An analysis of Hewlett-Packard Company com-
on stock in mid-1961. Here is Hewlett-Packard's record from
I56 to 1960:

Year	Earnings per Share
1960	$.11
1959	.10
1958	.07
1957	.07
1956	.05

Now we will evaluate Hewlett with the use of our guide.

1. Hewlett's earnings per share had grown 115% over this four-year span ($.11 − $.05 = $.06; $.06 ÷ .05 = 1.20 or 120%). The four-year-column for a 120% growth (see Appendix) shows a figure of 22%. Thus Hewlett-Packard grew at a 22% compounded annual rate over this period.

2. The company's basic trend should not change. Demand for electronic measuring instruments should continue to increase and Hewlett's reputation for quality is almost unchallenged.

3. The company will continue to bring out new products. In addition, Hewlett is interested in making acquisitions, any of which will no doubt increase its earnings per share.

4. Balancing these elements against the realization that as a company gets larger it is more difficult to sustain very high growth rates, one might conclude that H-P's rate over the next three to five years will approximate the past.

5. A growth rate of 20–25% seems attainable.

6. The company certainly deserves a Super Glamour rating.

7. A 20–25% Super Glamour company is entitled to a P/E of 30–40.

8. Risk was about medium for the company. H-P seemed to be advanced over its competition, but one had to assume potential obsolescence. Hewlett was at that time gaining institutional support—something that was fostered by a recent listing on the NYSE. This support, from a low base, might add an extra 5 to the multiple. Thus the stock should command a 35–45 P/E.

9. At the then-current price of $12, H-P stock was selling at an astronomical 110 times earnings ($12 ÷ $.11 earnings = 110).

10. It should be obvious that the public had inflated H-P stock. Despite the conviction that the company represented a solid and exciting vehicle in a rapidly growing field, the present price was simply "too rich."

RESULT: Certainly we did not need any guide to tell us that the stock was overpriced at that time and that it should be sold. Perhaps the thinking process described here, however, would have corrected the dangerous emotionalism that had obviously led to an overvalued stock.

A better proof of the value of our guide comes from an appraisal of its use in years subsequent to 1961. Just to trace the acts, H-P stock dropped from the $12 level to around $8 in a ix-month span. Quite interestingly, a full five years after 1961 he stock was selling at $9. By that time the company's earnings ad risen to 28 cents per share—for a 21% annual growth rate over the five years). The then-$9 market price amounted to 34 mes the 28-cent profit. Finally the stock had hit real buying evels according to our guide (which concluded that it deserved 5–45 times earnings). And from there the stock proved to be good value as it advanced to the equivalent of $22 in 1968, nd on to almost $50 in 1973.

This $50 price was more than 50 times the 95 cents H-P arned in 1973, once again signaling that the stock was overriced. So, according to our guide, we should have been a sell-r of H-P as it rose past $40. It subsequently fell to $28 in the 974 bear market, then rose to $60 in the ensuing recovery in 975, and then declined again to $30 in 1978. Let's see wheth-r this $30 price looked like a bargain in that year.

Here is H-P's record from 1973 to 1978:

Year	Earnings per Share
1973	$0.95
1974	1.54
1975	1.51
1976	1.62
1977	2.14
1978	2.64

Company growth from 95 cents to $2.64 per share amounted to 178% over the five years, or (according to the Appendix Table,) a 22½ annual growth. Interest rates had, how-

ever, risen to about 10% in the United States, which according
to our guide would have justified about a 17 P/E. Multiplying
the $2.64 earnings per share by 17 indicated an approximate
value of $45. Thus H-P stock looked (very) attractive once
again—which is exactly what it turned out to be. At the time of
this writing (1980), the stock is selling in the mid-$60 range
with anticipated earnings for the year of around $4.75, the P/E
is about 13½ times. Under our 11–15% interest rate table, a
20–25% growth company "deserves" a 13–16 P/E range.

EXAMPLE III. Here is an analysis of one of my favorite
growth companies of the past, Bristol-Myers, using as a base
the year 1961, which was a top for the general market over the
next few years:

Year	Earnings per Share
1960	$1.03
1959	.85
1958	.73
1957	.68

1. Bristol-Myers earnings grew from 68 cents in 1957 to
   $1.03 in 1960; this increase of 35 cents amounted to a
   51% increase over this three-year period ($.35 ÷ $.68
   = .51 or 51%). The Appendix shows that a 50%
   growth over three years (Column B) amounts to a
   14½% annual compounded rate.
2. There is no reason for any change in the company's basic trend.
3. A flow of new products, plus continued strong demand
   for existing lines, plus steadily rising product prices
   equals a good outlook.
4. Conclude that these elements will at least retain—and
   possibly enhance—the growth rate.
5. A 15% rate of increase is a reasonable expectation over
   the next three to five years.
6. Management image of this company is supreme; thus it
   is a Super Glamour stock.

7. A Super Glamour company with a 15% growth rate deserves 25–30 times P/E under prevailing (low) interest rates.

8. The company's business seemed to carry very low risk. Its institutional support was medium (193 owning about 11% of the company) but seemed to be growing. The combination of low risk and accumulation by large holders was enough to add perhaps a 5 P/E to the 25–30, giving a 30–35 "deserved" multiple.

9. Bristol-Myers stock is selling for $35 per share. In 1960 the company earned $1.03 per share. Dividing this $1.03 into the $35 market price gives a multiple of 34, right in line with our conclusion of 30–35 times above. Therefore the stock can still be purchased with the expectation that appreciation percentages will about parallel the company's earnings growth from here on.

RESULT: Four years later the company's net income had risen from the $1.03 figure to $2.65 per share. This increase of 157% over the five years was actually slightly above a 20% compounded gain. Over this period BMY stock rose from the $35 figure of 1961 to $95, an increase of 171%. The P/E based on 1965 earnings was 35.8, a slim premium over the 30–35 times range that our guide would have indicated a full five years earlier. Purchase of Bristol-Myers stock did work out well—and it did about parallel the company's profit growth.

EXAMPLE IV. Let's see whether our approach would have helped in the buying or (all-important) holding of what was once one of the nation's great growth companies, Xerox. Assume we were considering the stock sometime *after* the introduction of the 914 office copier in mid-1963. In the case of Xerox, it would be deceptive to go way back in the company's history and establish a growth rate; obviously the 914 precipitated a new pattern. In 1962, the first year of sizable deliveries of the 914, Xerox earned 72 cents per share. By 1963 quarterly results indicated that profits would rise to the $1.10–$1.20 range, up almost 60% over the previous year. Thus:

1. Xerox was apparently growing at a fantastic rate; many analytical projections pointed to a 50–60% compound growth rate over the next three to five years.

2. The above projections were feasible to substantiate because of the rental nature of Xerox's business.

3. New elements would obviously come into the Xerox scene (i.e., extensions of the 914, new products based on Xerography, etc.).

4. Certainly it would be difficult to anticipate a greater average rate of growth than 50–60% compounded because competition would no doubt build up.

5. Keeping our fingers crossed, we might have concluded that a figure of 50% was possible, realizing, however, that this high a rate could never be sustained for a very long period of time.

6. No question about glamour status for this company: Super.

7. 50% growth with Super Glamour allows multiples in the 60–65 range when interest rates are very low.

8. Despite the technological nature of Xerox's business, risk appeared to be quite low, because of the company's very advanced position vis-à-vis its competition. On institutional support, I could not determine figures for 1963—but 223 institutions owned about 16% of Xerox's outstanding shares a full three years later in 1966. So the stock was probably in its early stages of accumulation—especially since Xerox was "the only game in town" for an investor who wanted photocopy exposure in his portfolio. Conclusion: Could add a 5 P/E to 60–65 range.

9. Xerox stock at $60 per share was selling at 50–55 times the $1.10–$1.20 per share earnings forecast for the current (1963) year.

10. Despite the apparently astronomical multiple, Xerox stock was still within buying range and actually cheaper than our guide would indicate it deserved to sell at the moment.

RESULT: Xerox stock was, of course, a profitable performer over the next few years. In the following year (1964) profits rose from the $1.13 reported for 1963 to $1.88—an advance of over 66%. The stock proceeded to sell as high as almost $132 during the year; high as this looks, the resulting multiple of 70 times was still in the ball park of our 65–70 P/E conclusion in point 8 above. The year 1965 saw Xerox earnings rising to $2.78 per share, up 48% over the previous year; during this year the stock jumped to the $200 range—but once again the multiple was around 70 times.

Obviously the assessment of a company such as Xerox involves considerable guesswork. The risks of being wrong about growth rates are large, but our guide would have kept you on the Xerox track and allowed you to buy it along the line or retain it if you owned it—rather than allowing your emotions or the apparent high multiple to frighten you into deferring purchase or selling out.

Thinking of 70 P/E's today (1980) seems ludicrous, what with almost nothing in the stock market commanding multiples above 20 and with darned few stocks even above 15 times earnings. Interest rates, however, have changed tremendously since the mid-1960s. Under today's conditions, even if you could find a 40–50% growth company—which would be near impossible—your maximum multiple according to our guide would be 27–36 times.

The history of Xerox stock since 1965 is rather interesting. Although it doubled between 1965 and 1972, this was due to the enthusiasm (overenthusiasm) for a select number of growth-type stocks that rose in 1971 and 1972 to exorbitant P/E's *relative to their growth rates.* Our guide would not have "allowed" us to stay aboard for this "ride" since the very maximum P/E for a Super Glamour 15% growth company (which Xerox had become by the early 1970s) would have been 21–24 under the then-prevailing interest rates. Even adjusting to a 25–30 range would have forced you out in the late 1960s. In getting out then, you would have missed a 30–40% move in the stock—but this kind of move to unrealistic prices is something we never want to count on in stock ownership. Actually, Xerox stock sold in 1980 at about the same level it did back in 1965!

Time now for some additional and very pertinent comments about the use of our Compounding Growth Guide.

First of all, as the examples indicate, be sure to key into your thinking the kind of earnings expected for the *coming* year or two. Last year may well be an indication of the future, but it is ancient history as far as the stock market is concerned. Be sure to relate the present P/E to the immediate future—not to the past.

Second, an investor has to reassess his stocks against this guide (or any other) as time goes on. In other words, time flies and conditions change; the successful investor is the one who stays current and continues to anticipate the future. He alters his earnings estimates continuously—and he reassesses market prices and their potentials according to the new figures. Most important, he checks constantly to determine whether his appraisal of growth rates is on the beam or whether the company's pattern is changing.

Third, you can see from the examples that our guide is valuable mainly in evaluating *growth companies*. The next chapter will show the guide's usefulness in four specific money-making areas in the stock market, but many areas defy analysis by our guide. Nongrowth stocks, for example, generally sell on a basis of either yield or asset value (since there is no definable growth rate). In addition, typical cyclical stocks are difficult to evaluate with a guide such as this; and certain industries (e.g., the oils) have a heavy bias toward some deeply entrenched historical basis and do not generally sell at prices that relate directly to annual growth rates.

Last, I want you to realize that there is method in my madness of choosing very high P/E stocks as examples in this chapter. I did so because the premium multiple equities are most often the most difficult for people to buy (their fear that the premium might disappear inhibits them). Stocks that are cheap on earnings (i.e., 5–8 times earnings) do not pose the same "psychological block" as those that were in the 25–30 range when interest rates were low, or are in the 10–15 range today when there is much greater fixed-income competition. Obviously, it would have been simpler for me to present a raft of examples pinpointing the wisdom of purchasing stocks at 5–8 times earnings (at a matter of fact, I will give you such examples in the next chapter). By outlining the right procedure for buying growth companies, which unfortunately are rarely found at dirt-cheap multiples, and by understanding how money can be made in stocks that carry relatively high P/E's, too, I believe I have given you a well-rounded and sophisticated approach.

Needless to say, this approach requires some judgment on your part. But then, what successful endeavor does not! Furthermore, I want to make it clear once again that the stock market is not as precise as any formula or guide might make it out to be. I have felt it essential, however, to prove the point that the key to long-range success is in *paying the right price for what should be reasonably expected to occur in the near future*—and this is what my guide helps you to do. Over the long term, your largest stock market profits should come from companies that *are* growing, and the Compounding Growth Guide should be very valuable to you in assessing these growth companies correctly.

PART VII
How to Make Money in the Stock Market

25
Five Roads to Big Profits

The Compounding Growth Guide will help you to consider a company's growth rate against various interest rate conditions, and show you the effect of public psychology and institutional support on a stock's price. The guide will allow you to analyze companies of differing qualities and quantities.

When correctly used, the guide will help you to buy good values and to sell those stocks that have run up beyond a logical judgment of their intrinsics. The guide revolves around value, and in the stock market value will eventually prevail.

Let me show you five major ways to make money in the stock market and indicate how the Compounding Growth Guide is useful in all but one of these approaches. Let's consider these five roads to big profits separately.

ROAD NUMBER ONE: CYCLICAL STOCKS

Buying "cyclical" stocks when they're at the bottom of their cycles.
Certain industries go through definite cycles over the years. They have several years of very good business and then they go into the doldrums for a few years. Most cyclical industries follow the cycle of business in general: when the economy is rolling along at high speed, they prosper famously, but when the country's output starts slipping, they face sharp cutbacks. Automobiles, heavy machinery, copper, steel, and airlines are

some of the foremost industries that follow the economy in this way.

Other industries have their own cycles—not necessarily in line with business in general. Building (which can get a boost when *lower* business activity forces the Federal Reserve to grant easier money and lower interest rates), farm equipment, and insurance (fire and casualty) are a few cyclical industries that fluctuate in their own way.

All of these cyclical industries lack a strong enough growth trend for their products to overcome this sensitivity to ups and downs. You can be pretty certain that when business is booming, it will not be too long before the cyclicals are slipping once again. Automobiles are a perfect example! Autos are "durable goods"—they can be made to last a long time if necessary by their owners. When you run out of food, you have no choice but to buy more, but when your car runs down, you can make it workable by a motor overhaul, a new set of tires, and so on. Thus, people are not compelled to buy new cars. They do so in vast quantities when times are good, but the minute business and/or employment sloughs off, people defer new purchases. You can see from this that new car sales may enjoy one, two, or even three good years in a row, but it is almost inevitable that the booming sales will be followed by a decided dip, at least temporarily. Auto sales, then, are extremely sensitive to the changes in the business cycle and auto stocks must be classified as "cyclical."

This gloomy picture does *not* mean that people cannot make money in auto stocks or other cyclical stocks. They can. Stock prices will generally follow these cycles. Take steel, for example. When production is falling, steel stock prices generally go lower and lower and lower. Then it's only a matter of guessing how low steel production will go and *buying* a steel stock sometime *before* production improves drastically. (Remember, the stock market is always looking ahead. If you wait for production to rebound sharply, steel stocks will already have had a good part of their rise.) You can be sure that steel production will not remain at 50–60% of capacity for long. Barring a sharp general business recession, the country will need more steel than that, and thus the rate will have to be increased before too long.

The trouble with cyclical stocks is that you *do* have to plan to sell them, frequently, for maximum profits. Steel stocks are a buy when production is at very low levels, but they should be sold when the operating rate is very high. After all, what more can you expect when the industry has attained an operating level of 90–100% of capacity? Certainly not 150%.

Our Compounding Growth Guide will *not* help you in buying and selling cyclical stocks because the growth rates are so erratic that they cannot be depended on. You have to approach cyclical stocks by acting directly opposite to the way business is. You assume investors are not trained to buy when things are bad (on the contrary, they are probably selling their stocks in a state of panic), and then you have to fight your own emotions and *sell these stocks when things look their very best.*

This takes flexibility and strong convictions. It is not easy to buy stocks when the news is bleak, and it is even more difficult to sell them when everything looks rosy. This is one reason why cyclical stocks are not ideal for the average investor. The other reason is that a person will generally do better to buy a company with a stronger inherent growth trend, so that he doesn't have to be so nervous about selling. His chances for big gains are enhanced, especially in contrast to the smaller after-tax profits generally made by buying and selling cyclical stocks.

Incidentally, there are two chapters in *The Common Sense Way to Stock Market Profits* that I honestly believe are unique in their approach to cyclical stocks. For those who are intrigued by this area, Chapter 19 on "How and When to Sell Cyclical Stocks" is a must, as is Chapter 7, which deals with the uncovering of "cyclical-growth" stocks.

ROAD NUMBER TWO: MANAGEMENT "PLAYS"

Buying companies that have new, more aggressive, more efficient management.

Many companies are held back by poor management. With an infusion of new blood, the profit picture can change tremendously. Safeway Stores (see Chapter 19) was a good illustration of this, although not nearly so dynamic as Crown Cork and Seal, Raytheon, United Technologies, Whittaker, and some others over the past few years.

Beckman is a good example. Here was (and still is) a strong research company with many glamorous products. Management made the mistake of becoming so interested in research that it neglected the backbone of success—profits. Earnings in 1956 were $1.36 per share; by 1957 they had slipped to 16 cents per share, and by the end of that year the company was operating at a loss. Beckman stock had followed this trend: from a high of 47¾ in 1957 the stock had sunk to a low of 18⅛. The time had come for a change in managerial philosophy, and Beckman's board of directors set about to make just such a change. Some personnel changes were made and a complete housecleaning was accomplished. While these changes were being made, Beckman remained in the red and ended up the 1958 year with a loss of 70 cents per share. By the end of this year, however, the company started "turning the corner" and profitable operations were foreseen. In 1959 Beckman earned $1.30 per share and in 1960 net income was a fat $2.25. By that time, Beckman common stock had soared to over $100—a wonderful 5 times higher than its low of just two years before.

Our Compounding Growth Guide will help you to decide what price to pay for these "new management" companies. *In these cases, however, the past record is not a reliable indication of what lies ahead, so the proper procedure is to pick a normal earning power for the company and project a growth rate ahead for it in determining what price to pay.*

Let's look at International Telephone and Telegraph in 1960. This old established company had embarked on a management change (Mr. Harold S. Geneen, who did such a good job at Raytheon, joined ITT in 1959). ITT's earnings over the previous five years (1955–1959) averaged 83 cents per share, with 92 cents being the average for the last two years (1958–1959). The company had announced that it expected sales to double by 1965, and since Mr. Geneen's forte had been the improvement of profit margins, you could have assumed a 20% annual growth rate over this period. ITT would be a Super

Glamour company but for the risk of its large overseas operations. Thus we might have concluded that it deserved an Above-Average rating. Consult our guide and you can see that a 20% Above-Average growth company should have sold, in those days of low competitive interest rates, at 25–30 times earnings. Multiply this 25–30 P/E times last year's 90 cents earnings and you come up with a price of $22–$27, compared to a market price at that time of about $18. Obviously this "management-change" stock was very reasonably priced at that time, according to the guide. Interestingly, only a year later ITT stock was selling in the $25–30 price range, in line with our projection. Later ITT's growth rate diminished, and in 1973 and 1974 the company experienced earnings declines. You can imagine what happened to the P/E. The combination of higher interest rates, a reduced growth prospect, and the label "cyclical" drove the stock's multiple well below 10 times earnings.

ROAD NUMBER THREE: RECOGNIZED STOCKS

Buying a company that is correctly priced according to both glamour and growth rate and holding it for continued gains over the years.

On pp. 190–191 we discussed the stock of Bristol-Myers and concluded that it was selling right about where it should considering its glamour status and expected growth rate. In such a case, we concluded, the stock should be bought for consistent gains—about in line with the company's earnings progress over the years. There are many stocks like Bristol-Myers—stocks that are already selling at P/E mutliples that correctly evaluate their glamour status and growth rate. So long as they continue to increase their earnings and retain their glamour, investors can make money owning them.

Take the case of duPont (E. I. du Pont de Nemours, to be exact) stock. Back in 1946, duPont was recognized as a blue chip growth issue. The stock had a median price of $50 during 1946; it earned $2.36 per share that year and thus had a median P/E of 21 ($50 ÷ $2.36 = 21.2). As of 1960 duPont was selling for $195; the company earned $8.92 per share in 1959, so the P/E was 21.8 ($195 ÷ $8.92 = 21.8). Here's what had happened to duPont's earnings and to the market's evaluation of duPont stock over this fourteen-year period:

Year	Earnings per Share	Median Market Price	P/E Multiple
1946	$2.36	$50	21.2
1959	8.92	195	21.8
% INCREASE 1946–1959	277%	290%	

The stock market gave the same overall rating to duPont in 1960 as it did in 1946—a P/E multiple of around 21. Because of this, the growth in duPont stock *came mainly from the growth in earnings:* these earnings grew 277% and duPont stock grew 290% over this fourteen-year span.

For a more recent example, take Levi Strauss. Over the six-year span from 1974 to 1980, here is what happened to this fine apparel manufacturer:

Year	Earnings per Share	Median Market Price	P/E Multiple
1974	$ 0.80	$ 4.50	5½
1980	5.50 (est.)	35.00	6+
% INCREASE 1974–1980	587%	677%	

Levi Strauss stock appreciated about in line with its spectacular growth. Apparently, investor perception of the company changed little—the P/E in 1980 was almost exactly what it had been six years before. Actually, the fact that the P/E remained flat over a period in which many stocks were being accorded lower multiples was a sign that its recognition had improved somewhat, but the low 6 P/E indicates "not much."

It must be obvious that our guide would have suggested much higher valuations for Levi Strauss than the market was

willing to accord it. Investors in 1974 were certainly not expecting much from the company, assigning a 5½ average P/E. Of
course, 1974 was a disastrous year for the stock market and low
multiples prevailed practically everywhere. The strange thing is
that Levi Strauss stock carried average P/E's of 5 for the years
1975 through 1978 and not much more than 6 for 1979–1980.
What this means is that investors simply haven't "bought" anything near the company's growth record. They seem to be waiting for some sort of "negative shoe to drop"—assuming that
an interruption, perhaps sharply declining profits, is in store.
So the best we can say for our guide is that it would have kept
telling you the stock was underpriced so long as you anticipated anything near 10% annual growth. The company experienced around a 35% annual growth, but still investors
repeatedly refused to pay for anything resembling this.

At any rate, you can see how much money can be made
from owning companies that produce rising profits—and you
can prosper handsomely even without any change in P/E.

A few generalizations are appropriate here:

1. Whenever you pay a very high multiple for a stock, you
   probably should assume that your investment will increase at best about in line with its increase in earnings
   per share. Thus when you buy the equivalent of our du-
   Pont or Bristol-Myers examples, be satisfied with gradual but consistent gains as time goes by.
2. When you own securities that seem to be anticipating
   lower growth than might be expected, you may well get
   a "kicker" as investors recognize the fundamental improvement. Although our Levi Strauss example was not
   one where a higher P/E did develop, shareholders did
   fine without this; but just imagine the gains that would
   have been made if the P/E had risen, too. Let's look
   now at opportunities that present themselves when you
   get either improved image alone or the great combination of higher glamour status and excellent earnings
   growth.

ROAD NUMBER FOUR: GLAMOUR PLAYS

Buying companies when you can foresee an improvement in their glamour status.

In Chapter 23 we discussed the importance of sex appeal in stocks. If you can foresee an improvement in a company's glamour status, you can make big money without any appreciable growth in earnings. Many times an industry will lack appeal to investors for years on end. Then, all of a sudden, investors will fall in love with the industry's growth prospects and go on a buying spree that will hike up stock prices of the whole group. Stocks may double or triple in a short time despite the fact that actual growth prospects of a given company may not be much better than before.

Consider the stocks of B. F. Goodrich Company in 1946 and Crown Zellerbach in 1950.

At the end of World War II the rubber stocks had little following. Investors were concerned about the fluctuation of natural rubber prices in the world market and the industry's dependence on new car sales for growth. Because of this, rubber stocks were "cheap": Goodrich for one was selling around $11.00 with earnings of $2.95 per share, for a P/E of less than 4. A person with foresight could easily have become enthusiastic over the industry because: (a) synthetic rubber plants built during the war had lessened the dependence on natural rubber; (b) a large replacement demand for tires would build up as more autos were put on the road.

Thirteen years later (1959), Goodrich's earnings had grown only 42% (from $2.95 to $4.18), yet its stock had climbed from $11.00 to $90.00—an increase of over 8 times. *Despite very limited growth in earnings, Goodrich stock had advanced greatly because its glamour status had improved.* (This improved glamour status, which was aided by a rather general reappraisal of stocks in the market, brought about a higher P/E and it was this—not earnings growth—that accounted for the stock's appreciation.)

The case of Crown Zellerbach is similar. In 1950 paper stocks were not regarded as growth vehicles. Crown Zellerbach earned $2.73 per share in 1950 and sold for around $13.00—

at less than 5 times earnings. Nine years later Crown's earnings were still at the 1950 level—$2.76 to be exact—and yet Crown Zellerbach stock was now selling at $55.00. *Despite the lack of earnings growth, the stock had more than quadrupled.* Obviously this appreciation was due to an increase in the company's glamour status because net income had failed to advance.

A more recent example is that of Pneumo Corporation, a conglomerate-type company with interests in food distribution and retailing but with its greatest apparent potential in the expanding aerospace field. Here is what occurred at Pneumo from 1975 through 1979:

Year	Earnings per Share	Median Market Price	Median P/E Multiple
1975	$ 3.20	$ 8.50	2.6
1976	3.56	14.00	3.9
1977	3.30	17.25	5.2
1978	2.26	23.50	10.4
1979	3.25	37.50	11.5

Despite the lack of progress in earnings per share over the four years, the stock more than quadrupled and ended up at a P/E that seems totally unjustified by its recent record. In short, excepting the extremely low evaluations of 1975 and 1976 (multiples of 2½–4 times), it is hard to understand why Pneumo shareholders fared so well. One might assume that investors were anticipating the future would be much, much brighter than the recent past—and this turned out to be the case. In 1980, for example, analysts were forecasting earning power for Pneumo at $5.00–$6.00 per share for the 1981 year. Our guide shows that justifying P/E's of 11 or so in an 11–15% interest rate environment "demands" growth rates of 20% or 25% per year. So it is obvious that well before any such progress, investors were hyping the image—the glamour status—of this company.

While on the subject of glamour status, let's turn to a fad of the late-1950s—the vending machine stocks. With the introduction of an automatic bill-changing device in 1959, investors suddenly fell in love with this industry and two companies in particular, Automatic Canteen and Universal Match (both of which are known by different names today), became star performers through 1959–1960.

Early in 1959 Universal Match stock was selling as low as $12.00, or at about 10 times the year's expected earnings of $1.20 per share. The company had shown a growth rate of about 13% over the 1955–1958 period. According to our guide, a 10–15% growth company should have sold, under conditions then, as follows:

	Super Glamour	Above-Average Glamour	Average Glamour
10%	20–25	18–20	16–18
15%	25–30	20–25	19–20

It is obvious that the market felt Universal Match (at 10 times earnings) had only *below*-average glamour. As an investor in 1959, you only had to say to yourself: "Universal is engaged in an industry that should have at least Above-Average Glamour and possibly Super Glamour—because of its potentials."

On this basis alone, you would have bought Universal. After all, an above-average multiple of 18–25 (times the $1.20 earnings) makes the stock worth $22–$30, and a Super Glamour multiple of 20–30 makes it worth $24–$36 *without any increase in the growth rate at all.*

Thus our guide would have given you the go-ahead to buy, even if you took the most conservative approach and figured no increase in the growth rate. Had you allowed for an increase in the growth rate, too, you could have looked for spectacular results from the stock.

As it turned out, Universal ran into some severe operating problems in 1961 and earnings declined sharply. Before that, however, the stock had experienced the kind of gain the guide showed possible. I have used Universal to illustrate how stocks will advance or decline on the basis of what people *think* may occur. Long-term results, however, depend on what actually happens—hence, one hopes for actual performance from a company (not just image alone) for maximum results.

This leads us to the ultimate.

ROAD NUMBER FIVE: THE ULTIMATE—GROWTH AND GLAMOUR

Buying companies when you can foresee an improvement in both their growth rate and glamour status.

Here's the way to make really *big* money in the stock market. Find a company or an industry in which you can visualize both a stepped-up growth rate over the next few years *and* a re-evaluation of the glamour status (upward, of course). This double-barreled effect will lead to explosive profits for you.

Let's look at one stock that captured my imagination a number of years ago, American Photocopy Equipment.

Back in 1957 American Photocopy sold stock to the public for the first time (it had been a privately held company until then). The company's record of earnings from 1954 to 1956 and its 1957 earnings were as follows:

Year	Earnings per Share
1957	$.26
1956	.23
1955	.17
1954	.13

Apeco's earnings over the 1954–57 period had increased at an average annual rate of about 25% (a 100% increase over a three-year span equals a 26% compounded rate—(see Appendix table). Going through the procedure explained in the last chapter, it should have been apparent that the company's growth rate would at least continue at this 25% figure. This reasoning was based on the development of a decent product and hard-driving marketing. In addition, each photocopy machine sold "built in" an ever-increasing demand for photocopy *paper*—and this replacement demand was an extremely profitable item for Apeco.

Apeco stock was brought to market at a price—adjusted for stock splits that have taken place since then—of $1.50 per share. While a very limited supply of Apeco stock was available at this $1.50 price, I found there was a considerable supply of stock available around $2.50 per share, which was about 9 times the 26 cents per share earnings Apeco had achieved in 1957.

Now let's see what our Compounding Growth Guide shows you should pay for a 25–30% growth outfit like American Photocopy:

	Super Glamour Company	Above-Average Glamour Company	Average Glamour Company
25% Rate warrants	35–40 times earnings	30–35 times	25–30 times
30% Rate warrants	40–45 times earnings	35–40 times	30–35 times

The guide would have shown you how very cheap Apeco stock was at only 9 times earnings. Even if the stock had only Average glamour, it should have sold at 25–35 times earnings; as a Super Glamour company, the stock might sell at 35–45 times earnings, or at between $9 and $12 per share at that time (35 times $.26 = $9 and 45 times $.26 = $11.70), compared with the then-existing price of $2.50.

The results for Apeco stock were startling. The double-barreled effect of *increasing earnings and a higher glamour status* (as reflected by a rising P/E) brought the following results:

Year	Earnings per Share	Median Market Price of Stock	Median P/E Multiple
1957	$.26	$3	12
1958	.30	5½	18
1959	.47	12	25
1960	.57	21	36

At the close of 1961 Apeco stock was selling around $38 per share, which amounted to over 57 times the 66 cents earned for the year that ended in November. This very high multiple was the result of the public's expectation of even faster growth in 1962. The combination of a multiple that greatly exceeded the range indicated by our guide plus my fears about the advent of dry-process (Xerox-type) copiers caused me to alter my opinion of Apeco. By April of the following year all of my people had sold their shares in this company, most with gains of 10–20 times their original investment.

Aside from the fact that our Growth Guide would have prompted us to buy Apeco stock in 1957 *and in every year thereafter (through 1960),* there are other lessons to be learned from this great success story. First of all, the reevaluation, or upward revision, of the P/E did not occur overnight. As a matter of fact, it took a full three years for the P/E to get to the 35–45 level that the guide indicates it could have commanded right from the start. Therefore the investor had to have patience to realize the maximum gains on this fine stock.

Second, you can't expect the same rate of growth in earnings every year. For example, Apeco's 1958 earnings of 30 cents per share were up only 15% over the 26 cents earned in 1967; but 1958 was a recession year in the United States and a 15% increase under these conditions was remarkable (when business returned to normal in 1959, the company experienced a 57% increase in profit).

Third, the fact that Apeco had doubled or tripled or quadrupled in price over the two years from 1957 to 1959 did *not* mean that it had reached its maximum potential. Too often investors are scared away from buying a stock merely because "it already has tripled in the last —— years." Despite a quadrupling in price to $6 per share in the latter part of 1958, Apeco was still a great buy. This is a perfect example of how you should appraise a stock on the basis of its merits rather than on the basis of where it has been in price.

Fourth, you must constantly reassess your stocks. Industries and companies obviously change spots and you cannot assume status quo. Apeco was a classic example of an enterprise that lost a competitive battle—and investors had to be sensitive to this.

The private airplane industry affords another illustration of an improvement in growth rate and glamour status. In 1955 the private airplane stocks in general—and Cessna Aircraft in particular—could be purchased at about 6 times their earnings. The group had little glamour appeal! Over the next few years the net income of these manufacturers increased (Cessna outperformed the group) and suddenly investors took notice and began paying higher and higher P/E multiples for the stocks. Look what happened to Cessna:

Year	Earnings per Share	P/E Median Multiple	Price Range of Cessna Common Stock
1955	$1.12	5.7	8¼– 4⅝
1956	1.66	6.0	13¼– 6¾
1957	1.53	6.3	13¼– 5⅞
1958	1.87	6.3	16⅜– 7⅛
1959	2.47	9.9	34⅝–14⅝

Because of an improvement in growth rate and glamour status, Cessna provided gratifying results for its owners. Over this five-year period its common stock went from an average price of 6 in 1955 to a high of 34⅝ in 1959, and up to 40 in 1960.

Zenith Radio is another case in point—one that brought some worthwhile profits for my clients. Despite the company's then top management, quality product, efficient distribution system, strong financial position, and some interesting "kickers" from pay-TV and the advent of color TV, I found that Zenith stock in 1958 was selling at only 9 times its previous year's earnings. I strongly recommended the stock, which was then at only (adjusted for subsequent splits) $4.50 per share. In 1958, despite a recession in the United States, Zenith reported record profits of 68 cents per share and investors were attracted by this amazing performance. The year 1959 saw new highs in earnings, and the stock was spectacular. Here's what happened to Zenith in a period of less than two years:

Year	Earnings per Share	Median P/E Multiple	Price Range of Zenith Stock
1958	$0.68	11.2	11⅝–3⅜
1959	0.94	17.4	22⅞–9⅞

The combined effect of increasing earnings and a higher P/E multiple had shown Zenith stockholders a fast quintupling in market price. But that was not the end of this success story. The next year (1960) Zenith had a minor dip in earnings, but 1961 was on the up trend again and proving to be a dynamic performer:

Year	Earnings per Share	Median P/E Multiple	Price Range of Zenith Stock
1960	$0.85	21.5	21⅝–14⅞
1961	1.00	28.9	41⅜–16⅛

In a period of just three and a half years (from May 1958 to November 1961) my Zenith owners had seen their stock rise from $4.50 to $40.00 per share. This increase of almost 10 times their original investment was brought about by a combination of advancing earnings and a higher P/E multiple. Of additional interest is the fact that the person who bought Zenith stock through most of 1958 was taking very little risk. He had the assurance that he was buying the stock at a very reasonable price in relation to earning power; he knew that if Zenith's profits merely held around their existing level, the stock would not fall very far in price. Contrast this assurance with the situation of a person who buys a stock selling at 40 or 50 times earnings. The latter certainly could not expect any upward revision of the P/E; and if earnings fail to advance or if profits begin to trend downward, there will be a lot of "air" in the stock (having small earnings to begin with, the stock could retreat a long way before it becomes reasonable on a P/E basis).

A more recent, and interesting, example is Warner Communications, which had the following experience:

Year	Earnings per Share	Median Market Price	Median P/E Multiple
1975	$1.09	$5.75	5.3
1976	1.52	8.25	5.4
1977	1.92	11.12	5.8
1978	2.15	16.25	7.5
1979	2.65	20.50	7.7
1980	3.10	27.00	8.7

While Warner's increased P/E doesn't seem much—from 5.3 to 8.7—you have to remember that interest rates rose sharply over this period. Said another way, an 8.7 multiple in 1980 was the equivalent of 12 or so in 1975. If Warner continues its growth and if its P/E continues to expand, it will qualify as a classic "growth in earnings *and* P/E" situation.

What happened at Warner typifies what we would like to find in our investing. Five or six years ago the company was considered a fluffy movie and record concern; investors generally felt it had little solidity and expected either cyclicality or limited growth. As the years progressed, so did Warner and its image, to the point where in 1980 it is considered an intriguing entertainment vehicle with exciting potentials from cable television, programming "software" for cable, and so on.

Not all these rags-to-riches stories emanate from multiples of less than 10 times earnings. Take the case of Simplicity Pattern, a company that once had all the industry and company characteristics emphasized in Chapters 20 and 21. Earnings per share from 1960 to 1963 had compounded at a 20% annual rate, and the outlook for the future was apparently bright enough to consider this as a future trend objective. Referring to our guide, you can see that a mere Above-Average Glamour dictated, at that time, a 25–30 P/E. *Without* allowing upward evaluation for institutional support, the stock's P/E of around 17 times—as related to our guide—indicated its attractiveness. During the decade 1963–1973 Simplicity's profits about quintupled—at an annual rate of about 20% per year. And Simplicity stock went from a median price of $4 in 1963 to a high of $60 in 1973. After that the company experienced operating and management problems—to the point where investors question whether Simplicity qualifies as a growth company at all. Still, it serves as an illustration of how a great deal of money can be made from the right companies, even when the investor has to pay what looks to be a medium-to-high multiple for his purchase.

So you can see the potentials of road number five—of having a double-barreled profit-making effect working for you.

In all these examples our Growth Guide would have shown the value that existed in these stocks and given us a definite "buy" signal. Apeco, Cessna, Zenith, Warner Communications, and Simplicity Pattern were obviously not correctly valued relative to their growth rates or glamour status at the beginning. The important thing is that the guide would have given us the confidence to buy them *right along their upward trend.*

CONCLUSION

The Compounding Growth Guide gives you a tool to use in four of these five roads to big profits. You should find it valuable in assessing future profitable ventures in the stock market, though your imagination will certainly play a big role in selecting the star performers of tomorrow. The next two chapters will give you some food for thought and some ammunition to use in making such selections.

26
Spotting Growth Companies

So-called growth stocks have been in fashion for many years now. They have done far more than provide a hedge against inflation—they have built up small and large fortunes for their owners. The success of growth stocks has changed the theory behind investing in the stock market.

Years ago investors were advised to buy stocks for their yield—for the high current dividends they paid to their holders. The stock market represented a medium for achieving a higher current return than was available from various other investments. Buy stocks that yield 6%, 7%, or more! After all, a 6% return compounded (that is, with the dividends added to the investment each year) will double your capital in just twelve years.

Suddenly in the early 1950s many investors woke up to the realization that it was better to buy a growing company with a lower yield than to buy a nongrowth company with a high yield. One startling fact became apparent: Stocks of growing companies not only gained more in market price over the years, but *they actually provided more dividends for their owners over the long run.*

Remember our comparison of supreme and normal growth companies with stable and stagnant companies? To save you looking back, I'm repeating the table of earnings growth of the Supreme (30% growth rate) company with the Stable (no growth). For the sake of this discussion, though, let's see what might have happened to *dividends* of these two companies over the ten-year period. We'll assume that Supreme pays out one-quarter (25%) of its earnings to its stockholders in the form of dividends, while Stable pays out three-quarters (75%).

Year	Supreme Growth Company		Stable Company	
	Earnings per Share	Dividends per Share	Earnings per Share	Dividends per Share
Base Year	$ 1.00	$ .25	$1.00	$ .75
1st	1.30	.33	1.00	.75
2nd	1.69	.42	1.00	.75
3rd	2.20	.55	1.00	.75
4th	2.86	.72	1.00	.75
5th	3.72	.93	1.00	.75
6th	4.83	1.21	1.00	.75
7th	6.28	1.57	1.00	.75
8th	8.16	2.04	1.00	.75
9th	10.61	2.66	1.00	.75
10th	13.79	3.45	1.00	.75
TOTAL DIVIDENDS RECEIVED OVER 10-YEAR PERIOD	$13.88			$7.50

Supreme's growth allowed it to increase its dividends consistently over these years. By only the fifth year, this growth had brought the dividend rate to a level surpassing Stable (93 cents for Supreme versus 75 cents for Stable). Note that Supreme stockholders received $13.88 in dividends over the ten-year span compared to Stable's $7.50. Of even greater importance is the annual dividend rate of Supreme in the tenth year: the $3.45 dividend is more than 4½ times Stable's 75 cents.

Supreme stockholders have indeed benefited. And chances are they will continue to do so in the future. After all, Supreme in the tenth year looked like this:

Earnings per share	$13.79
Dividends paid out	3.45
Money left to be reinvested in the business	$10.34

By comparison, Stable is still earning $1, paying out 75 cents and still has a measly 25 cents per share to reinvest in the business.

You may think this theoretical example extreme, but I could cite countless cases to verify the point. To illustrate, let me show you how a $5,000 investment in 1958 in then-stable Consolidated Edison and Wrigley Company compares ten years later with normal-growth Sterling Drug, above-average-growth Bristol-Myers, and with (then) supreme-growth Xerox.

A $5,000 Investment in 1958 Would Have Bought	Which Would Have Paid You the Following Dividends in 1958	Here's What Your $5,000 Investment Was Worth in 1968	Your Yearly Income in 1968 Was
185 Con Ed at $27	$249.75	$ 6,100	$ 333.00
60 Wrigley Co. at $84	270.00	6,900	330.00
500 Sterling Drug at $10	170.00	19,000	350.00
900 Bristol-Myers at $5.50	162.00	61,200	1,080.00
1250 Xerox at $4.00	50.00	323,750	2,000.00

Despite the fact that both Con Ed and Wrigley paid (by far) the highest dividends in 1958, the growth of the other companies brought a *higher yearly rate* in 1968. It is obvious how much more successful Sterling, Bristol-Myers, and Xerox were market-wise. The $5,000 investment in Xerox, for example, was worth some $316,000 more than the same investment in Con Ed and Wrigley; at the latter two's current dividend rate it would take almost a thousand years to amass this amount.

While Xerox is hardly a standard case, the experience of Bristol-Myers is also startling. And even conservative-growth Sterling experienced market appreciation of around triple that of the two stable companies—and with more dividend return than either of them at the end of the tenth year.

History has proved over and over how profitable it is to buy growth companies. As I've pointed out before, investors are generally willing to pay premiums for growth stocks.

Corporate management has reacted accordingly. Most companies take great pains to point out to stockholders, security analysts, and the general public why their company qualifies as a growth company—hoping the label will stick and the company's stock will be better received (and qualify for a higher P/E) in the market. For this reason, many people are confused as to which companies are true growth vehicles.

Professional investors have found that there are certain fundamental elements that enable one company to outperform others, with the result that the stock of this one company will greatly outperform the general market.

So that you can distinguish a growth company on your own, here's a checklist to follow:

1. Growth companies have top management, which shows up as follows:
   A. They have a record of better-than-average increases in sales and earnings over the years.
   B. They have a record of introducing new products over the years and these products develop larger markets and good profits.
2. Growth companies spend a greater portion of their sales dollar on research and development than their competitors.
3. Growth companies earn a high return on their invested capital.
4. They plow back a good part of their earnings into expansion (new plant and equipment, etc.). This means that dividends paid out to stockholders may be very small at the beginning.

5. They have some great advantage over competition—
   e.g., patent position, manufacturing know-how, low-
   cost natural resources, strategic geographical location.

Whenever you find these characteristics in a company, you
will probably have to pay a premium for it in the marketplace.
*Timing is not quite so important in buying a growth stock as with non-
growth companies: the inherent trend of the growth company will usually bail you out even if (within reason) your timing is wrong.*

Let me warn you, however, that growth stocks are not resistant to declines. As a matter of fact, when public psychology
changes and the public becomes pessimistic, growth stocks may
well decline faster than the averages, which means that you, as
an owner, may have some uncomfortable months or years. Just
be sure that the company's growth is sufficient to give you profits *in the future*. Once again, let me stress the value of our
Growth Guide. It should reassure you in the event an original
purchase is ill-timed. Value will win out in the long run, and the
Guide allows you to make a value judgment for each stock.

PART VIII

Looking Ahead: A Forward View Toward Future Success in Stocks

27
Food for Thought

We have already determined that the logical approach to investing is to believe in *the industry* in which a company is engaged. Thus I thought you would be interested to know the basic characteristics of the major industries of our country. Look at the pros and cons as they appear today. Keep in mind that there may be some "sleeper" industries—ones that are not highly regarded today but that may turn out to be the Super Glamour babies of tomorrow.

Following is a summary of the industries. I have tried to be objective in giving you both sides of the coin. I've also tried to plant some seeds along the way. Let your imagination bring them to blossom.

Follow this procedure:

1. Read over the pros and cons of the industry.
2. Argue these points and conclude just how much the pros outweigh the cons, or vice versa.
3. Decide what glamour status you would objectively assign to the industry and what kind of growth you might expect *in the future.*
4. Look at the approximate P/E multiple the industry sells for in the market (which I have shown after the pros and cons).
5. Conclude that the market is undervaluing or overvaluing the group (or valuing it about the way you would).

Of course, you should be especially attracted to any industry group that is selling on a lower P/E multiple than you think it should. (Incidentally, the average P/E for the general market at the time of this compilation was about 9 times.)

6. Start investigating individual companies within the groups you like.

Here we go!

PRO	CON

AEROSPACE

Companies also heavily engaged in more glamorous electronic and other technological projects. Less chance of contract cancellation than in prior years (i.e., no duplicate programs awarded to more than one producer).	Remote possibility of world disarmament or reduced tensions in cold war.
	Heavy dependence on government spending.
	Possibilities of contract cancellations.
Government incentive contracts can mean greater profitability.	Profits subject to renegotiation by government.
Awareness of needs for military strengthening of U.S. (now reflected in federal budgets).	Massive R&D expenditures required.
	Heavy labor factor.

Average P/E Multiple: 7–12

AIRLINES

Tremendous growth in revenue since World War II.	Companies need huge capital to pay for new equipment.
Low saturation point (still very low percentage of adult population use the airlines).	Companies carry large debt.
Air freight in its infancy.	Operating earnings have been erratic.
Increasing leisure time.	Costs very difficult to control.
Deregulation allows more business flexibility.	High labor costs.
Some companies control interesting real estate (hotels).	

Average P/E Multiple: 4–8

PRO	CON

ALUMINUM

Lightweight, durable metal, easy to fabricate.	Sensitive to level of industrial and construction activity.
Making inroads with many new uses.	Industry temporarily plagued by oversupply.
Tremendous potential demands exist from aluminum engine blocks, aluminum cans, etc.	Government no longer buying for stockpile.
Doubling of demand expected over next decade.	Metal subject to price cutting on occasion.
U.S. dominating producer.	Government looks upon metals as inflation scapegoat.
Major companies are aggressive marketers.	
Use cuts down on weight and can be an energy saver.	

Average P/E Multiple: 5–8

AUTOMOBILES

More two-car families.	Autos are durable goods—they will last a long time if owners choose to delay new purchase.
Cars are a "status" symbol in U.S. (new car is a sign of success).	
Burgeoning "family-formation" population (ages 18–25 increasing rapidly).	Sales very sensitive to consumers' personal income, personal debt, savings, etc.
Expanded highway system.	Style changes expensive for producers.
Fairly "blind" price item (gives manufacturers firm price structure).	Hard to gauge which manufacturer's style will be popular.
	Foreign car competition is severe.

Average P/E Multiple: 5–7

AUTOMOTIVE PARTS

Those companies selling to replacement market benefit from increasing number of vehicles on the road.	Suppliers to Big Four forced to operate on low profit margins, are subject to fluctuations in new car sales. Always the risk that Big Four may manufacture parts for themselves.
	Possibility that new developments might outmode certain parts. High gasoline costs mean less driving and correspondingly low need for replacement.

Average P/E Multiple: 5–7

PRO   CON

BANKS

PRO	CON
Services being expanded. Mergers reducing overhead expenses. Most have shown consistent growth over the years. Mechanization of work is increasing.	Competition from savings and loan associations. Loan volume depends on business conditions. Labor costs are sizable percentage of expenses. Most employees earn less than in a comparable job in another industry. Heavy loan losses; question of adequate reserves. Apprehension about questionable foreign loans. Money market funds are tough competition.

Average P/E Multiple: 5–7

BROADCASTING

PRO	CON
Growing use of TV advertising. Home entertainment the most convenient; should grow in usage. Opportunity to automate radio broadcasting; following "master plan" for all stations leads to maximum efficiency. A strong cash flow business. Low labor costs.	Limit of radio and TV outlets for each company set by FCC. Have to operate within FCC requirements—which can mean nonincome guidelines. Advertising bound to be affected by general economy. CATV might infringe on markets. Pay-TV could change whole structure.

Average P/E Multiple: 7–10

BUILDING

PRO	CON
Represents an important segment of economy and thus government tries to avoid drastic declines. Family-formation age groups should create increased demand. Public construction should increase. Much potential in modernization of older buildings. Modular construction will lower costs and open up new outlets. Experience of homeowners has been favorable.	Easily postponed by consumer if he chooses. Been subject to ups and downs over the years (no steady growth). Labor rates are expanding sharply. Most materials lack uniqueness; this leads to excessive price competition. Question whether high construction costs make new dwellings out of reach of consumers. High interest rates hurt.

The building industry has many distinct segments (asphalt, cement, gypsum, plywood, paint, plumbing, etc.), and each requires a separate study.

Average P/E Multiple: 5–7

PRO   CON

CHEMICALS

PRO	CON
Production has grown almost twice as fast as the general economy.	Ample capacity in most lines.
Strong research continues to bring out new products and uses.	Subject to price competition.
Plastics are making inroads into countless markets.	Companies have high fixed-overhead expenses.
Takes considerable capital and know-how to operate—which excludes small competition.	European competition building up.
Many companies develop proprietary products for consumers.	Somewhat sensitive to business cycle.
	Pollution and other environmental costs are a real problem.
	Oil companies and producers integrating forward into chemicals.

As in the building field, there are many distinct areas, which have to be taken separately.

Average P/E Multiple: 5–8
(Specialty chemicals 7–12)

CONTAINERS

PRO	CON
Attractive packaging an excellent sales medium.	Aluminum foil and plastic film provide new competition.
Trend to supermarkets makes good packaging essential.	Possibility that customers might manufacture own materials.
	Few proprietary products.
	Ample production capacity exists.

Average P/E Multiple: 5–7

COPPER

PRO	CON
Most of the world supplies are controlled by a small group.	Demands are very sensitive to economic conditions.
Widely used in some attractive industries (i.e., electronics).	Aluminum is making inroads.
	Prices fluctuate widely.
	Persistent labor troubles and foreign government interference.
	Rising labor costs necessitate rising copper prices and the latter makes competing products more attractive.
	No control over prices because of sensitivity to world metal conditions.

Average P/E Multiple: 5–7

PRO   CON

COSMETICS

Expanding middle-income population.	Heavy advertising programs necessary.
No severe price competition.	Promotional expenses large.
Increasingly vanity-conscious population (both men and women).	Some products have seasonal patterns.
High return on invested capital.	Consumer buying patterns can be fickle; may also be more reluctant to pay very high prices.
Usage commencing at earlier ages.	

Average P/E Multiple: 8–12

DISTILLING

"Drinking age" population expanding.	Beer pretty much a nondifferentiated product.
Tax-free bonding period now extended; aged whiskey no longer dumped on market.	Little increase in per capita consumption over past 10 years.
	Industry has excess production capacity.
	Nationally advertised brands meeting severe competition from private-label merchandise.
	Many institutional investors will simply not own liquor stocks.

Average P/E Multiple: Beer: 7–9   Liquor: 6–10

DRUGS (ETHICAL)

Drugs protected by patents have firm pricing.	Heavy research expenses are necessary for company survival (products have rapid obsolescence).
Huge volume can be generated from new products.	Competition is severe and price cuts are common. Subject to occasional government investigations and criticism of high profit margins, both U.S. and abroad.
Breakthroughs in heart disease, cancer, common colds, etc., yet to come.	
Broadened medical insurance leads to increased use of drugs.	
Expanding old-age group will use more and more drug remedies.	Threat from greater use of generic drugs.
Expanding markets overseas.	Medicare and Medicaid could lead to more governmental intervention.
Labor costs insignificant.	
Not affected by fluctuations in general economy.	

Average P/E Multiple: 8–15

PRO   CON

DRUGS (PROPRIETARY)

Public now more "drug-conscious."   Heavy advertising outlays necessary.
Like ethical, have expanding old-age   Little prospect for dynamic break-
group and potentials overseas.   throughs.
Low labor costs.
Products have little obsolescence.
No price cutting.
Not affected by recessions.

Average P/E Multiple: 7–10

ELECTRICAL EQUIPMENT

Consumers using more and more   Growing foreign competition for
electrical appliances, which in turn   heavy electrical equipment and small
consume more electricity.   appliances.
Benefit from assured expansion of   Occasional price wars in heavy elec-
electrical utilities.   trical equipment and so-called white
Large companies working on atomic   goods
energy and countless electronic   Appliances sensitive to business cy-
items.   cle; heavy equipment subject to own
                                         cycle.
                                         Nuclear problems.

Average P/E Multiple: 6–10

ELECTRONICS

Countless new discoveries to be   Heavy research expenditures a ne-
achieved in the future.   cessity.
Fits in with definite trend in missiles, Obsolescence can be rapid.
space, automation, miniaturization,   Like most young industries, it is
etc.   flooded with many small companies.
Computers still at low saturation.
One of our country's greatest
strengths.

   This industry is highly fragmented. There are tremendous
disparities from company to company.

Average P/E Multiple: 10–25

FIBERGLASS

Constantly expanding uses.   Heavy reliance on textile and build-
Very flexible material with excellent   ing industries.
qualities.   Has been sensitive to business cycle
Growing use in missiles, space, etc.   (particularly the building cycle).
An energy saver.

Average P/E Multiple: 6–8

PRO   CON

FINANCE AND SMALL LOANS

Buying with credit now an accepted practice in U.S.

Former "luxuries" become "necessities" and people will borrow to buy these.

Unemployment and medical insurance make people better credit risks.

Amount of consumer credit now very high in relation to historical pattern.

Fluctuating auto and appliance sales represent large part of business.

More competition from banks.

More "captive" companies competing (i.e., auto companies, retailers).

Credit cards taking away business.

Average P/E Multiple: 4–6

FOOD CHAINS

Chains still eliminating smaller, marginal stores.

Taking on more profitable nonfood lines.

The "traffic center" for housewives.

Most areas now have ample supermarkets and thus it will be more difficult for the chains to achieve the rapid penetration they have had in the past ten years (many areas overstored).

Profit margins under pressure.

Independents have more flexibility to compete.

A low-margin business.

Average P/E Multiple: 4–7

FOOD AND LODGING

Restaurant business now being approached in more scientific way to save labor, lower food costs, etc.

Affluent society eating out more and traveling more.

Low-cost travel packages increasing demand for hotels.

Hotels, restaurants going into fewer and stronger hands.

Trend to higher rates (hotels) and menu prices.

Franchising is leading to proliferation of outlets.

Food, lodging should be sensitive to general economy.

Higher labor factor industries.

Sharply rising supply situation (large expansion in hotel rooms and restaurant outlets).

Rising minimum wage.

Higher gasoline prices restrict traffic.

Average P/E Multiple: 6–10

PRO   CON

FOOD PRODUCTS

A stable business—not subject to
wide fluctuations.
Trend to convenience foods increasing.
Lower than average labor costs.
Certain companies widening profit
margins.

Large advertising outlays necessary.
Sizes of crops vary, which affects
prices of raw materials.
Difficult to achieve dynamic product
breakthroughs.
Consumers seem to be more price
conscious.
Growing use of private labels.

Average P/E Multiple: 5–8

INSURANCE (FIRE AND CASUALTY)

Everyone needs insurance.
Have large investment income,
which is growing steadily for some.
Investment income has made dividends more secure.
Rate relief being granted or given
automatic "file and use."

Rates are regulated.
Lag in receiving rate increases harm-
ful.
Profits from insurance underwriting
have been cyclical; most often, large
losses occur.
Inflation not to their benefit.

Average P/E Multiple:
Top operating companies: 5–7
More marginal companies: 4–6

INSURANCE (LIFE)

Growing recognition of its impor-
tance by public.
Companies have aggressive sales
forces.
Prospects for broadening product
line (i.e., mutual funds, variable an-
nuities).
Longer life expectancy means more
premiums and profits.
Investment income growing.
Enjoy favorable tax shelter.
Higher interest rates help.

Large fire and casualty companies
and other financial service companies entering field.
Trend to group coverage means lower premiums per $1,000 of coverage.
Trend of higher interest rates hard
to duplicate in future.
People becoming more conscious of
equity (rather than fixed dollars) for
their future.

Average P/E Multiple: 5–7

PRO   CON

MACHINE TOOLS

Possibility of more governmental stockpiling.

More sophisticated equipment a necessity for businesses.

U.S. far advanced in producing specialized equipment.

Government spurring plant modernization through tax incentives.

Numerical control (N/C) tools revolutionizing industry.

No developed second-hand market for N/C tools.

Retooling of auto industry helps.

A function of capital spending; sensitive to business cycle.

Heavy competition developing as large companies pushing hard to get in N/C business.

Average P/E Multiple: 6–9

MACHINERY (FARM)

More large farms now, which become mechanized and need more machinery.

Government subsidies have favored farmers.

New kinds of machinery being developed.

Increasing labor costs force farmers to more mechanization.

Sales have been cyclical—according to farmers' income.

Public concern over huge subsidies to farmers.

Profit margins have varied widely.

Fight over control of farming by big business—attempts through proposed legislation to break up ownership.

Average P/E Multiple: 5–7

MACHINERY (INDUSTRIAL)

Highway programs require large equipment needs.

Tremendous potentials for mass rapid transit—and equiment needs for this.

Foreign nations have huge construction needs (i.e., dams, highways).

Sales subject to strong cycles.

Machinery quite durable and can be made to last (style not important).

Attempts to cut governmental spending may impact this group.

Average P/E Multiple: 6–9

PRO	CON

MOVIES

Film libraries great asset.
Getting higher prices at box office.
Large profits from lease of films to television.
Many companies have valuable real estate.
Industry's financial management improving.

Lower theater attendance because of competition from television.
Overseas markets will eventually get widespread television.
Risks of producing high-cost films.
Management often more concerned about awards than profits.

Average P/E Multiple: 6–10

OFFICE EQUIPMENT

Trend to automation.
Machines reduce dependence on labor, cut costs, are more efficient.
Unlimited potentials of new products.
Many companies have steadily growing rental business.
Supplies and forms business very profitable.

Many items are durable and purchase can be postponed.
Large research expenditures necessary.
Glamour has attracted new competitors.

Average P/E Multiple: 6–15

OIL

Fully integrated companies have shown consistent growth over the years.
Profitable byproducts exist (chemicals).
Decontrol of prices producing large earnings gains.

An inflation "scapegoat."
Price structure not firm.
Companies hold large reserves overseas—considerable risk of ownership in foreign countries.
Potential usage of atomic energy and possibility of electric or steam auto.
Possibility that depletion allowance will be reduced.
Increasing foreign pressure on royalty, tax structure.

Average P/E Multiple:
Fully integrated companies: 6–9   Refinery companies: 5–7
Producing companies: 8–12

PRO   CON

PAPER

Consumer paper products showing steady growth.

Companies with extensive timber reserves have a great asset.

Limited foreign competition.

Paper an expendable item that is used up rapidly.

Per capita consumption overseas increasing rapidly.

1970–1980 supply-demand position favorable.

Historically a poor "price discipline" industry (but improved now).

Industrial uses somewhat sensitive to business cycle.

Average P/E Multiple: 5–8

PUBLISHING

Expanding "middle class" in U.S.

More and more adults with greater education (more "readers").

Firm price structure for successful hard-cover books.

Growing need for reference books.

Good television programming would detract from reading.

Magazine publishing very difficult to make profitable.

Paperback book field crowded and difficult profit-wise.

Possibility of more paperbacks cutting into hard-cover sales.

Retailers can return unsold copies.

Demographics working against higher school enrollments.

Average P/E Multiple:
Magazine Publishers: 6–8   Textbooks, Business Services: 5–7
Normal Hard-Cover Publishers: 5–7

PHOTOGRAPHY

Benefits from increased leisure time activity, expanding middle-income group.

Film an expendable item—rapidly used up.

The more cameras owned, the more film sold.

Trend to more easily operated cameras.

A luxury item that could be affected by a drastic business depression.

Profitable processing business being proliferated with local competition.

Silver prices squeezing profit margins.

Average P/E Multiple: 8–10

PRO	CON

RADIO AND TELEVISION

PRO	CON
More older sets to be replaced.	Typical durable goods where purchase can be postponed.
More 2-3-4–set families.	Imports a serious threat.
Color TV first cycle replacement.	Severe price cutting at close-off of models.
Prospects for hi-fi, stereo, and home video recorders.	

Average P/E Multiple: 5–7

RAILROADS

PRO	CON
Vital part of our country's transportation system.	Inroads made by air freight.
Mergers should eliminate duplication of equipment, facilities, etc.	New pipelines taking part of traffic.
Transportation Act of 1958 beneficial to railroads.	Huge upkeep costs.
Advent of "piggyback," "fishyback," are very helpful to rails.	Need large amount of equipment to remain in business.
Possibility that unfair labor practices will be reduced.	Companies have large amounts of debt—are heavily leveraged.
Incentive freight rates have attracted considerable business.	Business very sensitive to general economy—very cyclical.
Many companies control extremely valuable assets (land, resources).	Burdened by unrealistic labor practices (feather-bedding, etc).
Many companies have diversification of assets.	Earnings records quite erratic.
Energy crisis has made rail very competitive (vs. trucking).	Competing forms of transportation get direct and indirect subsidies that railroads do not enjoy.
	High labor factor industry.
	Regulated by ICC.

Average P/E Multiple: 6–10

RETAIL TRADE

PRO	CON
Government payments make personal income more reliable.	Sales sensitive to change in disposable personal income, stores with large durable goods sales subject to wider fluctuations.
Consumer has been a reliable spender over post–World War II period.	Competition from discount houses.
Some automation procedures to help industry.	Highly seasonal business.
	Hard to increase productivity of labor.
	Variety chains (5 & 10's) losing business to supermarkets.
	Many new entrants coming into discount field, which is a low-margin business.

Average P/E Multiple: 6–9

| PRO | CON |

RUBBER

PRO	CON
More cars on road lead to more replacement demand. Major companies have own retail outlets. Numerous plant closings now taking place.	Large sales to auto manufacturers—fluctuate with new car sales. Tires now lasting longer. Compact cars, light in weight, use smaller tires and do not wear out so fast. Have occasional price cuts. High energy costs.

Average P/E Multiple: 4–6

SAVINGS AND LOAN

PRO	CON
Companies still attracting growth in deposits. Industry basic to all-important building industry. Many companies in fast-growing geographical areas (California in particular). Prospect for broadening lending areas. Enjoy favorable tax treatment. Participants in anticipated building boom in 1980s.	Have to offer higher interest to depositors to attract savings. Banks getting more competitive. Possibility of more normal taxation in future. Some companies engage in risky land and construction loans. Need for some sophisticated management. Money market funds attracting time deposits.

Average P/E Multiple: 4–7

SOFT DRINKS

PRO	CON
Very firm price structure on part of syrup manufacturers. Use of high-fructose corn syrup gives protection against sugar costs. Companies have strong balance sheets. Few firms enjoy exceptional brand loyalty. Recession-resistant. Low labor factor.	Increasing use of private labels by food chains. Need for heavy advertising. Weather can be a factor (i.e., cool summer a negative). Expensive to launch new products. Companies competing more on a price basis. Demographics no longer favorable.

Average P/E Multiple: 6–9

PRO   CON

SHIPBUILDING

Eventual conversion to atomic fleet
would mean tremendous business
for many years.
Continuous fleet replacement program, both in military and commercial (subsidies help this).

Foreign competition for commercial
shipbuilding.
High labor costs and continuously
rising costs have hampered margins.

Average P/E Multiple: 4–6

STEEL

Efficiency improvement possibilities
large.
Industry has well-disciplined price
structure.
Large earnings leverage when business good.
Plant closings now taking place.

Closely tied to autos and construction and other cyclically sensitive industries, thus quite sensitive to
economy.
Meeting stronger competition from
other materials.
Foreign competition.
Small per capita growth in consumption.
A very mature industry.
Government focusing sharply on industry's pricing practices.
Large unfunded pension liabilities.

Average P/E Multiple: 4–6

TEXTILES

A basic industry.
Companies modernizing plants and
getting greater productivity.
Industry has gone into fewer, stronger hands.
Industry trying to get more tariff
protection.
U.S. producers may be lowest cost
now.

Raw materials vary widely in price.
Foreign competition is severe.
High labor costs, especially with in-
creasing wage rates and minimum
wage laws.
Hard to control inventories.
Wide swings in prices.
Excess capacity exists.
Shifts in fashion.

Average P/E Multiple: 4–6

| PRO | CON |

TOBACCO

PRO	CON
Companies have reduced their costs substantially; low labor costs.	Product lacks growth potential.
Sales are really depression resistant.	Heavy advertising and promotional expenses necessary.
Disciplined price structure.	Companies introducing many new brands—could lead to inventory problems.
Most companies diversifying into other consumer products.	The health issue.

Average P/E Multiple: 6–8

TRUCKING

PRO	CON
Short-haul business cannot be replaced by other means.	Regulated by the ICC.
Can depreciate trucks rapidly and usually make capital gains when equipment is sold off.	Continuous labor difficulties in the industry.
Improved highways beneficial.	Long-haul business will eventually be dominated by the railroads (because of piggyback) or shippers (fishyback).
	Most companies heavily leveraged.
	Business very cyclical.

Average P/E Multiple: 5–7

Naturally a listing such as this cannot be all-inclusive. I have tried to list basic industries as they are normally shown. It is my hope that you will refer to this chart whenever you are considering a purchase or sale in the market. As you can see, there are arguments for and against *every* industry. The main thing is that this chart forces you into objective thinking—into the "vacuum" approach I talked about earlier. You will no doubt come up with some positives and negatives that I haven't listed (this is where your own imagination comes in). Then it's merely a matter of determining how much the pros outweigh the cons (or vice versa) and relating this appraisal to the P/E multiple the investing public has assigned to the industry.

Now that you've devoured this "food for thought," it's time for dessert—some further guidance on how you should aim your dollars for investing in the future.

28
Onward, Ever Onward

Much of your investment success is going to depend on what the future holds for our country. To be a better investor, you should know what trends are apparent. Economists differ in their opinions as to the future, but then it's a rare occurrence when economists completely agree on anything. As George Bernard Shaw put it so aptly, "If all economists were laid end to end—they would not reach a conclusion."

Still, certain developments appear certain to take place in the United States in the future. I've summarized these for you, with the hope that they will help shape your investments.

1. *The 1980s will witness an explosion in the all-important family-formation age group.*

No doubt you have heard about the burgeoning family-formation group in the United States. This term refers to those young people who have reached the age of marriage and parenthood. You might argue about the exact age that signifies the start of all this, but let's be practical and exclude cousin Jimmy who runs off at sixteen with the girl next door and let's not count on cousin Frank who thinks that nobody is good enough for him and waits till he is fifty to wed that long-legged beauty who was third from the left in the chorus line at one of Las Vegas's plushiest hotels.

The fact is that people get married and start to raise families when they reach twenty to thirty years of age—and this is extremely important to the economy because the newly married suddenly become large consumers of such items as appliances, furniture, and new housing. Invariably they have their additions, and these little joys necessitate spending on baby clothes, cribs, and new housing (again). In a nutshell, family formation costs money—enough to stimulate a great deal of business within the country.

Now why should I emphasize all this—and why did I highlight a prediction of an explosion in the family-formation group in the 1980s? Why hasn't this group "exploded" in size before?

The reason, of course, is the depression of the 1930s and the booming increase in births following World War II. The terrible state of affairs during the Depression reduced the birth rate severely, and this had a restraining influence twenty or so years later, when those who were born during the Depression reached family-formation age in 1950–1960.

After World War II, however, the birthrate in this nation rose sharply again—and these kids (now adults) will be banding together and producing offspring and related spending in the years ahead. No doubt the war in Vietnam and changing lifestyles delayed family formation to some extent, but it will happen. To place this in perspective, consider the demographic statistics. In the 1960–1970 decade, for example, the 25–34 age group in the United States increased by 10%; from 1970 to 1980, however, this age group grew by over 40%. As mentioned, life patterns have altered. Not only are people tying marital knots later, but they are having fewer children. Thus, while family formation looks favorable for most of the 1980s, the trend will weaken as time goes on—unless attitudes change and the nation's birthrate starts to rise again. Perhaps this is a good juncture to point out a second obvious development that should influence our investing approach for the 1980s, which is:

2. *There will be more two-person working families.*

Whether it was rising living costs brought on by high inflation or a stronger feminist trend, we left the 1970s with more husbands and wives sharing the monetary responsibilities of marriage. Frankly, it's hard to envision this trend diminishing.

It could mean changing apparel needs (if wives work, their wardrobe needs change), more eating out or fast-preparation home cooking, fewer children per family. In short, lots of things will be different because of the trend to two-person working families.

3. *The country has a rapidly rising middle-income group.*

Although it is hard to conclude what constitutes "middle income" because inflation has increased living costs so severely, certainly many people have experienced sharply rising income in recent years. It wasn't so many years ago that fewer than 10% of U.S. families were earning as much as $10,000 per year, whereas in 1978 the median household income was $15,000—and more than a third of all households earned above $20,000.

Whether this means that more of our citizens will have ample "discretionary income"—that is, dollars that can go into goods of their choice—will depend on the country's progress in licking inflation. If living costs can be tempered, the country will revert to higher living standards—and with this will come more luxury buying, more money spent on leisure-time activities, and the like. Your investing approach will obviously be influenced by whether or not this occurs. If inflation continues unabated, consumers will have to "trade down" and a different kind of product line (i.e., basics, no frills) will dominate.

4. *Energy trends will dictate the course of the United States as a world leader and our economic future.*

Whereas for most of this country's history it has been an independent economic force, the recent shift has been unfavorable for the United States. When a country has to pay $60 billion or $70 billion annually to others just to satisfy its energy appetite, it is obviously going to have trade-balance problems, just as the cartelization of an important commodity such as oil almost guarantees high inflation. Hence the kind of growth that is feasible and the rate of cost-of-living increases will depend to a large extent on greater energy self-sufficiency. If we muddle along as we have since the 1974 oil embargo, an investor should expect a so-called stagflation environment for the 1980s—a combination of lower-than-normal real GNP growth along with higher-than-normal inflation numbers.

A reversal of the energy imbalance (assuming this occurs without military conflict) holds exciting prospects. A dropping inflation rate and a shift of economic "power" back to the Free World industrialized nations (and away from the oil producers) would lead to the ultimate for the stock market. Just as in individual stock purchases the ideal climate for stock investors generally is the double-barreled prospect of higher earnings and rising P/E, this is just what should occur if the energy situation is reversed. Inflation and interest rates would decline, fear and pessimism would be replaced by hope and optimism— and P/E multiples, now very low, would increase.

5. *The United States is at last recognizing its underinvestment in "capital" equipment.*

For many years the emphasis in this country has been on "consumption"—on stimulating consumer purchases. Neglected in the process has been proper stimulus for making the United States cost-effective and just plain competitive in world markets. This is not to deny that many domestic companies and industries are world leaders; but most economists agree that the best cure for inflation is to create maximum efficiency at the production level; the result should be lower prices and a world competitiveness that hypes domestic employment, profits, and so forth.

Politicians today also seem to understand the necessity to encourage new and modern plants and equipment, but this understanding may lose out to the reality that it is more popular to continue the emphasis on consumption. We cannot therefore equate understanding of the problem with its solution because the political realities may work against it.

In a way, I feel apologetic about my estimate of the last two developments. Rather than predict, I have presented the parameters and suggested how you might proceed in your analysis of events. No one can truly predict the course of our economic future. Predictions in this area involve a lot of pure guesswork. The possible solutions to both the energy crisis and U.S. underinvestment in capital equipment are so crucial to the investment climate of the 1980s, however, that a delineation of possibilities is absolutely essential. I hope that by highlighting their importance I have given you an important clue to the economic—and investment—future in the 1980s. These conclusions, plus other trends discussed and a solid overall investment philosophy, prepare for our next discussion of where to invest.

WHERE TO INVEST

To begin with, I should warn you not to develop investment myopia. The last few pages concentrated on trends in this country, but there's a great big world out there—and many companies prosper handsomely from business done outside our borders.

For example, the demand for new technology exists practically everywhere—certainly in each and every industrialized nation. And this demand will increase, both because that's simply the way things happen and because rising labor costs and inflation make it imperative to achieve greater productivity. Whether it be the trend to miniaturization or rapid expansion in the uses of semiconductors and integrated circuits, there is no stopping the trend. If you think that so many items have already been converted from mechanical to electronic and that the saturation point is at hand—forget it. Many astounding developments are yet to come and the well-managed, strong research and development companies can expect tremendous demand for a long time to come. So many things will become computerized—automobiles, office work, communications, consumer items, you-name-it—that imaginative companies like Hewlett-Packard, Perkin Elmer, Digital Equipment, Intel, National Semi-Conductor, and Texas Instruments simply have to be represented in a growth-oriented portfolio.

Another obvious area is energy search and conservation. Here, too, technology will continue to make its mark. Whether it be deep and complicated drilling for oil and gas or controls that will allow us to conserve energy, the economics are favorable. Companies like Baker Oil, Schlumberger, and Honeywell are offering services that are desperately needed today—and should stay in strong demand until supply/demand relationships in oil and gas change from their present position. Incidentally, although the current view of this is negative—it assumes that we will never be free from the power of OPEC—the wise investor never accepts the most obvious without questioning. The energy search and conservation thesis looks solid at the time of this writing, but, like other trends, it has to be monitored. No cartel lasts forever and constantly rising energy costs are not inevitable.

The burgeoning of the family-formation age group in our population would normally spell a bright future for housing, particularly home building and related products. The trouble here is the sharply rising cost of new homes. The combination of exploding construction costs, high resale values of existing dwellings, and high mortgage rates throughout 1980 has pretty much priced a multitude of buyers out of this market. And while it can be expected that one or all of these factors will reverse themselves, there is a legitimate question of how much demand can be expected unless they reverse themselves significantly. Now, this sounds negative, and the purpose of our exercise is to think positive and isolate attractive areas for investment. In this case, there may be a fallout from the negative—remember, one industry's problem is usually another industry's opportunity. One beneficiary is the so-called mobile home nanufacturers. I say "so-called" because the demand I am forecasting is really not for the mobility at all. I am not thinking of recreational vehicles or anything intended to "hit the road." I am referring to the "manufactured house"—the one that is produced in assembly-line form and can be purchased at very low relative costs per square foot. The quality of these dwellings has improved dramatically in recent years, and they may well turn out to be the most practical way for many home buyers to satisfy their desires in the future. These products may be the "only way to beat the game" and companies such as Skyline and Redman, for example, which were very much depressed in price in 1980 because of the housing debacle, should have dramatic recoveries in the near future.

Speaking of demographics, don't forget about the rising population of older persons. Health advances have extended average life expectancy, and one result is a strong demand for wheelchairs (Everest and Jennings is the world's leader) and heart pacemakers (Medtronics has been dominant here). Another—a relatively new field—is home nursing care (Kelly Services, the employment firm, has been building a nationwide effort in the home nursing business).

While consumer activity was very strong during the late 1970s—as it has been ever since the end of World War II—stock buyers have been anticipating a decline in this area. The expectation is that government emphasis will be on capital formation, energy, and defense, to the detriment of personal consumption. Since consumers in 1980 appeared to be "spent up" anyway, the new governmental direction may have the force of a "double whammy." But, we might ask, will the government really allow a sharp shift away from individual consumption? Or will politics dictate simply more of what we have had?

My response is that the consumer is hardly "dead" and that investments in fine consumer-type companies will prove profitable. As with any field, though, the investor has to be selective. Let's mention a few specific areas that should do well. The first that comes to mind is entertainment. Human beings like to be entertained, and the 1980s will be no exception. As a matter of fact, the growing field of cable television holds terribly exciting prospects. One day soon you and I will be afforded such a variety of entertainment choices in our own homes that it will be mind-boggling. With this will come an eventual retailing revolution, as direct consumer response for purchasing will become a reality. Warner Communications' Qube system is a model for just such a combination "watch and respond" approach. Also involved will be a tremendous demand for "product"—for fine films, shows, athletic events, and so forth that will be "demanded" by viewers who will suddenly find themselves paying for entertainment they once received free. So the hardware involved represents only half the opportunity. So-called software producers—those that supply programming for the stations—will be good investments, too.

One clue for the investor in consumer goods: If unit demand promises to be above average, you have a good starting point for investment. For example, while I have never been terribly enamored of the beer business, demographics point to a 4–5% unit increase annually for the next five to ten years. While 4–5% is no bonanza, it is about twice the average real GNP forecast for the United States over this span. So if the beer producers do not expand too fast (which is a worry today), the market is there for at least a few strong brewers.

Last, I want to mention some decidedly unpopular fields that at least have a chance for resurgence. One is agriculture. If this country has one item to counteract our dependency on imported oil, it is food. We constitute the most efficient food producer in the world, and our grains give us a strategic non-military weapon of great importance. I anticipate that the fertilizer producers (International Minerals and others) and farm machinery manufacturers (Deere) will someday be looked upon favorably by investors again.

More controversial are two industries that have held little attraction to me over the years but which seem to be "shrinking down" to the point where investors can get a sharp, though probably short, play in the early 1980s. I am talking about steel and rubber—both of which have such poor unit demand that supply is being curtailed. Plants are being shut down right and left, which hints to me that the next upward overall economic cycle will produce startling earnings for the better companies (Inland Steel, Goodyear Tire). And while real growth entities with longer-lasting prosperity are to be preferred, investors should be conscious of contrary plays—industries that are poorly regarded and thus can benefit from improving image as well as fundamental changes.

I have ignored some very attractive industries in this chapter because we hardly have room here for a full discussion of investment opportunities. But, I hope the reasoning pattern will aid you in becoming a more thorough and sophisticated investor.

CONCLUSION

I have tried to give you some long-range, objective thinking. Naturally, projections and ideas are subject to change, especially when they are made well in advance of a publication— as these are. In other words, because of the time lapse, you should check my thinking to see if it is still valid.

As a summary, I thought you might like a recapitulation of the many industries as they might be viewed today. To be of greatest help, I have provided you with a grouping according to their "strength" characteristics. This should give you an excellent "feel" of the industries themselves and should point you to the areas where it seems logical that the best opportunities for the future exist

Industries and Their "Strength" Characteristics

To provide you with a better perspective, I have separated the industries according to their relative strengths and weaknesses. In doing so, I have used three broad categories: industries that are directly sensitive to general business cycles; those that are sensitive to cycles that are not necessarily tied to the general economy; and those that are not sensitive to cycles. Under these three headings I have assessed specific strengths and weaknesses and assigned ratings, with "1" denoting the greatest strength (or least weakness, as the case may be), "2" signifying above-average strength, "3" meaning less strength, and the "4" reflecting the least strength.

Needless to say, P/E multiples should reflect these strengths and weaknesses (if they have been properly assessed). I strongly believe that such an industry breakdown will be very beneficial to you now and over the years.

INDUSTRY STRENGTH GUIDE

CATEGORY I

INDUSTRIES DIRECTLY SENSITIVE TO GENERAL BUSINESS CYCLE

(1)	(2)	(3)	(4)
Air freight	Aluminum	Automotive	Lead, zinc
	Chemicals	Auto parts	Metal containers
	Department	(OEM)	
	stores	Copper	
	Machine tools	Discounters	
	Radio-TV	Glass	
	Railroads	Paperboard	
	(with other	Railroads (without	
	income)	other income	
	Synthetic fibers	Rubber	
		Steel	
		Trucking	

CATEGORY II

INDUSTRIES HAVING THEIR OWN SEPARATE
AND INDIVIDUAL CYCLES

(1)	(2)	(3)	(4)
Computers, software	Airlines	Aerospace	Finance (small loan)
Electronics	Auto accessories	Air conditioning	Home builders
Fiberglass	Broadcasting	Apparel	Petroleum refiners
Forest products (paper)	Coal	Building materials	Shipbuilding
Industrial gases	Computer, peripheral	Carpets	
Instrumentation	Construction equipment	Cement	
Natural gas producers	Electrical equipment	Electric utilities	
Newspapers	Farm equipment	Food chains	
Oil-drilling services	Hospital management	Furniture	
Petroleum producers	Hotels	Gold	
Pollution control	Nuclear power equipment	Heavy equipment leasing	
Reinsurance	Oil contract drillers	Home appliances	
Specialty chemicals	Petroleum domestic (integrated)	Insurance (property)	
Specialty insurance	Publishing	LPG distributors	
Uranium	Restaurant chains	Mobile homes	
	Semiconductors	Motion pictures	
	Soft-drink bottlers	Petroleum, international (integrated)	
		Printing	
		Rail equipment	
		Savings & loan	
		Textiles	
		Toys	

CATEGORY III

INDUSTRIES WITHOUT CYCLICAL TENDENCIES

(1)	(2)	(3)	(4)
Computers	Cosmetics	Banks	Canned foods
Drugs (ethical)	Drugs (proprietary)	Beer	Dairy products
Hospital products	Household products	Convenience foods	
Leisure time	Insurance brokerage	Distilling	
Photography	Office equipment	Finance (broad-based)	
Protection services		Life insurance	
Specialized services		Soft drinks	
Specialty retailing		Telephone	
		Tobacco	

PART IX
Utility Stocks

29

Back from Vacation (or, Making Money for and from Utilities)

The other day I returned home from a short vacation. On entering my house, I activated four conveniences we all take for granted—I turned on the lights, flipped on the heat, turned on the water, and picked up the telephone and made a call. All of us spend a sizable amount of money each year on these conveniences, which in investment circles are lumped together under the title "utilities."

In the last two chapters I gave you some food for thought about the many industrial fields that exist today. Aside from railroads, which constitute a separate and distinct field, the others are termed "industrial stocks." I didn't include utilities in those chapters because this group of stocks deserves a discussion of its own.

Although investors in utility stocks have not fared well over the 1970–1980 decade, there have been periods in which these have been very rewarding stocks to own.

UTILITIES AS A GROUP

As you already gathered from the first paragraph, utilities are the companies that supply us with electricity, telephone service, natural gas, and water.* While there are some basic differences among these four utility services, they do have certain common characteristics:

*Telegraph is a fifth utility, but I prefer to discuss it separately.

1. *All are noted for their stability of revenues.* Regardless of what happens to the general economy, you and I are going to heat our homes, stay clean, turn on the lights, and talk to our friends. In short, we're going to continue to use the utilities, therefore these companies can count on *stable revenues* (profits are not so reliable because of inadequate rates or the lag between the time when costs are incurred and when rate relief is granted).

2. *All the companies are regulated. The rates they charge are set by a regulatory body.* Utilities that operate within one state have their rates set by either their state public utilities commission or a local body; those that operate interstate are regulated by federal bodies (gas and electric companies by the Federal Power Commission and telephone companies by the Federal Communications Commission). Naturally, regulation is a negative for the industry, and it is doubly so in our era of consumerism.

3. *Utilities are granted franchises, which prohibit identical competition in their operating area.* The electric utility in your area has been granted a franchise to supply electricity to you, and no other company can offer you this service. Your utility may or may not also have the franchise for supplying natural gas, which, of course, is competitive for the home heating and cooking market. *If the utility supplies both electricity and gas, then it has really no competition at all.*

4. *All utilities have to install expensive equipment to serve you* (huge generating equipment, extensive pipelines and storage facilities, etc.), but *all can finance this through heavy borrowing because of the industry's stability.* A utility that is not heavily leveraged with debt and/or preferred stock is a rare exception.

5. *Utilities don't need as much cash on hand as industrial companies.* I mentioned earlier that utility companies get by with a current ratio of slightly over 1 to 1. This is because the companies have money coming in every month without fail. Their accounts receivable (the monthly bills mailed to you every month) are paid fairly

promptly because if customers avoid their bills too long, the utility can shut off its service—a devastating prospect.

6. *Utilities don't have the problem of carrying inventories.* Whereas General Motors has a sizable inventory of this year's cars—which are worth far less if they're not sold this year—a utility has no such problem. Electricity, for example, doesn't have to be produced far in advance of its sale and it never goes out of style.

7. *Utilities have pollution and other environmental problems, as well as fuel problems.* None of these problems is easily overcome.

8. *The quality of utility earnings has deteriorated in recent years.* Without going into accounting details, the fact is that many utilities have "bookkeeping" profits, which are reported to shareholders, that are overstated relative to "cash" profits. (In some cases, this accounting has been forced on the utility companies by the regulatory commissions and thus it is not deceptive on their part, but merely in conformance with regulations.)

Now that we know the similarities between the utilities, I think you'll be interested to know the differences. These differences should help you decide where you might put some of your investment dollars to work.

Electric Utilities

Sales of electricity to industries amount to almost half of the utility business. This industrial business can fluctuate, especially in geographical areas that are subject to wide economic swings. Residential customers seem destined to consume more and more electricity, however, because of the wide variety of electrical appliances that are finding their way into the home. Therefore electrical output is perhaps the most stable of all businesses and one that promises consistent growth in the future. It is estimated that electrical output will about double each decade through this century. Growth of air conditioning and the prospect of heating homes electrically (through use of the "heat pump") are all added benefits. Needless to say, rising energy costs are a detriment to future demands for both electricity and natural gas. Conservation should be the country's design for the 1980s.

Natural Gas Utilities

Natural gas has been accepted everywhere it has been introduced. As a fuel, it is clean and efficient; it has almost eliminated the anthracite coal business and has made great inroads into fuel oil. Residential business predominates and thus revenues are stable, but the industry has regulatory problems. The price of natural gas rises consistently and the utilities have to count on higher rates to compensate for these increases. Certain areas are not completely covered by natural gas and thus the market is not yet saturated. There is a question, though, as to whether natural gas reserves will hold out forever. Reserves have been depleted, many geographical regions are gas-short, and costs are rising rapidly—all factors that could create a more severe squeeze than we have so far witnessed (unless utility commissions grant automatic fuel adjustment clauses).

Telephone

Although American Telephone is regarded as the most secure of all stocks, the telephone business in general is more sensitive to a severe recession than the electricity business. AT&T certainly qualifies as among the most secure companies, however, because its business has not fluctuated (it has grown steadily) and because the company has much lower leverage than other utilities. Tremendous strides have been made in the mechanization of the telephone business and there are countless new fields of service that could produce growth in the future (microwave developments, mobile telephone, etc.) A recent Supreme Court decision has produced one important (negative) change. Utilities such as Ma Bell no longer hold monopolies over telephone communication. Equipment manufactured by others can now be substituted for standard telephones, and there is severe competition for long-distance business from companies such as Southern Pacific, Western Union, and MCI—at substantial discounts from normal telephone rates. On the other hand, AT&T is pushing to become a major factor in the burgeoning data communications business.

Water

Most cities own their own water facilities and the trend toward taking over private facilities continues. This is one utility that can (but seldom does) suffer from a shortage of its commodity.

Telegraph

The telegraph business is much more sensitive to changes in general business than other utilities. Competition from long-distance telephone has hurt, but a great deal of mechanization of the telegraph business has taken place (Desk-fax, etc). Labor costs are still much greater than for the other utilities. New-growth prospects stem from microwave systems and from greater use of private wire systems.

WHAT TO CONSIDER IN BUYING UTILITY STOCKS

There are certain keys to investment success in buying utility stocks. Here are the factors that make one utility stock a buy and another not such an attractive purchase:

1. *The geographical area in which the utility operates.*

A utility operating in a fast-growing area has much better opportunity for growth than one in a stagnant or slow-growing region. Use recent population trends to get an idea of what kind of growth to expect in the future.

It is also important to consider an area's "background." Certain areas are dependent on heavy industry (machinery, steel, etc.) and business is subject to greater fluctuation because of this. For example, during the 1957–1958 recession Detroit Edison suffered from sharply lower industrial activity and reduced earnings in 1958, while the utility in my backyard, Pacific Gas and Electric (not dependent on heavy industry), showed increased profits for the year. Utilities that are very dependent on one industry are obviously riskier than those serving a diversified community.

2. *The attitude of the regulatory authorities.*

Public utility regulatory bodies can vary greatly in their philosophy from area to area. Some authorities are tough as nails on granting rate increases while others are extremely liberal. One of the reasons for the great growth of utilities in Florida and Texas has been the attitude of their governing bodies. Utilities in these states have consistently been granted a higher rate of return than those in other states; therefore they have shown somewhat better growth than companies operating under less favorable regulation.* In contrast, a state such as Oregon is well known for its negative attitude toward private utilities. In 1960, for example, Portland General Electric was granted its first rate increase in eleven years. In more recent years such states as Louisiana, Alabama, Montana, Missouri, and South Dakota, as well as our nation's capital, Washington, D.C., have become known as "poor regulatory climate" areas. Utilities operating in these regions have to struggle to get adequate rate relief and, of course, their stockholders have suffered accordingly. Needless to say, it's of great benefit to stockholders to have the authorities on their side.

3. *The utility's past record of growth and future projections.*

As with industrial stocks, a utility company's past record of growth can give you a good indication of its future. Once again it's a matter of looking at a company's record of earnings per share over the *past* three to five years and then determining what

---

*Your first reaction might be that these higher profits are at the expense of the population, but liberal authorities claim that, in the long run, rate increases are to the existing population's benefit. After all, a utility that realizes its expansion will be profitable to it will do everything possible to promote growth in the region.

has changed to alter this pattern either upward or downward over the *next* three to five years.

Naturally you will be especially attracted to those utilities whose records indicate consistent and rapid growth in the future.

Frankly, rising energy costs, consumerism, and skyrocketing interest rates have made it exceedingly difficult for electric utilities to show any consistency of growth in earnings; natural gas has similar problems, although those companies that own large gas reserves possess good offsets. Telephone entities have shown less quarterly fluctuations than the other two major utility areas.

4. *The quality of earnings of any company considered for investment.*

As mentioned on p. 255, many utilities' earnings are "overstated." Many book interest income on construction in progress, on the theory that they (the utility) had to borrow to build such facilities and such interest costs are nonrecurring (so when the facilities are completed, income will eventually offset such interest expenses). *It is preferable to purchase utility or industrial common stocks that have the highest-quality reported earnings.*

5. *Energy sufficiency.*

It is preferable to own utilities that are energy-rich or energy-sufficient, as opposed to those that cannot control their fuel requirements as they would like.

6. *Environmental "purity."*

You certainly do not want polluters or "bad citizens."

7. *Strong balance sheets.*

Bond ratings provide a good insight into the financial strength of utilities. But you cannot rely on ratings alone because they are subject to change. Certainly you should prefer utilities that will retain high ratings and avoid those that are in fear of downgradings. And you do not want any more leverage (extent of bond borrowings) than can be afforded.

8. *Yield.*

In Chapter 21 I pointed out how high yield can limit your risk in a stock and how, in certain cases, high yield can signal that a stock should be bought for at least a temporary rise in price. I concluded, however, that yield is of little use if long-term growth of capital is your investment objective.

In the case of utility stocks, yield *is* of major significance in a majority of cases. This is because most utility stocks are bought by investors *who need income* and these people are naturally attracted by high yield. Many utility stock owners are widows or retired people who depend on their dividends to live; *many buy stocks on the basis of yield alone,* so we have to give this consideration when we analyze utility issues.

As with all stocks, correct timing of purchase can make a good deal of difference. It's true that you're not going to worry how safe the $5 dividend for American Telephone and Telegraph is, but it's certainly to your benefit to buy the stock at 50 or 55 instead of 65, if you can. It's hard to generalize about exactly when utility stocks should be purchased, but there are two important factors to consider: (1) *the level and* (2) *trend of money rates* (that is, whether interest rates in the country are high or low at the time and whether they are going up or down in the near future).

Interest rates change. One year you get 7% on your bank savings account, and a few years later you get only 4%; one year you can buy U.S. government bonds that yield 10% or 12% and a year later you can get only 8% on the same bond. But why does it make so much difference to the utility stock buyer where interest rates are and which way they are trending?

The answer: *Because many utility stocks are bought for income, which puts them in competition with other income-producing securities for the investor's dollar.* For example, suppose U.S. government bonds are yielding 12% today and utility stocks are yielding 14%. Many investors who ordinarily put their money into government bonds might well be attracted instead to utility stocks, and thus it might be a good time to buy the utilities. Likewise, if the bonds are yielding 12% and the utilities 10% many investors might switch out of utilities into bonds and this might be an improper time to buy utilities. The *trend* of money rates is equally important. Suppose interest rates in the country begin to come down; perhaps business in general in the United States is not so good and the federal authorities try to stimulate it by lowering money rates. If you buy a utility stock today with a 12% yield and six months from now money rates have come down sharply, chances are that your utility purchase will be up in price. The figures would be something like this:

Buy a $100 stock paying $12 a year, for a yield of 12% when 12% is the "going rate" for income investors. Six months later the "going rate" is only 10%. The stock, still paying $12 a year, might sell at $120 to yield 10%.

$$(\$12 \div \$120 = .10 \text{ or } 10\%)$$

Thus your $100 stock has gone to $120—solely because of the change in money rates. The reverse is true when money rates trend higher. Therefore we can make the following generalization: *Utility stocks are an especially good buy if you think that interest rates in general are going lower,* * *or if existing yields on industrial stocks are low.*

9. *Price-earnings multiple.*

Earning power is just as important in utility stocks as in industrials and thus it is also important to compare the P/E multiples of utilities you are considering. *Dividends are paid out of a company's earnings; therefore the more earnings you have per dollar of market price, the more potential dividends you have.*

Say you are comparing two utility stocks both of which sell for $50 per share. Company A pays out $5.50 per share in dividends for a yield of 11% ($5.50 ÷ $50 = .11 or 11%), while Company B only pays out $4.00 per share for a yield of 8%

---

*Low interest rates have a double-barreled effect on utilities. Public utility companies, which rely on raising needed cash through the sale of bonds and other fixed-income securities, naturally save money when interest rates are low (their borrowing costs are lowered and this leads to increased profits).

($4.00 ÷ $50 = .08 or 8%). Is Company A a better buy with a 11% yield than Company B with a 8% yield? Not necessarily. Let's compare the earnings of these two:

Company A is earning $6.50 per share, which gives a P/E of 7.7 ($50 market price ÷ $6.50 earnings = 7.7). Company B is earning $8.00 per share, which gives a P/E of 6.2 ($50 market price ÷ $8.00 = 6.2).

On the basis of earnings, Company B is a better buy than Company A. Company A's yield is much higher because the company is paying out almost all its earnings in dividends to stockholders (85% of its $6.50 earnings paid out). In contrast, Company B is paying out only 50% of its $8.00 earnings directly to stockholders. If Company B were to pay out 85%, its dividend would be increased from $4.00 per share to $6.80, which would give a yield of 13.6%. Company B has chosen *not* to pay out 85%. It is probably retaining the bulk of its earnings for more expansion than Company A, and this expansion will no doubt lead to higher earnings *and higher dividends* to Company B stockholders in the future.

You can see how important earnings are. Like industrial stocks, *the utility stock with the most potential earning power is normally the best buy for you.*

GROWTH UTILITIES

For years Florida Power and Light, Texas Utilities, and other "growth utilities" have been recommended to investors seeking capital growth. People are often amazed when a utility stock of any sort is suggested for dynamic gains over the year. They would not be amazed, however, if they had ever looked at the past records of companies such as those just mentioned. Here is what happened to these two companies over the 1950–1960 decade:

Indeed, the growth was both consistent and remarkable. And the performance of these two stocks in the market was equally remarkable. Both companies passed the first three tests I provided for you earlier in this chapter: they operated in fast-growing regions; they benefited from liberal regulatory commissions; they had good marks on the qualitative factors 4 through 7 and anticipated a continuation of their growth in the future.

Let's see how they stacked up, at the beginning of 1961, on tests 8 and 9, namely yield and P/E multiple:

	FLORIDA POWER & LIGHT			TEXAS UTILITIES		
	Earnings per Share	Dividends per Share	Mean Market Price	Earnings per Share	Dividends per Share	Mean Market Price
1950	$ .61	$.32	5	$ .60	$.24	6⅛
1951	.62	.35	6⅛	.67	.34	7⅜
1952	.71	.37	7½	.78	.43	9⅞
1953	.77	.40	9	.83	.48	10¾
1954	.88	.44	12	.97	.52	14
1955	1.03	.51	16⅞	1.03	.58	17⅜
1956	1.29	.61	21¾	1.17	.64	19⅜
1957	1.49	.665	26	1.28	.72	22
1958	1.75	.76	36½	1.37	.80	27
1959	1.93	.865	49⅜	1.47	.88	34¾
1960	2.11	.97	60	1.56	.96	39¼

	Market Price	Annual Dividend Rate	Yield (%)	Estimated Current Earnings	P/E Multiple
Florida Power & Light	65	$1.00	1.5	$2.15	30
Texas Utilities	45	1.04	2.3	1.63	28

Naturally, we have the benefit of hindsight here, so let's do a Compounding Growth Guide analysis of these two stocks as they should have been approached in 1961. First of all, let's see what the compound growth rates had been for the two companies.

Without going into the mathematics, here is how the recent past had stacked up:

Company	1955–1960 Annual Growth Rate (%)	1957–1960 (%)
Florida Power & Light	15½	12½
Texas Utilities	8½	7

An important lesson to consider here is the *most recent trend of events,* which in both cases shows some diminution of growth. Whereas, for example, FPL showed a 15½% annual growth rate from 1955 to 1960, the rate for the most recent three years was 12½%—and in the latest year (1960/1959) the rate had declined further to around 9%. In the case of TU, the five-year growth rate was 8½%, the three-year rate was 7%, and the latest year was only 6½%. Needless to say, these figures should have had a strong bearing on our all-important projected growth rate for the future. Granting some benefit of the doubt, however, let's assume that FPL qualified at that time as a 10% + growth company, and that TU promised about 7½% +.

Our next step would be to categorize the companies according to glamour. Since utilities lack the excitement of IBM, Xerox, Hewlett-Packard, and other glamour stocks (we reserve the Super Glamour category for areas and companies such as these), it would be logical to classify the slow-growth utilities as only Average Glamour stocks and the more rapid ones as Above-Average. Both FPL and TU were in the latter growth range. Looking to our guide (p. 000), we find that FPL (with assumed 10% growth) starts off with a P/E of 18–20 times and TU (with 7½%) with a P/E of around 18 times, under the 3½–5% prevailing interest rates during the early 1960s in the United States. Since both companies had recent institutional support, an additional 2–5 multiple would have given you a "buying area" of 20–25 times for FPL and 20–23 for TU.

Both of these assessments indicate that the two stocks were selling way above what our guide showed they deserved (the table on p. 263 shows a current 1961 multiple of 30 times for FPL versus our Guide's 20–25 and a 28 P/E for TU versus our assessment of 20–23). Thus, despite the great past record of these growth utilities and notwithstanding their acceptance by the investment community, our guide pinpoints their "richness"—both were selling way above what their combined growth rate-glamour image deserved.

This analysis does not refute the theory behind the purchase of growth stocks generally. In utilities, as well as in industrial stocks, investors can reap double-barreled rewards from ownership of the growth vehicle. They will not only end up with vastly superior capital appreciation, but *in the long run they will end up with more annual income from owning growth companies as opposed to those in the nongrowth or slow-growth category.*

Incidentally, our guide would have proved to be quite accurate. Some eight years later both FPL and TU were selling very little above their 1961 price—hardly the kind of performance you should be striving for. From 1969 to 1980, performance of the two was most discouraging, as was market action for all utilities. Interest rates had risen, leading to lower P/E's, and earnings turned decidedly cyclical.

All stocks have their right price, something our guide should help us with immensely. I think it only proper to close with the thought that utilities, which were once noncyclical and had consistent (though low) growth patterns, have developed decided cyclical tendencies. The problems reviewed in this chapter created costs that have hampered earnings progress. In short, utilities constitute a basically unattractive area for investment in the kind of rising-inflation environment we experienced in the 1970–1980 decade. So long as these conditions persist, our guide will be of little use in assessing P/E's and utility evaluations will be low.

PART X

Some Tax Advice for Investors

30
Ugh!

Perhaps you're thinking the letters "UGH" are a symbol for a secret stock that is going to be the IBM of tomorrow. So sorry! "Ugh!" is what people say when they start talking about income taxes. And that's what I'm going to talk about right now.

Not that I am an expert on taxes. "Only a fool is his own attorney," they said, and the same thing goes for the nonaccountant who thinks he can handle complicated tax problems by himself.

But I am familiar with certain tax items that concern the average investor and I think it only fair to relate these "tips" to you. They are elementary—but they can save you money.

DIVIDENDS

Very little discussion of dividends is necessary. At the present time you are exempt from income tax on the first $200 in dividends you receive each year. If you are married, you and your spouse are entitled to $200 each for a total of $400.

Interestingly enough, there are a select number of stocks that pay dividends that are either partially or completely free from taxation. A number of utility stocks are paying out tax-free dividends* but in almost all cases this tax-free status has a limited life. Philadelphia Electric, Pacific Gas and Electric,

---

*Usually only a portion of the dividend is nontaxable.

and Long Island Lighting Company are but a few in a long list of these utilities. Certain nonutility companies also offer tax-exempt income: Mesabi Trust and Standard Shares are examples.

Don't buy a stock on the basis of nontaxable dividends alone. This status can serve as a "kicker," however, if you've decided on the basis of other analysis that a stock is a good buy.

TAKING PROFITS

There's an old saying: "No one ever went broke taking profits." But I'm sure you're aware that Uncle Sam's money counter—the Internal Revenue Service—gets a slice of every profit you take when you sell a stock. It's indeed a pleasure to buy a stock at 10 and sell it at 20 or 30 or 40, but it's important to know how much of your gain belongs to the government.

There are two kinds of gains you can make as an investor:

1. A "short term" gain, which is when you sell a stock at a profit *within* twelve months of your original purchase date.
2. A "long term" gain, generally referred to as a "capital gain," when you make a profit on a stock you have held for more than twelve months (twelve months and one day is enough).

There is a considerable difference in the tax liability of a short-term and long-term gain. With the former, *your total profit is taxed as ordinary income*—that is, it is added *in full* to the rest of your income for the year and thus you can be taxed up to 70% on this income. When, instead, you have a capital gain, *you only have to declare 40% of the gain, along with your regular income.* Thus 28% of the total capital gain is the most anyone has to pay to the IRS (your state tax is extra)—e.g., 40% of the maximum 70% income tax rate = 28%. A 30% bracket individual will only pay 12% on a long-term gain (40% of 30% = 12%).

Take the case of Mrs. Ima Smart Investor. Ima bought 100 shares of Brooklyn Bridge stock on January 2 at $10 per share. Here it is December 15 and the stock is $20 per share. Ima sells the stock at $20. Very shrewd! Ima's $1,000 investment has gotten her $2,000—for a profit of $1,000. Comes next April and Ima is stewing over her Form 1040. She arrives at the summary of her stock transactions for the previous year. She proudly puts down the Brooklyn Bridge coup—and suddenly she discovers that she could have saved herself some tax money had she only waited until January 2 (twelve months and one day) to sell the stock. You see, Ima's in a 50% tax bracket and the difference between a short-term gain and a capital gain for this $1,000 profit is:

Short-term gain: $1,000 profit taxed at 50% = $500 tax to be paid.

Capital gain: only 40% of the $1,000 long-term gain has to be reported; this $400 taxed at Ima's 50% rate means a $200 tax to be paid.*

Thus there is a $300 difference in tax because Ima didn't wait for January 2. Maybe Brooklyn Bridge stock would have gone down between December 15 and January 2, but even if it had declined from $20 to $16.50, Ima would have realized about the same after-tax profit. And who knows, maybe the stock would have gone up over that two-week period.

You can see the importance of watching your acquisition and sales dates and being conscious of how long you have held a stock you are planning to sell. This is especially important to people in the higher tax brackets.

TAKING LOSSES

I hope you'll have very few stock market losses in your lifetime, but let's be practical. In the stock market, as in all forms

---

*If Ima were in a higher tax bracket, the saving would be even greater. If her bracket were 70%, the short-term gain would cost her $700 in tax versus only $280 on a long-term tax basis.

of investments, even the shrewdest of us will sometimes make mistakes and experience losses. While you will never make money by losing money, at least you can learn to take the fullest "advantage" of the losses you incur.

Our government is sympathetic about your losses—but only to a limited extent. Uncle Sam will let you subtract any losses you incur during the year from your gains, so losses taken will reduce the amount of tax you would have to pay on these gains.

If you haven't taken any gains during the year, a loss still can be helpful by reducing the amount of normal income tax you have to pay. You see, each individual is allowed to take a $1,500 net loss (over and above gains taken) each year and use this to reduce the amount of income reported to Internal Revenue. Suppose your yearly taxable income is $20,000. As you know, the tax rate gets higher as your income grows: you pay no tax on income below $3,300, but on the last $1,000 that hikes your income from $19,000 to $20,000, the rate is 34%. Thus, by taking a $1,000 loss, which in this case lowers your income from $20,000 to $19,000, you are saving the 34% tax you would have to pay on this last $1,000, for a saving of $340. Incidentally, if you take a loss by selling a stock, you must wait thirty-one days to repurchase the same stock if you wish to deduct the loss on your income tax statement. If you buy it back *within thirty days,* Internal Revenue calls it a "wash sale" and forbids your utilizing the loss.

BENEFITING FROM OTHERS' LOSSES

Most Americans hate to deal with tax forms. I agree that these forms are a nuisance. If you *don't* fill out your form correctly, you go to *jail;* if you do fill it out right, you go to the *poorhouse*!

Most people are procrastinators at heart. They put off unpleasant tasks and decisions as long as possible. This applies to investors, too. They have a loss in a stock early in the year, yet wait till the very end of the year to sell the stock in order to establish a tax loss. Suddenly in November and December people comb through their stock lists to see where they can establish a loss that will "save" them some taxes. Naturally they sell the stocks that are down in price. All of a sudden a great deal of "tax-loss selling" occurs in certain depressed stocks. *This concentrated selling further depresses the market prices of these stocks— many times to bargain levels.* Therefore you should keep your eyes open in December for these artificially depressed issues.

ONE IMPORTANT WORD ABOUT LOSSES

Suppose you bought a stock at $50 and it's now selling at $45. You have a loss of $5 per share right now. Some people contend there is no such thing as a loss until a stock is sold. They insist they have suffered no loss on this $45 stock because they haven't sold it yet. After all, the stock might go back up to $50 and then they'd be even again. True, indeed. But the stock might never go back to $50—it might instead go down to $40 or $35.

Believe me when I say that if you bought a stock at $50 and it is now at $45, you have a loss of $5 whether you sell the stock or not. Which brings us to the point in mind! So many times I've heard people say, "I can't afford to sell that stock—I'd have to take a loss." This is incorrect investment thinking. If conditions have changed in the company or the industry since you bought the stock and *if the stock has lost its attraction, it should be sold regardless of what your cost is.* The smart thing to do is to admit your mistake and buy another stock that does look attractive. I'm sure you've heard that *the most successful investors are those who minimize their losses and maximize their gains.* This axiom recognizes the reality that losses are inevitable. If you fail to recognize your mistakes, you cannot abide by this good advice.

SPLITTING YOUR GAINS AND LOSSES

Let's assume we're in the month of December and that you have two stocks you are considering for sale—one for which you will have a $1,000 capital gain, and the other for which you will have a $1,000 loss. At first thought you might conclude that both stocks should be sold *this year* so that you incur no extra taxes (because the $1,000 loss offsets the $1,000 gain, thereby giving you no gain at all to report). While this seems logical, in practice it is not correct tax thinking. Instead, you save some important tax dollars by splitting your gain and loss into *separate* tax years. Here's the way it works:

1. Sell the loss stock now. You will have a net $1,000 loss for the year and your taxable income will be reduced by this amount. Assuming you're in the 50% tax bracket, the $1,000 loss saves you $500 in taxes.
2. Wait till next year (only a few weeks away) to sell the gain stock. Since it is a long-term gain, you will be taxed on only 40% of the gain or on only $400. Your 50% tax rate taxes away $200 of the $500.

Thus, by splitting your loss and gain into separate years, you have saved yourself $300 in taxes, as follows:

Tax *saved* by taking $1,000 loss this year:	$500
Capital gain tax to be paid on $1,000 gain next year:	$200
Tax saving	$300

This strategy can be reversed—you can take the long-term gain *first* (this year) and take your loss the next year—but the above is the normal method.

Incidentally, if you want to establish a capital gain in one year, *you have to sell the stock within five business days* (exclude Saturday, Sunday, and holidays) of December 31. In contrast, to establish *a loss, you can sell the stock right up to and including the very last day of the year.*

MORE INVESTMENT ADVICE ON TAXES

Now that you understand the importance of knowing something about taxes as they relate to your investments, paradoxically the best advice I can give you is *don't let taxes influence your investment judgment.* If you think a stock is greatly over-priced, then it is usually better to sell it, regardless of tax considerations. Of course, the case of Ima was an exception—seldom can you not afford to wait a few weeks if it is to your tax advantage to do so.

If you own stock with an extremely low cost, you might be influenced in investment decision by tax considerations. If, for example, your cost on ABC stock is $1 per share and it is now selling for $21 per share, you may think you are "locked in" to owning this stock because of taxes. After all, you will have to report a capital gain of $20 per share if you sell it, and the taxes on this gain may run up to $5.60 per share—which is a pretty big hunk. You have to be convinced that ABC stock is selling way too high at $21 before giving consideration to selling it. Or you have to have a new purchase in mind that looks exceptionally attractive to switch out of ABC.

The case of Ima and ABC are the exceptions rather than the rule, however. Don't be afraid to pay some taxes if your investment judgment tells you a stock should be sold. Remember, unless you die owning a stock, you will eventually have to pay tax on your gain. In the ABC example, too often a person will refuse to sell, and argue that "after the $5.60 per share tax I am really receiving not $21.00 but only $15.40 a share for my stock." But all too often if the stock then proceeds to go down, the same person will sell it at a lower price—and then have to pay a tax that will net him far less than he would have received at the beginning.

PART XI
A Hard Look at Some Stock Market Theories

31

So You Want to Trade

"What I want is to make some quick profits."

I wish I had twopence for every time I've heard this expression over the years. Who doesn't want quick profits? I know I do. But *wanting* and *getting* are two different matters.

Perhaps you're disillusioned by my apparent pessimism about achieving quick gains in the stock market. After all, I am an investment adviser and therefore should know when the market is going up or down—specifically, I should know whether XYZ stock will go up or down 3 points over the next few weeks. Or should I?

My reply to people who assume that I know these answers for sure is: "If I knew for sure, I wouldn't be working—I'd be on the beach at Waikiki right now. And so would all the other investment experts in the world."

Don't misunderstand me. I'm in favor of quick profits and I've made some fabulous gains for both my clients and myself in a very short time. But I think it only fair to say that there is a certain amount of *luck* involved when one achieves one's price objectives on a stock in a very short period.

Let's explore this! As you know, *stock prices go up when there are more buyers than sellers, and they go down when the pressure from sellers exceeds buying interest.* When you choose an attractive stock for the future, you are in essense saying, "I believe that this company's earnings will rise over the years", or "I believe the glamour status of this company will improve as time goes on," or "I expect the understated asset value to be recognized"—or a combination of these three statements. You conclude that these favorable fundamentals (understated asset value, increased earnings, and/or improved glamour status) will create more buyers for the stock than sellers and that the stock will therefore go up in price.

When you choose a stock for quick profits (say for a few weeks), it is another matter. Then you are saying, "I believe there will be more buyers than sellers in this stock *in the next few weeks.*" How can you know such a thing? How can you know what people all over the country are going to do with XYZ stock over a few weeks? To be truthful, you cannot.

Just when you're convinced that a mass of buying interest will build up in a stock over the near term, someone with a very large block of that stock may decide to sell. Perhaps a large estate has a block of 150,000 shares and has to liquidate in these few weeks you are aiming for. Countless elements make it difficult to foretell what will happen to a stock (or the market in general) over a very short period of time.

If you don't think it's difficult to gauge where the market is going, try reading the sage comments in the periodic market letters published by most of the large brokerage houses in the United States. It's normal for these letters to hedge, so that they don't put their feet in their mouths, but some are really absurd. Here's one that really caused me to chuckle one day:

> The market has had a sizable advance, one which indicates investors should take a cautious attitude. On the other hand, stocks appear on firm ground, because of improving earnings. As corporate earnings reports are released investor confidence should be strengthened, but the release of these reports may well invite profit-taking.

You tell me which way the market should go after reading this mumble-jumble from the mouth of a supposed expert!

Have you ever been to a gambling casino? How would you like to own one of the dice tables at one of these casinos? My guess is that you could retire in peace by owning just one. But suppose someone offered you ownership of one table for only an hour. Could you rest in peace with that? Certainly not! That one hour could be disastrous. Some lucky fellow might make twenty passes and the table might show a huge loss for this one hour. Still, over the years this table is certain to show a good profit because the percentages and statistics work in its favor. The same principle applies to stocks. Choose a good stock and the statistics will work in your favor as time goes by—but don't count on making a quick killing.

I hesitate to compare a gambling casino to the stock market, but when we talk about trading in and out of stocks *day in and day out,* the comparison is not so farfetched. Trading really is gambling, and I don't like to confuse it with investing for gains over a longer period of time.

There are many traders in the market—people who buy a stock one day and sell it the next for a small profit. This is about the toughest way to make a living I know of. *I wholeheartedly advise you against this kind of gambling.* I feel very strongly about this, so I think it only fair to tell you why:

1. You will pay a fortune in commissions to your broker. A broker should tell people who ask about day-to-day trading that "it will make *me rich, not you.*" I doubt whether your objective is to make your broker rich.
2. You are trading against professionals. There are hundreds of men on the floor of the exchanges who specialize in trading. They have the advantage of not paying commissions, so they can survive with very small profits every day. Their position on the exchange gives them a better "feel" for trends than you could ever hope for sitting in a brokerage office or wherever. In addition, you are at a time disadvantage; the professionals are on the spot and can act instantly. You are a minute or so away, and this can make a big difference (in the case of frequent "late tapes" you may be five, ten, or even thirty minutes behind them).
3. Trading involves making many decisions. It takes far more time than long-term investing and can detract from a person's everyday vocation.
4. Commissions and other execution costs (you may have

to buy at the offer price on the specialist's book and ultimately sell at the bid price) make your breakeven point higher than you might think. For example, if the normal spread between bid and ask on a $30 stock is one-half of one point (50 cents) and if your commission is 30 cents per share to buy and the same to sell, your total cost (execution plus commissions) is 50 cents + 30 cents + 30 cents + 50 cents = $1.60 or over 5% of the $30 stock price. This is the move upward you need to break even.

5. All your gains will be subject to ordinary income tax. You will never benefit from the advantageous capital gain rate because you are not holding stocks for twelve months.

6. You will *never have big winners.* Traders who are happy to make a few points will never own stocks that will double, triple, quadruple, etc.

Many people envy traders. They hear them brag about their fabulous turns in the market. But I ask you—do you suppose they would talk about their losses? No, sir. Perhaps the best comment on the wisdom of trading was made by a man who had spent his whole working lifetime in the stock market. He said simply, "I know a lot of millionaire *investors,* but I *don't know one millionaire trader.*"

So now you know the way I feel about day-in and day-out trading. Still, there is a middle road between trading and long, long-term investing. Investors shouldn't have to wait a lifetime to realize worthwhile profits on their money. For the sensible, realistic investor I suggest the following:

1. Realize that your judgment will not be perfect and that you will have to take losses on occasions.

2. Buy stocks you "can sleep with." Don't buy junk.

3. Do not buy stock for small gains. Set your sights for good-sized profits.

4. Do not concern yourself after "the race is over." If you have decided on an investment philosophy of taking occasional profits, do not consider jumping off the near-

est building if a stock goes way up after you have sold. It's part of your game.

5. Do not be impetuous and overeager to take down profits. Try to let them run.

CONCLUSION

Trading is gambling—not investing. The latter is both the easiest and the most profitable way of making money, so concentrate on it. You'll be glad you did! (Note: In our next-to-last chapter [38] on "Common Stock Commandments," I make reference to an important chapter from *The Common Sense Way to Stock Market Profits*—the one entitled "How to Amass Large Amounts of Capital." The philosophy here is diametrically opposed to trading—and I strongly recommend it to all investors, particularly those who are considering, or actively involved in, trading.)

32
Beating the Market

Human beings constantly strive to come up with schemes that
will make them money. Because the stock market itself is a ve
hicle for making money, you can imagine the number o
schemes that have been invented to "beat the market."

Formerly there were plenty of illegal ways of moving stock
prices to one's favor through manipulation. Fortunately the Se
curities Exchange Act of 1934 set up the Securities and Ex
change Commission in the United States and most of thes
illegal practices are now a thing of the past.

Legal schemes, of course, remain, and every investo
should be conscious of what they have to offer. Let's take a loo
at a few of the widely used stock market theories to see wha
merit they have.

THE DOW THEORY

The most widely publicized theory of all is the Dow theory
One Charles Henry Dow, who was the first editor of *The Wa
Street Journal,* wrote some editorials in that paper from 1900 t
1902. These editorials were later interpreted by W. P. Hami
ton and Robert Rhea to formulate the Dow theory.

Actually the originators of the theory did not contend tha
it would allow you to "beat the market." They suggested mor
modestly that it would tell you whether the stock market was i

an overall upward trend (a bull market) or in an overall downward slide (a bear market). The originators were confident that their barometer could predict business conditions many months in advance. They were not interested in analyzing any of the economic indicators I discussed in Chapter 8. Instead, they contended that the action of the stock market itself would tell you where business was headed.

The Dow theory is based strictly on certain interpretations of the Dow Jones Industrial Average and the Dow Jones Railroad Average. This is one weakness of the theory, for the Dow Jones Industrial Average is a very limited one and the railroad stocks carry significance different from years ago (many are today considered more for their natural resource ownership than for their transportation services).

Like all theories, the Dow is subject to all sorts of interpretations and assessments. Also like all theories, it is sometimes right and sometimes wrong. It had a wonderful record in "predicting" a downfall in 1929. W. P. Hamilton published a now-famous editorial on October 25, 1929 entitled "A Turn in the Tide" in which he stated that the action of the averages on October 23 signaled the end of a long bull market and the beginning of a bear market. Had an investor sold all his holdings on October 23, he would have saved himself a fortune. He would already have seen the market on industrial stocks drop about 19%, but after October 23 it was to fall another 70% from its high to its low in 1932.

On the other hand, the Dow theory did not forecast the fantastic bull market that preceded the 1929 crash: the theory in early 1926 gave very bearish indications and the three and a half years that followed were the most profitable in history.

An objective appraisal of Hamilton's work was made by the economist Alfred Cowles III in 1933. Cowles studied Hamilton's editorials for the twenty-six-year period from 1904 to 1929. During this span Hamilton made ninety recommendations for a change in attitude toward the market (55% were bullish, 16% bearish, and 29% doubtful). In retrospect, forty-five of the ninety forecasts were correct and forty-five were incorrect—an investor might have done as well by flipping a coin. Cowles also concluded that an investor would have had a better performance from outright ownership over these twenty-six years than from buying and selling on Hamilton's signals.

CHARTS

Many stock market students adhere to charts to predict which way the market is going and the trend of individual issues. There are countless chart systems, and most of them attempt to correlate a relationship between market price action and the volume of trading. The idea is that it is a sign of strength when a stock advances on a large volume of shares traded; conversely, when volume in the market or on one stock enlarges as a stock declines, it shows that the pessimism is mounting and that the trend is for lower prices.

In essence, the chartists contend that a study of a stock's behavior not only tells you where a stock had been but also where it is going. Say, for example, a stock has risen to $50 twice in the last few months and each time the stock has backed down from this $50 price. The second time it falls off from $50 the chartists conclude it has formed a "double top," and it is assumed that it will have a very difficult time going up through this price in the near future.

Or a chartist might keep a trend line on a stock's behavior just as you would on a company's sales trend. From this chart he will try to judge just where the stock is going.

Chartists have scores of terms to designate price action. "Head-and-shoulders top," "dormant bottom," "scallop and saucer," and "rounding top" are some of them. They all assume it is possible to predict a stock's future by charts—*with no regard whatsoever for its fundamental values.* Pure chartists couldn't care less about earnings, dividends, industry position, new products, overall outlook. All they care about is what the charts tell them.

I can't help but think of charts and the position of the market on September 16, 1960. At that time the Dow Jones Industrial Average was hovering about the 600 level. The market had already retreated to this level three times and each time it had rallied upward—thus the 600 level was a "triple bottom."

Chartists were saying that the market would meet tremendous support at this level. Why? Because business was getting better? Certainly not! Only because the charts told them so. Now I ask you, what should be so magic about 600 on the Dow Jones average? If people were becoming more pessimistic, the market would go lower regardless of "triple bottoms." It was only a matter of days until the magic number was pierced. This penetration below 600 caused many chartists to liquidate their holdings and this heavy selling forced the market lower still. By October 25, the average hit 566 and this proved to be the bottom of the decline—from which the market commenced a dramatic upsurge. In other words, the people who were frightened by the penetration of this ridiculous magic number sold out within 5% of what proved to be the market's low. The interesting thing is that most of these chartists had no idea what the outlook was for business, earnings, inflation, political climate, and all the important considerations that affect and even determine the level of the stock market. All they were concerned with was the Dow Jones Industrial Average—and they were so completely fooled by its action.

Interestingly enough, a sharp decline in just *one* of the thirty stocks that make up the average might have caused the DJIA to go below 600. I ask you—should isolated declines like this speak for the whole market? Of course not.

Interpretation of charts is very much a personal affair. In a way, it's like abstract art. Take an abstract painting and show it to ten people and you'll get at least eight different interpretations of what is seen. Take one set of chart figures and show it to ten chartists and you're liable to get almost as many interpretations of which way the stock is going.

The trouble with most chart patterns is that they cause their followers to change their opinions so frequently. Chart services change like the wind. One day they put out a strong buy signal; two weeks later they see a change in the pattern and tell their clients to sell; then two weeks after that they tell them to buy again. The result is that the chartists' followers are forced in and out of the market time and time again. This is great for brokers' commissions, but not so great for the investor.

Another disadvantage to charting—and a great one—is what I've already mentioned about decisions made on the basis of the *chart alone*. Most buyers under this method have no idea *why* they are buying a company's stock, hardly a condition that fosters contentment or relaxation.

As you have no doubt gathered by now, it is the *way* in which charts are used (I should say "misused") that I object to. I admit that charts *can* be helpful. They can point out to the potential investor that "accumulation" is going on in a security— that some supposedly knowledgeable people are quietly buying stock for investment purposes. (Or that "distribution," or concentrated selling, is being done by insiders—by people who know best what is really going on.) But upon discovering such accumulation, should one become a sheep and follow the action blindly? I say *no*! Never buy a stock "blind"—ignorant of the important facts I have stressed in this book. It's true that my insistence on sound reasoning may cause you to delay action and thus miss out on some winners, but this approach will help you avoid many more losers—and you will have a much better performance over the years. And no doubt you will sleep better at night because nothing is worse for the nerves than having no idea in the world why your stock is retreating.

I never buy a stock "blind" and I have *never* regretted sticking to this principle.

One further comment about the use of charts in common stock selection: I already mentioned the major thesis regarding charts, i.e., that they can be useful in pinpointing what "insiders" or other knowledgeable people are doing with their securities. There comes a point, however, when *too many* people are using charts—which is another way of saying that the chart no longer tells the tale. If, for example, a multitude of investors start basing their decisions on chart patterns, they begin to "feed" on one another. A chart may have bullish implications at the beginning, but as more and more chartists follow it, then there are simply more and more owners of the stock who really have *no* special information or reason for owning it. The buyers (or sellers, as the case may be) are perpetuating the chart pattern, and one day in the future, when the values start to tell, the chart will suddenly change from bullish to bearish (or vice versa) and one heck of a rush for the exits will commence. Then, with no chartist support any longer (as a matter of fact, just the opposite), a truly disastrous result can occur.

Therefore I implore you to be especially wary of charts in widespread use. In my first revision of *Primer*, I warned readers about the excessive use of charts in 1968. I stated that "the heavy charting of 1968 will be in large part responsible for some painful losses in lower quality issues sometime in the 1969–1970 period." Certainly this proved true.

BACK TO FUNDAMENTALS

Most of our great football coaches have stressed fundamentals. A team that cannot block and tackle cannot be expected to win! After a disappointing loss the top coaches don't run helter-skelter looking for a magic play to beat next week's opponent—they put their boys to work and cry, "Back to fundamentals!"

In buying stock you must be conscious of the fundamentals of potential earning power to achieve success. If you forget your "blocking and tackling," you're asking for trouble. Whenever I think of charts versus fundamentals, I am reminded of a true story of a woman who was very much involved in charting stocks in the 1920s. She was a master at it, and was making a handsome living from it. As she gained confidence in herself, she started selling some of the blue chip stocks she had owned for years and put the proceeds into stocks that looked good on the charts. One stock in particular had the most assuring chart pattern of any she had ever seen. That stock was Kolster Radio, which was then listed on the San Francisco Stock Exchange. Despite the fact that Kolster's fundamentals would not encourage buying it, the stock was zooming upward and was a chartist's dream. Higher and higher it went and by the end of 1928 Kolster was 73¼ and this lady chartist was up to her earrings in the stock. By January 1929, the trend of Kolster stock reversed itself and the bottom fell out suddenly. By May of the same year, the stock had plummeted to 25½. Then came a rally in June, but by October it was down to around 11 and by December it was $3. In January 1930 Kolster announced it was in receivership and went through bankruptcy proceedings. The worst part of this tragic story is that the lady had nothing left— no earning power, no dividends, no fundamentals on which she could at least hope for the future.

As you've gathered from both my earlier discussions and this illustration, I believe in buying value. This does not ensure you won't make an occasional mistake, but it does guarantee you won't end up with stock certificates that are useful only as wallpaper.

PART XII

Investment Trusts: Pro and Con

33

Putting Your Dollars in Someone Else's Hands

About sixty years ago a number of men decided that many investors wanted *someone else* to make their investment decisions for them. To accomplish this, they sold shares in an *investment trust*. The idea was simple: They would invest the money they received in stocks and bonds and each owner of the trust would share in any profits or losses the trust incurred.

The idea was indeed sound. The originators found that many people preferred to have experts do their thinking for them, consequently many dollars rolled in to buy these trusts.

Today investment trusts (or investment *companies*, as they are more commonly called), constitute a multibillion-dollar industry. Let's look at some of the characteristics of these trusts.

There are two main advantages of an investment trust: *professional management* and *diversification*. The first of these is obvious. The people who run the trusts and make the investment decisions are professionals; you expect people who spend their working life studying investments to do a superior job. In addition, an investment trust retains a large staff of experts, so you have the advantage of the judgment of many versus the judgment of one (you!).

Diversification is an equally important advantage. When you buy a share of an investment trust, you are buying all the stocks and bonds they own and thus you have your eggs spread around rather than all in one basket. It's interesting to note that there have been about 1,500 automobile manufacturers in the United States since 1920—and now there are only four (maybe three). If you had placed all your eggs in any one of the 1,496 that failed to survive, you'd have gone down the drain with them.

Investment trusts are *convenient* to own, too. If you had your own portfolio of twenty or thirty stocks, you'd be deluged with dividend checks from all the companies you owned. When you invest in a trust, which may own fifty or more different securities, you receive one check every three months (they lump all their dividends and interest received together for you).

There are a few other advantages. First, a trust supervises its investments constantly, whereas you as an individual owner might not have the time or inclination to do this religiously. Second, trust management is more flexible than the average individual. They are more inclined to take profits on occasions, whereas individuals often "fall in love" with their stocks and lose their objectivity in appraising them. Third, trust shares are not as volatile—they do not move up and down as wildly—as most individual stocks do. The advantage of this is that their owners are not prone to panic in a declining market because the trust shares will usually decline rather gradually. Of course, this lack of volatility is a two-sided coin since trust shares may not rise very fast in a good market. Many trusts are so widely diversified that they end up with only mediocre performance; a trust with fifty stocks, for example, may see twenty-five go up, ten go down, and fifteen remain the same on a strong day in the stock market.

Now for the *disadvantages*. Aside from mediocre performance, which may or may not apply, depending on the specific trust, the *major drawback of investment trusts is their costs of ownership*. All trusts charge a *management fee*, which generally runs around ½ of 1% of the trust assets per year. Now, ½ of 1% doesn't sound like much, but this management fee is charged against the income received by the trusts (the dividends and interest earned on the stocks and bonds held) and reduces the ordinary income paid to shareholders to the point where *trusts generally pay lower yields than can be obtained from owning individual stocks outright*.

The most valid and glaring criticism of the trust involves

the large sales commission charged to buy them, but this criticism has to be confined to one type of investment trust—the "open-end trust," more commonly known as the "mutual fund." I'll discuss this in a minute, when I talk about the mutuals separately.

Another drawback of the trusts involves their size. Most trusts (especially the mutual funds, which continue to grow in size) accumulate large blocks of stocks. When these stocks are going *up* in price, the trusts have no problem in disposing of them, if they seek to do so. But what happens if the market is tumbling or if a company's business turns sour and its stock is being actively sold by the public? How can a trust with 400,000 or 500,000 or more shares get rid of them without driving the price down unmercifully? This problem was encountered in 1929. While we can't compare anything since to 1929, the principle holds. This is one hidden, little-publicized risk of a large trust.

There are two more facts you should know about investment trusts. The first involves a special kind of dividend usually distributed once a year—a *capital gain dividend*. This distribution comes from profits the trust takes during the year. Suppose, for example, your trust bought IBM a number of years ago and this year sells off some of the stock for a large gain. These profits are lumped together with others taken during the year and are paid out to you. As with any other capital gain, you will only have to pay tax on 40% of the profit, with a maximum federal rate of 28%. These capital gain dividends are bound to fluctuate, depending on how good the market is each year. They can be sizable and they can be nothing. Some investors get very excited about the high yield they receive when they add their regular investment income (the ordinary dividends from the trust) and the capital gain income together. Say you get a 3% yield from the regular dividends and then you get a capital gain dividend that, when related to the market price of the trust, amounts to another 12% yield. Total yield for the year looks like 15%. The Securities and Exchange Commission wisely prohibits security salesmen from combining these yields and quoting prospective customers on this combined basis because of the variable nature of the capital gain distribution, and because this payout may be termed simply a return of your own capital—and thus not "true yield."

A second question should also be answered for you, namely: How does one judge management's performance in an investment trust? In an individual company you judge performance by the company's earnings record. *In an investment trust you judge performance by its growth in net asset value per share.*

Don't worry, you don't have to figure this net value; the trusts figure it for you and usually compute it once or twice a day. What they do is add the market values of all the securities held and divide the sum by the number of trust shares outstanding. This net asset value per share tells you how much each share would be worth if the trust were to liquidate completely. If management does a good job and buys stocks that go up in price, then the net asset value per share will go up. By noting the trend in net asset value per share (plus the capital gain dividends they pay out), you can judge management's performance. Incidentally, some investment services summarize the performance records of the trusts for you. The best known of these is the Wiesenberger service.

Time now to distinguish between the two basic types of investment trusts—the closed-end and the open-end.

CLOSED-END INVESTMENT TRUSTS

These are called closed-end because the *number of shares of the trust outstanding is limited.* Let's say a new closed-end trust is brought to market today. One million shares are to be sold at $10 per share. This one million shares is the total amount the trust is planning to issue. A year from today you want to buy shares in this trust. It may be listed on one of the exchanges or it may be traded over-the-counter. Its price will depend on its net asset value per share at that time, but it may sell a little above this value (at a premium) or a little below it (at a discount). Whether the trust shares are selling at a premium or at a discount will depend on investor attitudes toward stocks generally and on what people think of this trust's management. In other words, like other stocks, it will sell at a price determined by supply and demand.

The same thing applies if and when you want to sell the trust stock. You have to depend on the market to sell your holding—you cannot require the trust to redeem the shares for you (as you will see, stockholders in an open-end trust do redeem their shares with the trust).

Closed-end trusts may differ in their philosophy and/or approach from open-end trusts. Closed-end trusts often can leverage themselves—they can borrow money to buy stocks. Likewise, they may or may not be limited in what kind of investments they can make (some are permitted to own large interests in companies that have no public market for their stock).

Some prominent examples of closed-end trusts are Lehman Corporation and Madison Fund, both listed on the New York Stock Exchange, and Standard Shares, which is listed on the American Exchange.

OPEN-END TRUSTS—MUTUAL FUNDS

The number and size of mutual funds in this country has grown like Topsy. In 1950, for example, investors had $2.5 billion invested in the funds; by 1961, the figure exceeded $20 billion, and by year-end 1979 it had skyrocketed to over $50 billion. This mushrooming can be attributed to the public's growing desire to put their dollars to work, to a rising stock market for part of this period, to burgeoning sales of money-market funds, and to imaginative and aggressive sales efforts. This brings us to the *major disadvantage of the mutual fund—the high selling commission involved.* Whereas the commission you pay to buy a stock on the New York Stock Exchange might be 1–2%, many mutuals have a "sales load" ranging from 6 to 8¾%. A person can buy $1,000 worth of stock on the exchange for a commission of $15.00 (you could buy a closed-end trust for this amount, too), while a similar purchase of a mutual fund might cost you $60.00 to $87.50. You can see why security salesmen eagerly seek mutual fund purchases.

There are a few redeeming factors to consider, though. Of real importance is the fact that the sales load on a mutual fund takes care of your cost for *both buying and selling.* In other words, you pay the 6–8¾% commission when you buy, but you *pay no commission* (or, in some cases, only ½ of 1%) *if and when you sell the fund.* This, of course, is *not* true of the commission you pay to buy and sell an investment security on the exchange. You pay your 1–2% when you buy and another 1–2% when you sell. To be completely objective then, you should cut the mutual sales load in half to 3–4⅜ in comparing it with other investments. Therefore, on average you pay two to three times as much to buy the mutual fund and there is no question but that this is quite a premium to pay. And if you are the type of investor who almost never sells a stock (one who "buys and dies" with an issue), then you are probably paying about five times as much to purchase the mutual fund as you would if you bought a security on the stock market exchange. All of this commission figuring is very approximate. With the negotiated rates now in force, you may be able to buy and sell with lower rates than indicated; but then, you may have to pay more, too. The best I can do is provide the comparisons and let you insert the percentage commission charges that are appropriate to you. Incidentally, mutual fund charges are also changing. Some funds, in an effort to attract more investors, have lowered their sales charges substantially. So you have to check this, too, in your comparison of outright ownership of individual securities versus mutual funds.

Commission rates on funds, however, do drop sharply as the amount of purchase increases. Whereas the sales load might be 8½% on purchases up to $25,000, the rate might be about 7% over $25,000, 5% over $50,000—gradually working down to 1% on purchases over $500,000.

In the financial section of your newspaper you will see a long list of prices quoted on mutual funds. These prices show like those of the over-the-counter (unlisted) stocks—with a bid and an ask price shown. Here is a typical quotation as it might appear in the paper:

	Bid	Ask
XYZ Mutual Fund	$10.00	$10.75

The bid price represents the net asset value per share of the fund. The ask price is merely the *net asset value plus the sales load*. In this case, the sales load is 7½%, or 75 cents, on a 10.00 net asset value for a total of $10.75. You buy mutual fund shares at the ask price; if and when you sell, you do so at the bid price.

As you can see, it's going to take time for you to break even after your purchase. It may be a year or so before XYZ net asset value rises to $10.75 per share—where you can get out without any loss. Thus *mutual funds should only be bought by long-term investors.* If you're investing money you think you might need in a year or two or even three, don't put the money into the funds.

Before I give you some other conclusions and my opinion of mutuals, let me point out a few more characteristics. You remember that in the discussion of closed-end trusts I said that the latter have a limited number of shares outstanding and that a buyer or seller has to contend with market conditions of supply and demand. This is *not* the case in open-end trusts. They are called open-end because they have no limit as to the number of shares they will sell. Mutual funds want to sell as many shares as possible, and they stand ready to do so at the asset value plus sales commission. By the same token, mutuals must stand by to redeem their shares in cash at the asset value in unlimited amounts. This gives you a little protection, for even if the market goes down sharply, you know you can get the asset value as it stands on the day you redeem. In a closed-end trust, on the other hand, a sharply declining market might take the stock to a substantial discount from its asset value and you might have to settle for this if you want out.

You might be thinking now: Suppose a large number of mutual fund stockholders decided to redeem all at once. The mutual might have to sell a lot of stocks very suddenly to get the cash for redemption, and these forced sales would tend to lower the asset value very sharply. Or perhaps the mutuals couldn't be able to raise the cash right away. This is a legitimate thought. Fortunately, redemptions of this type over the post–World War II period have not been that severe. But the risk, although not probable, does exist.

Types of Mutual Funds

There are many types of mutual funds. Some seek very a[g]gressive capital gains and invest in growth stocks and some [of] the smaller companies that, while more speculative, could b[e]come the "Polaroids of tomorrow." Dreyfus, Fidelity Capit[al] and Putnam Growth are representative of these. Some fun[d] have growth as their major objective, but take a more conse[r]vative approach—they concentrate mainly on already prove[n] companies. Typical of these are Investment Company of Ame[r]ica, Massachusetts Investors Trust, and Affiliated. Then y[ou] have the very conservative funds, whose major objective is [to] provide good income and very gradual gains over the year[s] these are usually "balanced funds," which means that they ow[n] a large amount of bonds and preferred stocks in addition [to] their somewhat conservative common stocks. Eaton and Ho[w]ard Balanced Fund, Boston Fund, and Wellington are good e[x]amples.

In addition, there are certain funds that concentrate [on] one or two industry groups, such as Chemical Fund. If you a[re] enthusiastic about one segment of our economy but have [a] hard time making a choice of one stock in the group, you c[an] solve your problem by purchasing an industry fund.

How Have the Funds Performed?

The test of theory is performance. Countless invento[rs] knew the story behind flying before the Wright brothers. Th[e] latter were heroes because their airplane didn't end up in [a] heap—it performed.

The same thing goes for mutual funds. The theory behi[nd] professional management, diversification, constant superv[i]sion, flexibility, and so on is fine, but has it proved itself or h[as] it ended up "in a heap"? The answer cannot be generalized b[e]cause there are so many funds doing business; some have be[en] quite successful and others have been unsuccessful. Just as [in] choosing individual stocks, you have to analyze the perfo[r]mance of the individual funds to determine whether they'[re] worth considering.

Let's see, however, how an average of the funds performed from 1969 to 1979. Using the Wiesenberger compilation of mutual fund management results, which incidentally allows for both dividends and capital gain distributions made to shareholders but does *not* account for the sales charge made at the initial time of purchase, here is how a $1,000 investment would have grown from December 31, 1969, to December 31, 1979. I will present four broad categories of funds: (1) the large growth funds; (2) middle-of-the-road "growth and income" trusts; (3) funds that emphasize higher-income common stocks; and (4) very conservative balanced funds, which hold decent amounts of fixed-income securities along with common stocks. Repeating the fact that the sales load has not been deducted and thus the figures should be somewhat *lower*, here is how the mythical $1,000 would have looked after its ten-year life:

Categories:	(1)	(2)	(3)	(4)
	$1,476	$1,838	$2,230	$1,704

Frankly, these figures are not very impressive—annual compound returns range from 4% to only 8½%—not high considering that inflation in the United States was exploding. Markets for both stocks and bonds were very disappointing over these ten years, however, so the fund managers hardly had an ideal climate in which to operate.

Some funds did a lot better than these averages indicated—and some did a lot worse. The idea, of course, is to buy fund management that will outperform both the market and other funds.

You might have outperformed the statistics I've shown above by buying certain individual stocks. If you had put your money in certain big winners, you probably would have had far better success in much less time. But would you have been smart enough to buy these "stars"? And, just as important, would you have been smart enough to stay with them, or would you have sold out for small gains?

One final, important, caveat. Just as in individual stocks, do *not* assume the past is any guarantee of the future. Be careful not to lose your objectivity because of a trust's magnificent recent performance. Its style of investing, perhaps its industry bias, may have just completed a dramatic move upward—resulting in exaggerated price levels. You certainly don't want to buy overvaluation, so be sure to investigate the reasons for its success and do not simply react to the record.

OPEN-END NO-LOAD FUNDS

One final form of investment trust is the so-called no-load fund, which is the same as the mutual fund *with the exception that there is no sales charge to the buyer*. This vehicle is open-end in that it continuously offers shares and stands ready to redeem them whenever requested. All transactions revolve around the trust's net asset value and there is no sales charge to either buyer or seller. Thus, in the case of our example on p.   , the $10 net asset value is the figure used for purchases and sales.

You are probably wondering why anyone would buy a mutual fund when he might find the same diversification and management without the significant sales load. For one thing, the no-load trust might charge a higher annual management fee than the normal $\frac{1}{2}$ of 1% the mutuals generally charge; a larger fee would eventually negate some of the advantage of no initial load. Aside from this possibility, the only reason an investor should choose a load over a no-load fund is the all-important management consideration. Good portfolio supervision and management can overcome the sales cost. If this stewardship is really superior in the mutual, the load should not stand in the way.

An investor should definitely look into the no-loads. Outfits such as Johnston Fund, Energy Fund, and some emanating from investment counseling organizations have compiled good investment records over the years. Given a continuation of such management, an investor considering investment trusts might heed the famous slogan from the clothier Robert Hall "Why pay for overhead when you can't wear it."

CONCLUSIONS

When are funds suitable and preferable to direct owner-ship of individual securities? They seem most logical when: the investor does not have a great deal of time to study his invest-ments; he doesn't have enough money to afford some diversi-fication of stocks; he doesn't have an adviser who can guide him correctly; or he hasn't found an adviser who has his best interests at heart.

If you are in one of these categories, then you should con-sider investment trusts. Naturally, you should concentrate on superior management to offset the aforementioned additional costs. The right kind of "stewardship" can mean a lot to you and can overcome the additional costs fairly fast under the right conditions.

Mutual funds are ideal for periodic investment programs (i.e., monthly investment plans). I will discuss this in Chapter 35.

PART XIII

Some Specific Help in Planning for the Future

34

The Four W's

All newspaper writers are taught to emphasize certain facts in the first paragraph of a story. For one thing, they are taught to answer the "Four W's":

WHO (is involved in the story)?
WHAT (was the action which took place)?
WHERE (did the action occur)?
WHEN (did it happen)?

In the field of investments we have our own Four W's. Just as a journalist has to ask his basic W's to make an article complete and successful, an investment adviser has to answer these:

WHO should invest in the stock market?
WHEN is a person ready to make the plunge?
WHAT is the investor's objective?
WHERE should the money be invested?

Let's look at the W's one by one.

WHO SHOULD INVEST IN THE STOCK MARKET?

There is room for *every* investor in the stock market. After all, there are as many types of stocks as there are types of in-

vestors, ranging from the most conservative to the most speculative.

So the market has a potential for everyone. There remains,
though, the important question of just *when* a person is ready
to take the plunge. Therefore we have to tie in the next W of
when in deciding just *who* is suited for stocks.

WHEN ARE YOU READY TO INVEST?

A good investment adviser should be able to tell you when
you are ready to buy stocks. It goes without saying that you
should have all your necessities and a lot of the luxuries you desire before you think of investing. After all, our basic purpose
is to live and enjoy life, and we should be doing this before we
start thinking of fortune building.

Please don't forget two necessities that you should certainly have before investing. First, be sure you have adequate *health
insurance* for yourself and your family. If you've spent a few days
in a hospital of late, you'll know the tremendous costs involved.
I'm especially strong on so-called catastrophe health insurance,
which protects you against the big expenses. Most families can
afford bills that run to a *few hundred* dollars—it is the *thousands*
that can create insurmountable problems. If you have normal
health insurance *plus* the protection against catastrophe, you
will be relaxed about your investments and this is important.

The second necessity is *life insurance.* Some people call it
"death insurance," and I suppose that's a more apropos title
because life insurance is best bought for what it can do for your
heirs *after* you're dead. Since we're all certain to die someday,
"death insurance" is a basic part of our future planning.

I've been asked many times, "How much life insurance
should I carry?" There is no one answer to this question. If you
knew you were going to die tomorrow, you'd put all your dollars into life insurance and not one penny into stocks, real
esate, and other investments. On the other hand, if you knew
you were certain to live to be eighty, you'd put all your money
into investments and not a penny into insurance. Some insurance salesmen stress the unpleasant possibility that you could

be snuffed out tomorrow and therefore should carry $200,000 or $300,000 worth of insurance to provide an adequate income for your family. To carry these amounts would cost you a small fortune in annual premiums and you'd be "insurance poor." As the saying goes, life insurance is a plan that keeps you poor all your life so you can die rich.

As with many other things in life, you are probably better off striking a happy medium in your life insurance buying. Have a program whereby you increase your coverage as time goes by and as you can better afford the premiums. Life is always something of a gamble, and the best bet is that you will enjoy some years of good health and that you can buy insurance progressively over the years.

Let me repeat: *No one* should think of investing in the market or real estate until he has adequate health and life insurance. In addition, almost every family should have a cash reserve—an emergency fund—before investing. Most home economists suggest that you put at least three months' salary into a savings-type account and never touch it. I heartily agree.

This advice will vary according to circumstances. For example, if you're a bachelor or a career woman, you have little use for life insurance. Or if you know you're going to inherit a lot of money in ten or twenty years, you should protect yourself for now (through cheap term life insurance) instead of for the distant future. Or if your business will carry on regardless of your state of health, you require less life insurance and a smaller emergency fund than the next fellow.

WHAT IS YOUR OBJECTIVE IN INVESTING?

People invest their money for different reasons. Some want to get a higher return than they can obtain from bank interest so they can live better. Some want to see their money grow so that they can drive Cadillacs instead of Chevrolets. And some (a large percentage) are looking ahead to retirement and invest so they can have security and comfort in their later years. In Chapter 36 I'll show you how to plan for the future, but now I just want to stress that it's important for your investment adviser to know what your objectives are.

There are two basic questions you should ask yourself and answer honestly. Then make sure your adviser knows the answers, too.

1. *How important is current income to you?*

Some people have a fixation about receiving a certain yield on their money and yet they never spend or use this income. As we've already seen, some of the most successful stock investments have been the growth companies, which pay a low yield.

On the other hand, you may need additional income to live and higher dividends may be of great importance to you.

Determine which category you fit and let your broker (or counselor) know whether high dividends are necessary.

2. *How many years ahead are you looking for the major benefits of your investments?*

If you're looking ten or twenty years ahead, you can buy the growth companies. If, instead, you're already seventy years old, you're interested in today and should buy stocks that give you safety, security, and income now.

WHERE SHOULD YOUR MONEY BE INVESTED?

You've satisfied yourself that you have adequate health and life insurance and an emergency fund; you've set your investment objectives and determined how important current income is to you and how far in the future you are looking for the real fruits of your investments. Now we're ready to pull the trigger!

Where should you put your money? Here again, there are a few questions you should ask yourself and then relate the answers to the person who's helping you with your stock decisions.

1. *When will you be investing again?*

If the capital you now have is all you expect to invest for quite a while, it's safer to stagger your purchases over a period of time—perhaps a few years. If instead you plan to invest sums consistently over the years, you don't have to worry about automatically spacing your investments.

2. *What is your personal temperament?*

Your investments are intended to make money for you, but it is extremely important that they also make you happy. Some people are poor gamblers by nature. Losses upset them greatly. It goes without saying that people who fall into this category should avoid volatile stocks, stocks that fluctuate wildly in the market. By the same token, aggressive investors who are looking for quick gains are not generally going to be happy with Consolidated Edison.

I recall an investor who owned conservative stocks, but who had become unhappy with her stable holdings and decided to put her next invesment dollars into a growth stock. She did—and she bought a good one. A few days after she purchased her growth stock it had risen from 64 to 71. Her broker didn't hear from her. Then one day the stock dropped sharply from 71 back to 68½—a loss of 2½ points. That day the broker's phone did ring. She was concerned over the drop, even though she still had a 4½ point profit after only owning the stock ten days. The anxious calls continued for a few days until he finally advised her to sell the stock—on the basis that it was making her unhappy. She simply wasn't temperamentally equipped to own volatile stocks (even though she could afford losses) and the wide price movements were disturbing her. Living with a stock that bothers you is like living with a mate who makes you unhappy. So it's best to analyze a stock's "personality" before you "marry" it.

Decide how much risk you are willing to take when investing. I usually put it this way: Decide whether you want to *sleep well* or *eat well*. The "sleep well" stocks should never hurt you;

they will provide you, not with spectacular gains, but with peace of mind. Your "eat well" stocks are intended to put steak and caviar on the table.

> Don't try for steak
> If it keeps you awake.

Or, put another way:

> Caviar's indeed a delicate dish,
> But the worrisome type should settle for fish.

35
Stocks for People

I don't mean to imply by this title that there are stocks for animals as well as for human beings. But certain stocks have consistently met the different objectives of investors over the years. Every investment adviser has his own favorites. I have compiled a list of stocks that have proved rewarding for my clients in the past and that *I believe will continue to do the job for them in the future.*

In presenting these securities I have separated them according to the individual's investment position. Determine under which category you fall and concentrate on those comments. I hope they will be helpful to you in shaping your investment decisions now and over the years. (Remember, though, that we are living in a changing society and the stock market changes accordingly. These stocks have to be reassessed according to outlook and according to market price at the time of your reading.)

Just one comment before starting. You will notice that I make reference in each case to the amount of fixed-income securities (bonds and preferred stocks) that are suitable for each portfolio. In our business we call this apportionment of fixed-income securities the amount of *balance* the investor wishes to achieve. The more conservative the investor's objectives, the more balance we strive for. An elderly widow, for example, might have 50% of her money in fixed-income securities (the other 50% in common stocks) and we would say she has a 50–

50 balance. On the other hand, a young professional who has no need for immediate income and is looking twenty or thirty years away for the benefits of his or investment program might have *no* bonds or preferred stocks—and have *no balance* in the portfolio. *Balance refers solely to how the capital is divided between fixed-income securities and common stocks.*

We've talked about not having all your eggs in one stock; it is safer to have spread them around into different stocks. When we talk about *diversification,* we are talking about *how the common stocks are divided.* A certain percentage of the common stock portion of a portfolio might go into chemical stocks, a certain percentage into electrical equipment, foods, oils, utilities, and the like. This is diversification by industries. In addition, an investor will generally have some geographical diversification; in a large portfolio, for example, it is wise to have utility stocks from a few geographical locations (if you own utilities at all, that is).

While we're on the subject, let me warn you against *over-diversification.* This is a common ill among investors. Too often I've seen a person with $20,000 or $30,000 with a list of stocks as long as your arm. Many people think it is safer to keep diversifying and adding new companies to their portfolio. This is untrue and can actually lead to dangerous consequences, because:

1. There are only so many companies that are truly deserving of investment and too often an investor ends up lowering standards merely to achieve diversification.
2. A long list of stocks is difficult to supervise. It's hard enough to keep current with ten or fifteen stocks, much less to have to keep up with twenty or thirty or more.
3. It's a nuisance to receive small dividend checks from a multitude of companies.
4. You pay greater brokerage commissions to buy many securities than you would if you concentrate on a lesser number.
5. You'll no doubt end up with very mediocre performance with too long a list. Even on a strong day in the

market, you might see, say, twenty stocks go up, ten go down, and ten remain unchanged.

6. Too much diversification can lead to laziness. When you concentrate on fewer issues, you take the time to analyze correctly. But when you choose ten stocks instead of three, your attitude is bound to be that you can afford a mistake or two.

The most successful portfolios are those that concentrate to a degree rather than "buy the board" and try to own everything. If you really want complete diversification, perhaps you're better off putting your money into someone else's hands—into an investment trust.

Now—on to stocks for people.

TOCKS FOR THE ULTRACONSERVATIVE

As for all the categories covered here, much will depend on just how much current income is needed. Fixed-income securities might account for as much as 50% of the list; 50% is conservative, however, and most advisers will put between 30% and 40% in bonds and place the remaining 60–70% in conservative common stocks such as the following:

Utilities such as American Telephone
Paper, with UnionCamp
Foods, such as Standard Brands, Quaker Oats
Proprietary drugs, like American Home Products, Sterling Drug
Banking, such as Wells Fargo, BankAmerica
Tobacco, like American Brands
Oil, such as Exxon, Shell, or Standard Oil of California
Household, with Procter & Gamble
Retail trade, like Federated Department Stores
Also, a moderate amount might be invested in solid high-yielding industrial companies such as General Motors.

MIDDLE-OF-THE-ROAD OBJECTIVES OF GRADUAL GROWTH WITH GOOD SAFETY

This category is for those who have enough money to liv on, but want a moderate current income to supplement the needs—and who need a feeling of security while planning fo the future. If you won't retire for ten or twenty years, then suggest little if any balance. Instead, I would choose the follov ing common stocks:

Utilities, including American Telephone and Florida Powe
    and Light
Household, such as Procter & Gamble, Revlon
Proprietary drugs, like American Home Products
Ethical drugs, such as Merck, Pfizer
Services, including Dun and Bradstreet, Marsh and McLenna
Oil, including Standard Oil of Indiana
Insurance: Connecticut General
Electrical Equipment: G.E.
Photography: Eastman Kodak
Forest products, like Boise Cascade, Georgia-Pacific
Banking: First Int'l Bancshares (Dallas)
Miscellaneous: MMM, Cleveland Cliffs, Schlumberger

AGGRESSIVE GROWTH

These suggestions are for people who are investing build up capital. They have ample income and, as a matter fact, would prefer not to add any more direct income; instea they want capital gains. They want their money in commo stocks and are not attracted by fixed-income securities. The people should build up a foundation of growth stocks, such a

Forest products, such as Potlach
Office equipment and computers: IBM, Digital Equipment
Chemicals: Air Products, Nalco
Energy: Standard of Indiana, Superior Oil, Schlumberger, He
    merich and Payne
Drugs, like Johnson and Johnson, Merck, Pfizer

Hospital services, such as Humana
Electronics, like Hewlett-Packard, Tektronix, Perkin-Elmer
Photography: Eastman
Services: Marsh and McLennan, Dun and Bradstreet
Leisure time: Warner Communications, Time Inc.

HOW ABOUT THE KIDDIES?

Before we leave the subject of how to invest for different people, let's pause to consider what you might want to do for your children, grandchildren, nephews, or others. Anyone making a gift to a child or having the responsibility for investing a child's money has good intentions, yet this is perhaps the least understood area of investment. Many grave errors have been made here.

Think, for example, of all the dollars that have flowed into annuities for children. Take little Junior, age three months. You don't want him to get his little mitts on any substantial money for eighteen or twenty-one years lest he squander it on a souped-up racing car with mink cushions. You want the money to grow so that it will pay for college or for furniture when he marries. Putting money into an annuity is like putting it in the bank at 3–6% interest. You wouldn't consider that a good investment, I'm sure. I subscribe to the belief that money for children should be placed in stocks.

But which stocks? Amazingly, the first reaction of most parents is to put the money into the safest stock they can think of—with little regard for growth. My contention is that you should look instead to the solid growth companies. After all, even if the child is ten years of age, you are looking about ten years ahead and you want growth over this period. A child is an ideal growth investor because he has time and because he won't be reacting to the ups and downs of the market. If you believe in the growth of our country, then you must believe that a ten-year investment in a solid company in a good industry will achieve excellent results for your child. For this reason, I suggest you consult the stocks of either the middle-of-the-road or aggressive growth investor and put them in the safe deposit box for Junior.

36

How to Reach
That Pot of Gold

There are very few of us who don't dream a little. Our dreams,
of course, take different forms. Some of us still see ourselves
scoring the winning touchdown for dear old Peduka Sub Normal; others picture relaxing by the ol' fishing hole with not a
care in the world; and still others dream of building mansions
and owning yachts. Aside from scoring the touchdown—which
is impossible to do at the age of forty anyway—most of our personal dreams have one thing in common: *they require money.*

Please don't misunderstand me. I know that money can't
buy happiness and that countless joys and dreams are void of
materialism. Yet it does take capital to live now and to retire
later in life. Regardless of what you want for yourself now, it
is important to build yourself a pot of gold at the end of your
working years so that you can enjoy retirement. This involves
planning for the future, and I hope to be able to help you do this.

"Planning for the future," I had a man growl to me, "is
frustrating. You work and work and save your money all your
life so that when you're old you can have the things *that only the
young can enjoy.*" He had a good point, but it doesn't rule out
the necessity for looking ahead and determining just what you
will need when you do retire.

Ask yourself how much *income you will need* when you stop
working. Then look at how you will get this income. More often
than not, people find that they haven't provided enough for

themselves. And more often than not, they find out *too late* that they're short on capital.

Pick a monthly income figure out of the air. Assume you will need a minimum of $1,000 per month to retire twenty years from now and live the way you want. But will $1,000 per month in 2000 buy you what $1,000 per month will buy you to-day? Not if inflation continues. Thus you'd better account for inflation in your figuring. There's no way of estimating how much the cost of living will increase over the next twenty years. From 1958 to 1966 it was a little under $1\frac{1}{2}\%$ per year; since then it has been on the upswing and the recent rate has been in the frightening 8–18% range. Disinflationary measures are being administered, however, so let's hope for a return to the low part of this range—to around 8%. Eight percent over twen-ty years is 160%. Thus we should add on 160% of $1000, or $1,600, to bring our monthly requirements to an unbelievable (how frightening inflation is!) $2,600 for the year 2000.

Now that we've decided how much you'll need, we'd better see *where the money's going to come from*. Most of us are entitled to Social Security, and this might provide about $600 per month—the amount will no doubt be raised as time goes by. Let's assume that it is raised in line with inflation to about $1,600 per month by the year 2000 (I know this sounds astro-nomical, but the figure comes from tacking on the same 160% to our $600 base).

Next we should figure any other income you will be receiv-ing at that time. Let's assume you will receive a pension from your company of about $500 per month when you retire.

Here's the way you stand right now:

In 2000, you will get:	$1,600	Social Security
	500	Pension
	$2,100	Total
In 2000, you will need:	$2,600	
You are lacking:	$ 500	

You have to count on some form of investments to bring you that extra $500 per month in 2000. The logical question is: How much capital will you need in 2000 to give you an income of $500 per month, or $6,000 per year?

This is hard to answer because we don't know what kind of return after taxes we can count on from stocks or real estate twenty years from now. But assuming an average after-tax return of 7% on your money, you will need almost $90,000 in stocks and bonds to give you this $6,000 per year (7% of $90,000 = $6,300). Or you can turn over about $55,000–$60,000 in cash to a life insurance company and they'll guarantee to pay you $6,000 a year for the rest of your life (in this case, however, you will have no capital to leave to your heirs—the $55,000–$60,000 is no longer yours). Or you might find a piece of property that will net you 8% on your money and you'll need $75,000 (8% of $75,000 = $6000).

Thus, depending on how you want to do it, you will need between $75,000 and $90,000 in 2000 to bring your income up to where you want it. Let's say that you need about $80,000 to live in the style to which you're accustomed twenty years from now.

Now the big question: How are you going to accumulate $80,000 in the next twenty years? The answer: Through *saving*. Now don't run away. I, too, know that the number of people who are able to save $80,000 during their lives is small. But I also know that the reason so few are able to is that *they don't start early enough.*

You know that money compounds as it sits collecting a return. Take $100.00 and invest it at 6%; the first year your investment will grow to $106; the next year it will grow to $112.36. By the twelfth year it will be $201.22—it will have doubled. Thus the secret to accumulating capital is to start early and let your money compound itself.

Even though I know the figures, I never cease to be amazed at *how little a person has to save every year to accumulate a huge amount of money later in life.* To illustrate the point, here's a table that shows you *how much money you have to save each year to end up with $10,000 in fifteen, twenty, twenty-five, thirty, thirty-five and forty years.*

| | Yearly Saving That Will Produce $10,000—If Money Is Invested at a Compounding Rate of Return of | | | |
Number of Years	6%	8%	10%	12%
40	$ 65	$ 40	$ 23	$ 13
35	90	60	37	23
30	133	90	61	41
25	182	135	102	75
20	272	220	175	139
15	430	370	315	268

The 6% column could represent money put in a bank savings account; the 8% column could represent net return from corporate bonds; and the 10% column should be achieved by putting your dollars into stocks. Naturally it's hard to generalize and predict just what rate of return (including both dividends and capital gains) you will get from stocks, but 10% looks very attainable over the next five to ten years since you are starting from a market that has languished for about a decade. Historical returns from common stocks have average 8–10% per year. And today, with U.S. government bonds returning yields as high or higher than these historical stock returns, there had better be very favorable overall conditions favoring equity ownership lest stocks become *un*attractive alternatives (after all, government bonds should carry less volatility and less basic risk than stocks). Because of this warning, and because some of the figures in this book on investor needs twenty years hence have probably been understated, I have assumed low rates of return for all investments as a basis for your future planning. It is certainly better to err on the side of conservatism.

Now let's go back to your problem of amassing $80,000 over twenty years. The table tells you how much you'll have to invest to accumulate *$10,000* in twenty years:

At   6%—$272 per year
At   8%—$220 per year
At 10%—$175 per year

Since we need $80,000, we have to multiply these figures by 8—which produces the following sums to be set aside (invested):

At   6%—$2,176
At   8%—$1,760
At 10%—$1,400

If you take the most conservative course and put all your money in the bank (ridiculous, of course, with even Treasury bills yielding well over 10% today), you will have to save $181 per month ($2176 per year) to amass $80,000 in twenty years.

If stocks perform at the 10% rate, *you will only have to put aside $116 per month ($1,400 per year) to achieve your pot of gold.* Chances are you can save at least a portion of this amount and can count on a pretty good hunk of investment capital in 2000. The main thing is to *get started now* and let your investment snowball as time goes by.

If you're fortunate enough to have forty productive, saving years ahead of you, your pot of gold should be a cinch to reach. The table shows that you need set aside only $40 *per year* to accumulate $10,000 over forty years at the 8% rate of return. To amass $40,000, you will need four times as much, or $160 per year ($13.30 per month). I ask you—how many people cannot afford to do this?

The idea of investing money regularly in stocks has been widely publicized by both the New York Stock Exchange and the many mutual funds. The idea is simple. You send in your money periodically just as you would deposit money in a Christmas Club savings account in your local bank. Investing small amounts is "painless"—you will scarcely miss the money—and these small amounts can grow to large sums over the years.

Once people thought that stocks were only for the very rich, but the mutual funds have made a strong play for the small investor in recent years.

The funds have plans, which they usually call "periodic" or "cumulative" investment plans. Generally, there is an initial investment requirement of $300 or $500—after which you can invest in periodic installments as long as you contribute a minimum of around $300 per year. These plans normally call for automatic reinvestment of dividends (regular dividends at the fund's price with commission; capital gain distributions at net asset value without commission).

I recommended the fund periodic investment programs in Chapter 33 because they are generally cheaper than buying small amounts of individual stocks outright. Investing up to $100 at one time on the exchange will generally entail a hefty commission; $200 at one time might cost 6%—and these are all "one-way" commissions (you have to pay another commission if and when you sell the stock). In contrast, you pay commission generally only when you buy a fund—the 6% or 8% commission covers both buying and selling. *Unless you are investing over $200 at one time, it is normally as cheap or cheaper to buy the funds than it is to buy a stock on the New York Stock Exchange.* If you are investing less than $200, you may as well avail yourself of both the lower cost and the professional management provided by investment trusts—and this is where I believe the funds are most useful. They are ideal for a long-term periodic savings program and I strongly recommend them to anyone wanting to build a pot of gold.

DOLLAR AVERAGING

Periodic investment programs have many advantages. When you buy a stock at different intervals over a period of years, you will buy some at very low prices, some at high levels, and some in between. When you buy on a consistent basis, you are not trying to outguess the market—you are only trying to establish a reasonable average cost for yourself. As a matter of fact, a person engaged in systematic investing *actually benefits from declining prices* along the way. Say, for example, you have decided to invest $100 per month in a stock or an investment trust that sells at $10 per share. The first month your $100 buys you 10 shares. By the next month the stock has declined to $9, but is this drop cause to shed tears? Absolutely not. Just the opposite. Why? Because now your $100 buys you $1\frac{1}{10}$

shares of the same stock. You are getting more shares for the same amount of money. If the stock eventually sinks to $5, your $100 will buy you 20 shares. Now you are getting even more for your money. This is great—*provided that the stock eventually recovers and goes way up in price.* In other words, the problem of *timing is eliminated*—the only problem is selection of the right stock.

Many large investors, such as insurance companies and colleges, adhere to investing fixed amounts on a periodic program. In essence, they are saying, "We believe in the future of this company. We want to own the stock, and rather than try to pick out the low points (and maybe never get them), we aim for a reasonable average cost." They practice what we call "dollar averaging," and this can be a wise policy for individuals as well as institutions. Dollar averaging forces you to buy your stock or stocks just when you might hesitate to do so—when the outlook for the market is gloomy and stock prices are low. This is, of course, precisely the time when you should be buying.

PART XIV

An Explosive Area for Profits

37

"Bikini" Stocks

Bikini bathing suits have become the rage of the beaches throughout the world. There's only one reason for their popularity, namely that these small suits provide the male population with maximum exposure to feminine pulchritude. The more curvaceous a woman is, the more she benefits from the small bathing suit.

It stands to reason that common stocks that provide maximum exposure to pleasant things will be popular, too. The more curvaceous a company is (with exciting products and developments), the more it benefits from "a small bathing suit"—in this case a *small amount of common stock outstanding*.

Take, for example, a company that has a new product with dynamic possibilities. Assume this product has a sales potential of $10 million, on which the company should show a profit of $1 million. This $1 million sounds big, but everything is relative: to a very large company with 100 million shares outstanding, $1 million is peanuts (only 1 cent per share), whereas to a small organization with only 100,000 shares, $1 million amounts to a gigantic $10 per share.

Thus you can see the possibilities that exist in a growing company with only a small number of shares on which to compute its earnings (a "small capitalization," as they say in investment circles). A company like General Electric, which has over 226 million shares, *has* to come up with *countless* new discoveries that will produce a large volume of sales and profits to keep earnings per share growing, while companies with only a few hundred thousand shares can grow rapidly with only one or two new developments. The experience of Mead Johnson and Company with its weight-reducing formula Metrecal was a perfect example, although it was short-lived. Mead Johnson had a little over 1¾ million shares outstanding (a relatively small capitalization) when it introduced Metrecal, and this one product was primarily responsible for the company's earnings ballooning from $3.02 per share in 1959 to $7.25 per share in 1960. This magnified effect was, in turn, responsible for Mead Johnson stock going from a low of 60 to a high of 164¾ during this one year.

Of course, there are two sides to the coin. Just as gains are magnified, so are losses. A small company that spends a great deal of money on a new development only to see it flop will experience large losses on a per share basis.

Still, because of the dramatic results that can be shown by small capitalization companies, investors should be willing to pay a premium to own the promising ones. But you do have to be particular about which bikini stocks you buy.

RESULTS OF FIRST-EDITION (*PRIMER*) BIKINIS

In the first printing of *Stock Market Primer* (1962) I compiled a list of eight bikini companies that had proved successful for me in the preceding years and that still appeared attractive. For the sake of example, I summed up the potential developments to which an investor had what I considered maximum exposure in each stock. Following is an *exact* reprint from the 1962 edition, showing my chosen "bikini" companies, the number of shares they had outstanding at that time, and the major developments that appeared to be the source of potential future excitement.

"BIKINI" STOCKS

Company	Shares Outstanding (No.)	Developments That Could Be Magnified
American District Telegraph	651,000	ADT, approximately 80%-owned by Grinnell Corp., is the nation's largest factor in the field of burglar and fire-alarm protection. Rising costs of employing round-the-clock watchmen plus constantly rising insurance rates (large discounts come from having efficient alarm systems) invite growing use of ADT services. Government has instituted antitrust suit against Grinnell; if ADT spins off to become a completely separate entity, its stock would become popular. True earnings hidden by heavy depreciation charges.
Dymo Industries	442,000	Company has a unique labeling tape (used in conjunction with its own machines) that could have wide application by both consumers and by industry.
Heli-Coil	698,000	Has patented fastening device with increased strength, which could open up unlimited markets for a wide variety of uses.
Interstate Hosts (now Host International)	841,000	Provides participation in the future of air travel without being subject to regulation by CAB. Provides restaurant, beverage, snack bar, gift shop, and newsstand services in many airports. Los Angeles airport (a major installation for Interstate) to be open completely in 1962.

Company	Shares Outstanding (No.)	Developments That Could Be Magnified
Masco Corp.	734,000	Masco manufactures the Delta faucet, one of the top selling one-lever faucets in the U.S. Delta has only one moving part and has been strongly merchandised by management. Trend in bathroom construction is toward the single-lever faucet.
Paddington Corp.	1,191,000	Exclusive distributor of J&B liquors, which have not yet been introduced into certain geographical areas (low saturation point).
Raychem Corp.	1,001,000	One of the few companies in the U.S. well advanced in the treatment of wire insulation and tubing by radiation. This method imparts certain qualities to materials (rubber, plastics, etc.) that add to temperature resistance, strength, etc.
Howard W. Sams	501,000	Leader in supplying technical diagrams of electronic equipment to repair and maintenance people. Recently bought Bobbs-Merrill, book publishers.

Just for the record, here is how these eight companies performed over the ensuing six years (all prices adjusted for subsequent splits, stock dividends, etc.):

Company	Sept. 1962 Price	Subsequent High	% Gain to High	1968 Year-End Price	% Gain to Present
A.D.T.	12½	42	237	39¾	218
Dymo	18⅝	52⅛	180	26½	43
Heli-Coil	11½	39⅜	251	23⅜	103
Host Int.	3½	48	1270	39	1015
Masco	5½	48⅜	780	41¼	650
Paddington	23¾	45⅝	84	40*	68
Raychem	29½	323	995	299	915
Sams (Howard)	20	62	210	58¼†	190

*Now merged into Charing Cross Importers, Ltd.
†Merged into International Telephone and Telegraph; price reflects 1968 value of ITT stock.

As you can see, the overall performance of these bikini equities was pretty dramatic. The eight stocks showed an *average gain of 400%—they quintupled in value.* Within the group, we find *two that multiplied over 10 times their September 1962 levels* (Host International and Raychem), one (Masco) that went up 7½ times, and two more (ADT and Sams) that about tripled. Their owners would have derived an even higher return if they had been able to sell near interim high points.

One further point should be stressed here—something that spells out the philosophy of many investors who seek out high-reward situations. Successful venture capitalists and special-situation stock buyers take the approach that a few big winners will achieve their goal. Realizing that it is difficult to predict exactly which individual stocks will succeed famously, they take a package approach and buy a handful (or so) of situations. Within the package, they hope to have selected a few like Hosts, Masco, and Raychem that will appreciate sufficiently to bring about a very high return. *Most important, this philosophy dictates holding on for the huge returns those several situations might produce.* As I hope you have already gleaned from your reading, the secret to success lies in thinking *BIG* and not being satisfied with small profits (if amassing large amounts of capital is your goal). Unless you absorb this philosophy, this chapter—or any other on common stock selection—will be of limited value to you.

Although the performance of these bikini stocks was dynamic, in many cases, the experience shown constitutes but a part of the story. So you can understand the approaches necessary to bikini selection and see just how large the potential rewards are, let me trace the reasoning and the results of four of these companies—ones that I uncovered and recommended strongly to people at one time in the past.

Dymo was first brought to market in June 1960 at $9 per share. I knew absolutely nothing of this company at that time but a few weeks later I saw its product in action and was impressed by it. I proceeded to study Dymo and found that it had many growth-company characteristics: management was aggressive, honest, able, and hard-working ("hungry," as we say in our business); its labeling machine was well engineered and the specialized Dymo tape had patent protection; the tape was expendable, meaning that repeat sales would be large; and competition was almost nonexistent.

Equally important was the fact that Dymo had less than 450,000 shares outstanding. At the time Dymo stock was selling for $14 per share, and I had only to ask the following question to conclude the stock was a great buy: Can Dymo some day soon earn $1 million? This question was so important to answer because with less than 450,000 shares outstanding, a net profit of $1 million meant per share earnings of over $2. Obviously these $2 per share earnings would guarantee far higher prices for Dymo stock than the existing $14 per share (under P/E multiples common at that time).

My analysis concluded that Dymo had at least this earning potential in the near future, and it was on this basis that I became enthusiastic about this stock.

Before long the company had reached the $1 million level in earning power—and Dymo common stock soared to $120 per share. In a span of a few years the stock appreciated over eight times. The combination of a growing and profitable product and small capitalization had indeed produced spectacular results. Incidentally, Dymo is an example of a bikini company that required real flexibility. The company did not capitalize on its success as it should have; it failed to develop new products to complement its line—and, as was to be expected, competi-

ion soon appeared on the scene. Because of this, I changed my
position on the stock (very luckily, near its high).

Another successful bikini stock of mine was Masco Corporation. In contrast to Dymo, which had just come on the market
as a new issue and was trading over-the-counter, Masco had
been publicly held for many years and was listed on the Detroit
Stock Exchange. As with Dymo, I was attracted to Masco because of its product—the Delta one-lever faucet. I had learned
that one-lever faucets were becoming the trend in certain types
of new residential construction and modernization, and I soon
discovered that Masco's Delta faucet was increasing its accep-
ance and popularity. Masco had engineered a quality product—one that had only one moving part (an important sales
feature)—and had also developed strong merchandising. It was
one of the top two manufacturers in its field.

I was amazed when I learned of Masco's growth record
since it had introduced the Delta product in 1954 (the company
had previously concentrated on serving the major auto manufacturers with auto parts—basically an unattractive business).
Here's how the company's record looked in January 1961 when
I first became interested in it:

Year	Earnings per Share
1956	$.06
1957	.15
1958	.17
1959	.48

You can imagine how amazed I was to find that Masco stock
was selling at only $3.50 per share. Here was an ideal bikini
stock—a well-managed company with a fine product line, increasing business, and only (*not* adjusted for splits) 367,000
shares outstanding—and it was selling for less than 7 times
1959 earnings (more than a year before).

My analysis (which, as in the case of Dymo, included contact with management) led me to believe that profits in the year

just completed (1960) were higher than those of 1959, and that 1961 would show even better results. Some months later Masco reported 1960 net income of 65 cents per share. Yet the stock was still relatively unknown and was selling for a very reasonable $6 per share.

The rest of the story is certainly gratifying to me. Thanksgiving Day of 1961 (less than a year after my discovery of Masco) found Masco stock at (adjusted) $27 per share—or almost 8 times its worth in January. A little over four years later Masco had doubled again in price and was thus up about 16 times over its original "discovery" price. And today the stock is selling for about 100 times our entry price.

The attraction of Host International should have been fairly obvious. As the description on page 329 indicates, the company had successful service operations located in airports that were certain to see increasing traffic over the years. In short, the thesis behind this bikini company was that it offered participation in the growth of air traffic without the vagaries of federal regulation.

Typical of so many bikini situations, Host International took a number of years to blossom and become fully appreciated for what it was. As a matter of fact, I lived with this stock for several years without finding any acceptance of its real worth. Once accepted, however, the stock found higher and higher evaluation by the investment community, which of course, meant a higher and higher P/E multiple. At any rate, the stock multiplied more than elevenfold over the period 1962–1968.

Raychem was a company that had an unusual technological know-how in an area that held startling possibilities. It had a tremendous lead time on potential competitors—something that is hard to come by and is especially important in a bikini capitalization. Like Host International, Raychem took some time to develop. As a matter of fact, my research department published the "bible" on Raychem in July 1963 (some eighteen months after I completed the writing of *Primer*'s first edition) and the stock was actually lower then than before. A few years later, significant profits started to show at the company and the combination of these figures and a real acceptance of Raychem by investors took the stock up to the $300 level (since then, the stock has been split the equivalent of 6-for-1 and its $60 market price in 1980 is equal to around $360 on the original recommended price). Once again, concept plus earnings plus small number of shares outstanding brought unusual happiness to those who recognized bikini thinking.

BIKINIS, 1976 STYLE

In the last revision of *Primer* (1976) I submitted another set of bikini stocks—although then I used larger bathing suits. I stated then that "I found it difficult to isolate a representative list of companies with extremely small capitalizations." This, I commented, brought up "an important investment point: that one should never 'strain' to produce investment ideas. If they come naturally after study, then they should be utilized; but if they do not, a person makes a mistake trying too hard."

I then listed seven companies of varying sizes that seemed to possess unusual prospects. Here is a description of these as they appeared in the 1976 *Primer* and the subsequent performance of the stocks as of mid-1980:

"BIKINI" STOCKS, 1976

Company	No. of Shares Outstanding	Developments That Could Lead to Exceptional Growth
Beverage Management	1,713,000	Small but rapidly growing bottler and distributor of soft drinks. Opportunities for both geographical expansion and extension of product line.
Hanes Corp.	3,979,000	Company has built a strong consumer franchise through its L'Eggs division. Has recently survived entries in packaged hosiery and pantyhose from larger companies—none of which have been able to penetrate the L'Eggs market domination.
Martin Processing	1,967,000	Possesses unusual know-how in the processing of nylon and polyester yarns for carpets. Ties in with trend toward multicolored tufted carpets.
LA-Z-Boy Chair	4,643,000	The "Cadillac" of the little-known but rapidly growing reclining chair market. Very low saturation level of recliners in homes here and abroad. Unusual features of LA-Z-Boy chairs plus strong distribution. Now entering recliner-rocker and office furniture market.
Neutrogenia	934,000	Company has successful skin-care product line, which it is now broadening. One successful new product could have strong impact on earnings, with existing small capitalization.

Company	No. of Shares Outstanding	Developments That Could Lead to Exceptional Growth
Pittway Corp.	3,259,000	Whereas part of Pittway's business is unexciting, more than 75% of earnings now come from Alarm Device Manufacturing Company—one of the most successful manufacturers of burglar, smoke-detection, and other security products. This business is growing very rapidly and has a very exciting future.
WD-40 Company	1,217,000	Admittedly a one product company, but WD-40 has ever-growing uses as lubricant, rust preventive, etc. Still very low sales base and potential for significantly higher market saturation.

Company	Average 1976 Price	Subsequent High Price	% Gain to High	1980 Price	% Gain to 1980
Beverage Management	5¾	26	+352	12	+108
Hanes	21½	61*	+184	*	+184
Martin Processing	20	28	+ 20	10	− 50
LA-Z-Boy	18	21	+ 16	10	− 44
Neutrogena	10	35	+250	30	+200
Pittway	30	45	+ 50	30	—
WD-40	8	42	+425	37	+362
		Average	+185		+108

*Merged into Consolidated Foods in January 1979 at $61 per share (cash) to Hanes.

This list, like our first Bikini group, produced good results. Four of the seven stocks have done well (three exceptionally well), and the average return of 108% was substantially better than stocks did generally over this period.

But enough backward glances. Since this book is devoted to putting theory into practice, it's time to place my neck on the proverbial chopping block again, as I did in 1962 and 1976. So here is a list of ten companies of varying sizes that I believe have unusual prospects for the near future. *Caution:* Both company progress and market prices can change sharply between the time when this is written and when you read it.

"BIKINI" STOCKS, 1980

Company	No. of Shares Outstanding	Developments That Could Lead to Exceptional Growth
Alpha Industries	2,511,000	Leader in millimeter technology, which will be used in "smart weaponry"—an important area of concentration in the future.
Chas. River Breeding Labs	2,641,000	Holds proprietary position in breeding, raising, and selling of animals for laboratory testing of all sorts.
Crawford & Co.	8,052,000	The country's leading independent adjuster of property and casualty claims and losses for insurance companies. An interesting service company, not well known in investment circles.
Moog Inc.	2,193,000	The world's leading producer of high-performance valves, which are critical to important and growing aerospace and industrial applications. One interesting way to invest in the future of industrial robots—rapidly increasing in usage here and abroad.

Company	No. of Shares Outstanding	Developments That Could Lead to Exceptional Growth
Pay'n Pak Stores	4,426,000	Fast-growing retailer in the home improvement (do-it-yourself) field. Located in fast-growing regions.
Perini Corp.	3,363,000	A major contractor, but this is of little interest; company owns substantial real estate, which is undervalued on its balance sheet. Company is using its cash to repurchase its own shares.
Pinkerton's	2,360,000	Leading company is security services. Once a recognized growth company, it has gone through a flat period but seems to have made changes that promise renewed growth.
Peoples Drug Stores	3,689,000	A self-service drugstore chain; in good locations and with strong management (which owns a large share of the company).
Trus Joist Corp.	3,600,000	Manufacturer of patented structural components for buildings. Large cost advantages make for interesting future for Trus Joist products.
Twin City Barge	1,604,000	Should participate in increasing barge business which facilitates grain shipments both domestically and overseas. (Barge shipment is cheaper than either truck or rail.)

PART XV

Do's and Don'ts in the Stock Market

38

Common Stock Commandments

The preceding pages have given you some fundamentals about investments and the stock market. In addition, I have provided rules in each chapter that I believe will guarantee you greater success in your ventures. Now I have some further comments that should be equally helpful to you. I call these "common stock commandments" and here they are:

1. *Do not make hasty, emotional decisions about buying and selling stocks.*

   When you do what your emotions tell you to—on the spur of the moment—you are doing exactly what the "masses" are doing, and this is not generally profitable. It is better to wait until your emotions have returned to normal, so that you can weigh the pros and cons objectively. Never allow yourself to be pressured into buying or selling securities by anyone. Hard-sell techniques hint there may be "'stale merchandise on the shelf," and that's not what you want. If you're in doubt about buying, my advice is to *do nothing*.

2. *If you are convinced that a company has dynamic growth prospects, do not sell it just because it looks temporarily too high.*

   You may never be able to buy it back lower in price and you stand to miss a potential *big winner*—which is just what you should be looking for. Perhaps the gravest error I've seen made over the years is selling great companies with bright future prospects just because they temporarily looked a few points too high. While on the subject of big winners, let me suggest the chapter on "How to Amass Large Amounts of Capital" from *The Common Sense Way to Stock Market Profits.* The philosophy and the approach detailed there are essential reading for growth-oriented investors.

3. *Do not fall in love with stocks to the point where you can no longer be objective in your appraisal of them.*

Stocks are different from human beings. You'd be a fool to think of your spouse all day the way he or she looks the first thing in the morning—maybe it's best that you think of your spouse as he or she appears all dressed up. But you do have to scrutinize stocks and think of their worst points; you have to reassess your feelings constantly and you must be brutal and unemotional in your appraisal.

4. *Do not concern yourself as much with the market in general as with the outlook for individual stocks.*

Oftentimes you will see a fine stock come down to an unquestionable bargain price, only to let your feeling about the general market dissuade you from buying it. As they say, it's not the stock market that counts, but the market for individual stocks. Buy a good value when it appears and do not let the general market sentiment alter your decision.

5. *Forget about stock market "tips."*

If you learn to exercise good judgment, you won't have to rely on unreliable information. This is hardly an original point, but still, it's often ignored. I'll never forget the day I was visited by a certain client at my office. He wanted a recommendation on a good stock and I suggested he buy American Photocopy Equipment, which looked very attractive to me. I related my reasoning to him about the industry, the company, and so forth, and I showed him all the facts and figures I had on the stock. I spent ten or fifteen minutes extolling the glowing outlook of this company, and then my client told me he would think about it and let me know. The next morning he called me and placed an order—for an entirely different stock, one of the "Happyjack Uranium" type. He explained he "had heard some very good things" about this stock and he wanted to own it. A year or so later his purchase was about half of his cost and he visited me again. This time he told me the "source" of his information: he had spent an hour at a very fancy cocktail lounge the evening of our original meeting and had overheard a very confidential conversation about this stock. A fine thing, I thought (and my client agreed). Here I had spent hours researching American Photocopy and had given him the benefits of these hours—and he turned around and disregarded this in favor of a hot tip he overheard between two strangers who had consumed an ample supply of martinis. This is such a common temptation that I can't resist warning you against following tips in the stock market.

6. *You get what you pay for in the stock market (as in everything else in life).*

Some people consider a $5 stock good just because it's low in price. Nothing could be further from the truth. High-priced stocks usually provide far better value than low-priced stocks; they generally have more earnings, dividends, and so on behind them than the low-priced issues. Likewise, high-priced stocks go into "better hands" (many are purchased by large institutional investors and other long-term holders), while the low-priced issues most often go into the hands of speculators and gamblers, who may be less informed and inclined to occasional panic selling. Also remember that high-priced stocks carry one potential that cheap stocks do not—they are all potential split candidates.

7. *Remember that stocks always look worst at the bottom of a bear market (when an air of gloom prevails) and best at the top of a bull market (when everybody is optimistic).*

Have strength and buy when things do look bleak and sell when they look too good to be true.

8. *Remember that you'll seldom—if ever—buy stocks right at the bottom or sell them right at the top.*

The stock market generally goes to extremes: when pessimism dominates, stocks go lower than they really should, on the basis of their fundamentals, and when optimism runs rampant, stocks go higher than they deserve to. Knowing this, don't expect your stocks to go up in price immediately after you buy them or to go down after you sell them, even though you are convinced that your analysis of their value is correct.

9. *Do not buy stocks as you might store merchandise on sale.*

No doubt you've seen people scrapping and clamoring for goods on sale at stores like Macy's. They fight to buy this merchandise because of the reduced price and limited supply of the merchandise. Too often shoppers buy things they don't need or don't like, and then find they haven't made a "good buy" after all. *But they simply couldn't resist the urge to join others in competing for goods that are in limited supply.*

Actively traded common stocks are not in limited supply. Therefore I advise you not to rush to buy as though the supply is going to dry up. If you've ever sat in a stock brokerage office and watched the "tape" (which shows stock transactions as they take place), you'll know what I mean. A certain stock might suddenly get active and start rising in price: one minute you see it at 35, a few seconds later it's $35\frac{1}{2}$, then 36, $36\frac{1}{4}$, $36\frac{1}{2}$, 37. By the time it has hit 37, it is human nature to feel an almost irresistible urge to buy the stock (regardless of its fundamentals of earnings, dividends, future outlook, etc.)—to get in on the gravy train, to join the rest of the flock who are clamoring to buy the stock as though it is "sale merchandise." Resist this urge. Only buy "goods" that you're sure you'll like and that meet your objectives.

10. *There is no reason always to be in the stock market.*

After the stock market has had a long and sizable advance, it is prudent to take a few profits. Too often, after selling, the money from the sale "burns a hole in the pocket" of the investor. It's like working in a candy shop: no matter how much will-power you have, after a few weeks the bonbons look awfully good. Go slowly—there are times when cash can be a valuable asset.

11. *Seek professional advice for your investment.*

Find a broker who is honest and who you are convinced will have *your* best interests at heart. Make sure he knows your financial status, your objectives, and your temperament. If you don't know a good broker, consult your bank or your friends and then go in and meet the person recommended to you. Take the same pains to find the best broker as you would to find the best doctor for yourself. I strongly recommend reading pages 185–204 of *The Common Sense Way to Stock Market Profits*, which deal with establishing a *profitable* relationship with a broker.

12. *Take advantage of the research facilities your broker has to offer.*

Certainly you'll agree that *analysis is a better market tool than a pin.* The top brokerage firms spend millions of dollars every year to find the most attractive investments for their customers. Read the reports that are published—they will give you insight into the investment firm with whom you are dealing. Keep track of their performance over a period of years (performance over a few months may be deceiving, both because the general market may be against them and because you can't expect recommendations to bloom overnight). (Note: Part of the section of *Common Sense* referred to in Commandment 11 discusses research reports—their functions, advantages *and dangers.*)

13. *Remember that the public is generally wrong.*

The masses are not well informed about investments and the stock market. They have not disciplined themselves to make the right choices in the right industries at the right prices. They are moved mainly by their emotions, and history has proved them to be consistently wrong. If you don't believe this, I recommend that you get hold of a book entitled *Extraordinary Popular Delusions and the Madness of Crowds*, written by Dr. Charles

Mackay and published in 1841. The book is filled with concrete examples of the irrational behavior of human beings. Dr. Mackay's descriptions of the famous tulip mania in Holland in the 1630s and the famous South Sea Bubble about a century later are eye-opening, to say the least. Just in case your high school or college history is not vivid in your mind, let me tell you what happened in these two historical events.

Tulip bulbs in Holland in the early seventeenth century were originally sought by collectors and horticulturists, just as orchids and other rare flowers are sought today. As the prices of tulip bulbs rose in the 1630s, people commenced speculating in them. One thing let to another, prices rose further, and suddenly everyone from the downstairs maid to the chimney sweep was speculating in markets that had sprung up solely for trading in tulips. Higher and higher went the prices of tulips—till there was absolutely no relationship between price and the tulips' intrinsic value. As usual when a wide discrepancy exists between price and value, it was not long before prices came tumbling down. Fortunes that had been made speculating were quickly wiped out and the great majority suffered miserably from their emotional speculation.

In the eighteenth century similar speculation and failure occurred in shares of the English South Seas Company, and thereafter there were bursting "bubbles" in all types of stock companies set up for every conceivable venture. To illustrate how emotional and irrational people became, the records show that one company was able to sell its own shares to the public even though it stated that its objective was "to carry on an undertaking of great advantage but nobody is to know what it is."

Dr. Mackay wasn't alive to describe the almost unbelievable hysteria that overcame otherwise sensible people in our country in the late 1920s. In this generation, we have witnessed boom-and-bust experience in uranium, boats, bowling, titanium, small business investment companies and an absolute host of others that resulted in large losses for their emotional followers.

A wise investor should be wary of public overenthusiasm for anything. Don't *you* become "one of the herd." Resist the temptation to follow an exaggerated trend, no matter how assured it appears.

14. *Beware of following stock market "fads."*

I want to emphasize separately this idea of following fads in the market. Remember the "sack" dresses that became the fad fifteen years ago? This fashion was ill-conceived from the very beginning (it didn't make sense in such a vanity-conscious nation as ours). Women who rushed to buy the sack outfits found themselves with a useless wardrobe a short time later; and the retail stores that cluttered their racks with this merchandise suddenly found that their inventory was worth very little. This is but one of many examples of the fads in our country. Twenty years ago it was hula-hoops; sixteen years ago it was trampoline centers; eleven years ago it was "Batman," three years ago it was CB radios, and next year it will be something else. As a general rule, if you get in early on a fad, you stand to make money. But if you come along after it is in full swing, you are asking for trouble.

The same thing goes for the stock market. Just like sack dresses, hula-hoops, trampolines, tulip bulbs, and the rest, the stock market occasionally develops fads for certain industries. In almost all cases a sudden rush to buy the fad stocks pushes them to truly unwarranted price levels. *When you buy at the height of popularity, you almost always pay prices that have little relationship to value.* As I have emphasized so often in this book, you are only asking for trouble when this situation exists, so remember to do some vacuum thinking and pay prices that correspond to the values emphasized in this book.

15. *Don't be so concerned with where a stock has already been; be concerned with where it is going.*

Many times I've heard people say, "It must be a bargain now—it's down 20 points from its high." Where a stock *has been* is history, it's "spilt milk." Investors may have bid up ABC stock to $100 last year, but the outlook for the company may have changed entirely since then. Or it may have been emotional speculation (fad buying) that forced it up to an unreasonable price. *The important thing is what lies ahead, not what has already transpired,* and previous market prices have no bearing on the future.

16. *Take the time to supervise your stocks periodically.*

Needless to say, conditions constantly change. Don't shut yourself off from the outside world; take an objective look at your holdings periodically, with the thought of weeding out the "weak sisters" and adding stocks that have more potential. Your broker should be willing to make an analysis of your portfolio for you on a regular basis, and I encourage you to take advantage of this service.

17. *Concentrate on quality.*

While big profits are often made through buying and selling poor-quality common stocks, your success in the stock market is far, far more assured if you emphasize quality in your stock selections. Too many investors shy away from the top-notch companies in search of rags-to-riches performers. This approach is fine for a certain portion of your investment dollars; most people can afford an *occasional* "flyer." But a person who starts out looking for flyers usually ends up, not with just one or two, but with a host of poor-quality stocks—most of which turn out unsuccessful. These low-grade issues are certainly no foundation for a good portfolio; instead, the fine, well-managed companies should form the backbone. And don't for a minute think you can't make money without wild speculation—fabulous fortunes have been made over the years in such high-quality *non*speculative stocks as Carnation, Coca-Cola, and Procter & Gamble. In other words, place your stress on the elite, not on the "cats and dogs" of the marketplace. "Remember," said one wise stock market philosopher, "if you sleep with dogs, you're bound to get fleas."

39
Final Financial Formulae

At the beginning of this book I discussed finding an effective formula for successful investing in the stock market. Unfortunately there is no pure mathematical formula that will solve all the problems of investing. You can't do as the mathematicians do and say $X = Y + Z^2 (4 \times Y^3)$ and be sure that X will be correct 100% of the time. But you should strive for a high batting average and the preceding pages have instructed you on how to lead the league in making successful purchases and sales of stocks.

Sometimes the simplest rules are the best. I could summarize all the sage advice that successful speculators and investors have passed down to us over the years in a simple rhyme:

> *Here's the money-making lullaby:*
> *Buy stocks low and sell them high.*

But I'm afraid that's oversimplification. There *is* one bit of sincere advice that will bring all that we have covered so far to a conclusion, and it can be stated in one significant word:

PATIENCE

Patience is often the secret to success in any form of investment. Whether you own stock or real estate or your own business, you cannot expect success to come overnight. Obviously, there may be times in your investment life when some of the stocks you own are not moving up the way you would like. But remember, Rome wasn't built in a day. And patience is indeed an investment virtue. So don't be fidgety with your stocks. Don't be concerned with the day-to-day fluctuations that occur in the stock market. I always think of a statment made by one very successful investor. He contended that he made more money *by the seat of his pants than by his agile brain.* In other words:

If you believe in reasonable future growth of this country,
If you can locate the companies that will lead and share in this
    growth,
If you can isolate quality stocks representing top management
    and buy them at reasonable prices (i.e., buy value),
Then you should have patience and be willing to "sit" on the
    good stocks.

The result should be: real success in the stock market!

   The preceding pages have given you the tools you need. I have given you the background and the hindsight necessary for success. I've given you food for thought that prepares you to add foresight to hindsight. And I've supplied you with many basic rules that should keep you from making mistakes and a Compounding Growth Guide that enables you to judge a stock's fundamental value. In short, I think we've covered the bases and have both a solid defense against unnecessary losses and a potent offense for making sizable gains.

Appendix

How to Arrive at a Company's Annual Compound Growth Rate

The basis of our Compounding Growth Guide lies with the investors' appraisal of a company's future yearly rate of growth. The procedure involves:

1. Determination of a company's annual compound rate of growth over the *past* three to five years.
2. An analysis of whether this growth rate will increase or decrease over the *next* three to five years.
3. Allowance for the kind of institutional support a stock commands.
4. Conclusion of the "proper P/E," according to our guide.

Because the annual compound growth rate in the *past* and in the *future* is so important, I want to make it easy for you to be able to figure this rate. The mathematical formula for doing this is rather complicated, so I have done all the figuring for you (that is, I had an electronic computer do it). The result is a very simple table for you to use.

All *you* have to do is figure what a company's *total increase in earnings per share* has been (or is going to be) over a three to five year period, and then the table will tell you what the company's annual compound growth rate has been (or is going to be). Your computation is very simple but, just for review, here is how total increase over a period of time (on a percentage basis) is computed:

First of all, subtract the earnings per share for the first year you are using (your base year) from the *last* year you are using. EXAMPLE: You are analyzing ABC Company, which has had the following record over the last four years:

1979	$1.50
1978	1.37
1977	1.10
1976	1.15
1975	1.00

In this case, subtract the first year (the 1975 base year) from the last year (1979):

$$\$1.50 - \$1.00 = \$.50$$

Next divide this answer ($.50) by the base figure ($1.00):

$$\$.50 \div \$1.00 = .50 \text{ or } 50\%$$

This is the total percentage increase in earnings per share over the period you have chosen. ABC's total growth from 1975–1979 was 50%.

Once you have arrived at this simple calculation of the percentage increase, it becomes only a matter of consulting the following table to determine the *yearly compound growth rate.* Simply:

1. Find the column in the horizontal A headings that delineates the number of years you have chosen for your growth calculation.

2. Glance down the vertical column from that point until you reach the approximate percentage figure that your calculations of growth have produced.

3. Look to the far left—to the vertical B figures—to determine what the compound *annual* rate of growth amounts to.

In your ABC example above, you start by locating the "4 Yrs." column in A; then look down until you come to as close to 50% as you can (the 4 Yrs. column does not show 50 exactly but you can see that your answer lies between 46 and 52); look to the left to B and conclude that the 46% growth equals 10% per year compounded and 52% growth equals 11%. The answer, therefore, for ABC annual growth from 1975–1979 is about 10½%.

Let me caution you about figuring growth rates. Be sure not to start with a year that is either greatly depressed or greatly inflated. Instead, choose a year that is more normal, or use the average of a few years, as a base and compute growth from this.

COMPOUND GROWTH TABLE

B. Then the Compounded Annual Rate of Growth Is:

A. If Total Growth over the Below-Specified No. of Years Has Aggregated:

	1 Yr.	2 Yrs.	3 Yrs.	4 Yrs.	5 Yrs.	6 Yrs.	7 Yrs.	8 Yrs.	9 Yrs.	10 Yrs.	15 Yrs.	20 Yrs.	25 Yrs.
1%	1%	2%	3%	4%	5%	6%	7%	8%	9%	10%	16%	22%	28%
2	2	4	6	8	10	13	15	17	19	22	35	49	64
3	3	6	9	13	16	19	23	27	30	34	56	81	109
4	4	8	12	17	22	26	32	37	42	48	80	119	167
5	5	10	16	22	28	34	41	48	55	63	108	165	239
6	6	12	19	26	34	42	50	59	69	79	140	221	330
7	7	14	22	31	40	50	61	72	84	97	176	287	440
8	8	17	26	36	47	59	71	85	100	116	217	366	590
9	9	19	29	41	54	68	83	99	117	137	264	461	760
10	10	21	33	46	61	77	95	114	136	159	318	573	980
11	11	23	37	52	68	87	108	130	156	184	378	710	1260
12	12	25	40	57	76	97	121	148	177	211	447	870	1600
13	13	28	44	63	84	108	135	166	200	239	525	1050	2020
14	14	30	48	69	93	119	150	185	225	271	614	1270	2550
15	15	32	52	75	101	131	166	206	252	305	714	1540	3190

16	16	35	36	81	110	144	183	228	280	341	830	1850	3990
17	17	37	60	87	119	157	200	251	311	381	950	2210	4970
18	18	39	64	94	129	170	218	276	343	428	1100	2640	6170
19	19	42	68	100	139	184	238	302	378	470	1260	3140	7640
20	20	44	73	107	149	199	258	330	416	519	1440	3730	9440
21	21	46	77	114	159	214	280	359	456	573			
22	22	49	82	121	170	230	302	390	498	630			
23	23	51	86	129	182	246	326	424	544	692			
24	24	54	91	137	193	264	351	459	593	760			
25	25	56	95	144	205	282	377	497	646	832			
26	26	59	100	150	219	300	404	535	700	908			
27	27	61	105	160	233	318	430	572	754	984			
28	28	64	110	170	242	340	462	622	825	1082			
29	29	67	115	176	258	360	492	665	888	1175			
30	30	69	120	186	271	383	528	716	961	1279			
31	31	72	125	195	286								
32	32	74	132	206	305								
33	33	77	135	215	318								
34	34	80	142	224	335								
35	35	82	147	234	350								
40	40	96	175	285	440								

Index